Pollution and Reform
in American Cities, 1870–1930

Pollution and Reform in American Cities, 1870–1930

Edited by Martin V. Melosi

University of Texas Press, *Austin & London*

Library of Congress Cataloging in Publication Data

Main entry under title:
Pollution and reform in American cities, 1870–1930.
  Bibliography: p.
    1. Pollution—Social aspects—United States—
History. I. Melosi, Martin V., 1947–
TD180.P63 1980   614.7' 0973   79-13863
ISBN 0-292-76459-6

Requests for permission to reproduce material from this
book should be sent to Permissions, University of Texas
Press, Box 7819, Austin, Texas 78712.

To Mom and Dad—
for their love and their love of life

Contents

Acknowledgments

Pollution and Reform in American Cities was a collaborative venture from start to finish. Most of the contributors, at one time or another, had raised the idea of an anthology of original scholarship that would deal with the burgeoning field of urban environmental studies. My own interest in this area began at the University of Texas in a graduate seminar conducted by H. Wayne Morgan. He encouraged Ray Smilor and myself, among others, to pursue the study of the urban environment and constantly prodded us to publish our findings. Professor Morgan's inspiration was essential to this volume. I also wish to thank the Rockefeller Foundation and the Department of History of Texas A&M University for their financial support, which not only made possible my own research but also allowed me to gather the eventual contributors to this volume to discuss our mutual interests at meetings in St. Louis, Atlanta, Washington, D.C., Wilmington, Delaware, and Tempe, Arizona. Special acknowledgment must go to Barbara Burnham of the University of Texas Press for her encouragement; to colleagues at Texas A&M, Roger Beaumont, Keith Bryant, and John Lenihan, for their constructive criticisms; and to my wife, Carolyn, for her constant support. Our departmental secretaries, Carole Knapp, Rosa Richardson, Mary Watson, and Gloria West, all contributed to the completion of this study. Thanks to them as well.

Martin V. Melosi

Preface

Pollution and Reform in American Cities is the first volume of its kind. It is meant to fill a void in the study of the American city by examining the environmental impact of industrialization on urban growth during the nineteenth and early twentieth centuries. The essays highlight the extent of specific pollution problems, the emergence of environmental consciousness in the cities, and the efforts of reformers to improve the quality of urban life in the wake of massive pollution.

Since scholars have just begun to analyze urban environmental problems in historical context, this volume represents a departure point for understanding some of the forces that produced the first environmental crisis in the cities of the United States and how urbanites coped with that crisis. The essays are largely narrative and provide a basic chronology about urban pollution and the response of reformers. They are also national in scope—not narrow case studies —and offer a broad overview of significant environmental trends.

The chapters are of three types. The first attempts to establish a historical context for understanding the impact of pollution on American industrial cities. The next five deal with specific pollution problems. Stuart Galishoff's "Triumph and Failure: The American Response to the Urban Water Supply Problem, 1860-1923" treats how American cities were compelled to develop new water supplies and how they acquired new sources of pure water. "The Development and Impact of Urban Wastewater Technology," by Joel Tarr, James McCurley, and Terry Yosie, complements Galishoff's article and discusses the widespread adoption of water-carriage systems between 1850 and 1930 and their limitations. R. Dale Grinder's "The Battle for Clean Air" details the conflict between demands for limitless industrial growth and the abatement of smoke pollution. "Refuse Pollution and Municipal Reform" by Martin Melosi examines the extent of solid waste pollution in the industrial cities and the evolution of refuse reform. And Raymond Smilor, in "Toward an Environmental Perspective: The Anti-Noise Campaign, 1893-1932," discusses how reformers attempted to cope with the elusive, but multifaceted, problem of noise in the inner city.

The last two essays examine two important groups that had a profound effect upon environmental reform in general: municipal engineers and women. The piece by Stanley Schultz and Clay McShane analyzes the motives and roles of municipal engineers in a variety of environmental reforms. Suellen Hoy's " 'Municipal Housekeeping': The Role of Women in Improving Urban Sanitation Practices, 1880-1917" discusses how the dual role of housewife and mother influenced women to become involved in sanitation reform and the results of that improvement.

We hope that this book will not only provide a better understanding of the impact of pollution on industrial cities in the United States but will also help establish the foundation for more comprehensive and speculative historical studies of the urban environment, broaden the study of American environmental history to afford more attention to the cities and urban life, and provide essential background for those individuals grappling with current environmental problems.

The Context

1. Environmental Crisis in the City: The Relationship between Industrialization and Urban Pollution

By Martin V. Melosi

The industrial city was the most visible sign of the nineteenth-century economic revolution in the United States. Between 1870 and 1920, it became the dominant urban form in the country. As Sam Bass Warner, Jr., has suggested, "The ubiquity of power and machines in the late nineteenth and early twentieth centuries had profound effects on the American urban system."[1] In earlier times, large American cities had chiefly been centers of commerce and finance. As early as 1820, urban development and industrial growth were becoming immutably linked. Relatively new cities, such as Pittsburgh, Cleveland, and Milwaukee, began to experience rapid growth and vast economic prosperity by producing such products as iron and steel, petroleum, and beer. Industrialization also transformed many older commercial cities, such as New York, Boston, and Philadelphia, which attracted major industries of their own.[2]

As the undisputed centers of economic dynamism in the United States, industrial cities flourished. Yet their overcrowded tenements, congested traffic, critical health problems, smoky skies, mounds of putrefying wastes, polluted waterways, and unbearable noise levels attested to the price they had to pay for such success. Unlike the commercial cities, which had not suffered such massive physical defilement (because agriculture, decentralized manufacturing, and trade had dominated the preindustrial economy), the industrial cities were experiencing an environmental crisis on a scale not encountered before in America.

In *The City in History*, Lewis Mumford argues persuasively that the growing tendency of cities to concentrate on economic activities to the virtual exclusion of other functions had a devastating effect on the physical environment. He asserts:

> If capitalism tended to expand the province of the marketplace
> and turn every part of the city into a negotiable commodity, the
> change from organized urban handicraft to large scale factory

production transformed the industrial towns into dark hives,
busily puffing, clanking, screeching, smoking for twelve and fourteen hours a day, sometimes going around the clock. The slavish
routine of the mines, whose labor was an intentional punishment
for criminals, became the normal environment of the new industrial worker. None of these towns needed the old saw, "All work
and no play makes Jack a dull boy." Coketown specialized in
producing dull boys.[3]

Mumford's assessment of Coketown applies as well to the early industrial
cities of the United States. As the sites for rapid industrial expansion, their
economies thrived, indeed depended, on the burgeoning factories, retail stores,
and railroad lines, while their physical surroundings continued to deteriorate.
In a competitive age when economic growth meant progress, most people
attached little importance to preserving the quality of the environment—at
least in the beginning. Quantitative, rather than qualitative, measures of progress dominated the thinking of those who advocated unlimited growth.

The magnitude and nature of industrial expansion in the nineteenth and
early twentieth centuries are major reasons for the environmental crisis that
occurred. Especially important was the sophistication of manufacturing after
1820. New machinery supplanted hand tools and muscle power in the fabrica-
tion of goods, while the harnessing of water power to drive that machinery
allowed production to be centered in large factories. In addition, mechaniza-
tion undercut the need for workers with strong backs but required a large labor
force with specialized skills or, at least, the agility to operate the myriad equipment. Rapid increases in the population helped provide this labor force. Technological achievements, ranging from advanced communications and transportation to interchangeable machine parts, encouraged the expansion and concentration of manufacturing. An organizational revolution brought about
better coordination between management and production functions in various
business enterprises and encouraged the formation of large, integrated companies, which began to exploit regional as well as national markets. Also, by
mid-century factories were concentrating in milltowns and other urban areas
at an increasingly rapid pace.[4]

Later, between 1870 and 1920, American industry retained the basic features of the preceding decades but underwent substantial changes in detail
and scale. In the 1880s, the value added to goods by manufacturing and processing exceeded the value of agricultural products for the first time. About
1890, the United States surpassed Great Britain in the volume of its industrial
output, thus becoming a world leader in that field. American economic success

in this period can be attributed primarily to superior natural and human resources. Coal, iron ore, lumber, and petroleum were abundant and provided
the raw materials necessary for extensive economic growth. Steel production
served as a yardstick of industrial primacy, and the United States became a
major international producer after 1870. The exploitation of its petroleum resources led to extensive distilling and refining of lubricants, kerosene, and
other commercial fuels. By 1914, electricity would revolutionize industry in
America and replace water and steam as the major source of commercial
power. A vibrant agricultural system, exceptionally adaptable to mechaniza-
tion, became increasingly productive, even though industrial expansion came
to dominate the economy. Population growth continued at a steady pace, and
the demands for labor were met without serious setbacks throughout the
period.[5]

Many of these factors, which did in fact encourage industrial expansion in
the nineteenth century, also contributed directly to the creation or aggrava-
tion of urban pollution. Chief among these were the use of coal as a major
industrial energy source, the nature of the factory system, the process of industrial specialization and concentration, and the steadily increasing labor
force.

The smoky skies of the industrial city were a constant reminder of the
dominance of coal as an energy source in the late nineteenth and early twentieth centuries. The need for a plentiful, inexpensive, and effective source of
energy to provide power to run factory machinery and locomotives led to the
preeminence of coal. In the early 1830s, the discovery of huge anthracite (or
hard) coalfields in Pennsylvania furnished a high-quality fuel for industrial
use, especially in the expanding iron (and later steel) industry. After 1850, a
growing demand for iron in railroad construction and operation led to the
shift from charcoal to mineral coal as a metallurgical fuel. Although wood
was abundant and inexpensive west of the Mississippi, it was no longer available in large amounts in the vicinity of the eastern ironworks, especially in
Pennsylvania. By 1895, coal consumption began to surpass wood use, because
of the high demand for bituminous (or soft) coal by the steel and railroad industries. Wood continued to supply a substantial portion of the energy for
domestic heating, but coal became the primary fuel for manufacturing and
transportation.[6]

Using coal as a major energy source, industrial development increased markedly, which, in turn, contributed to the severity of air pollution in urban areas.
The most serious problem with coal, especially bituminous coal, was its devastating smoke, which left its mark on buildings, on laundry, and in the lungs
of urbanites. Since only a small portion of bituminous coal was consumed in

the generation of heat or power, much of the residue went directly into the air. The problem was greatest for cities with high concentrations of primary industries, such as Pittsburgh or St. Louis. Without vigorous regulation of pollution standards or the installation of adequate anti-smoke equipment, the smoke menace became critical.[7] The Edison Company, which generated electricity for New York City, was a constant source of smoke pollution in the 1910s and was repeatedly cited by sanitary inspectors. During times when hard coal was in short supply, New York Edison would use soft coal, thereby increasing its smoke output markedly. Often, to deter sanitary inspectors from photographing Edison's smokestacks for use as evidence in legal proceedings, the company placed scouts on the roof who warned the engineers to stop feeding the coal into the furnaces. Even so, the New York Health Department was able to institute twenty-eight actions against the company in the early 1900s.[8] Not until alternative fuels, such as natural gas, replaced coal, did the smoke problem begin to dissipate.

Coal provided the basic source of energy for large-scale industrial development, but the factory system created the managerial and operational means for the mass production of goods. By the 1850s, factories had become the dominant form of industrial enterprise, and they continued to expand in size as well as number into the twentieth century. In 1899, 40 percent of the approximately 500,000 industrial establishments of the country were factories. The scale of production was no less spectacular. Between 1879 and 1899, production of shoes and boots, for example, increased from 64,053 to 136,313. Between 1876 and 1899, raw steel production increased from 597,000 to 11,227,000 short tons.[9] As Blake McKelvey has suggested:

> The most important contribution of the industrial cities was the mounting output of their factories. Statistics show that the value added by manufacturing doubled between 1859 and 1879 and more than doubled again in the prosperous eighties, and yet again, despite two depressions, by 1909. The value added by manufacturing increased ten-fold in the half-century, almost trebling the increased value of farm products.[10]

By its very nature, the factory system encouraged the centralization of production in or near urban centers. Modern factories produced goods on a large scale, and location was of primary importance. Factories had to be near, or have ready access to, sources of raw materials, a sufficient labor force, and sizeable markets. Efficient transportation could compensate for some deficiencies, especially access to raw materials, but for the most part proximity to large cities meant the difference between economic success and failure.

These requirements for location of factories and their operational practices, however, contributed greatly to urban pollution. Factories, especially those in the textile, chemical, and iron and steel industries, were often constructed near waterways, since large quantities of water were needed to supply steam boilers or for various production processes such as cooling hot surfaces of metals or making chemical solutions. Waterways also provided the easiest and least expensive means of disposing of soluble or suspendable wastes. Studies of the impact of factories upon the environment suggest that, in 1900, 40 percent of the pollution load on American rivers was industrial in origin. (By 1968 that figure had increased to 80 percent.)[11] The "death" of New Jersey's Passaic River in the late nineteenth century was a classic illustration of how factories defiled their environment. Before it became badly polluted, the Passaic was a major recreational area and also the basis for a thriving commercial fishing industry. As urbanization and industrialization expanded after the Civil War, the volume of sewage and industrial waste that poured into the river forced the city of Newark to abandon the Passaic as a water supply. Pollution also ruined commercial fishing in the area, and soon homes along the waterway disappeared. During hot weather the river emitted such a stench that many factories were forced to close.[12]

Factories found simple methods of disposal for other forms of waste, too. Rubbish, garbage, slag, ashes, and scrap metals were often indiscriminately dumped on land. Referring to similar practices in England, Lewis Mumford notes, "In the Black Country of England, indeed, the huge slag heaps still look like geological formations: they decreased the available living space, cast a shadow on the land, and until recently presented an insoluble problem of either utilization or removal."[13] In the United States, slaughterhouses and meat packers were major land polluters. Meat packing, which began on farms or in small rural slaughterhouses, eventually concentrated in such cities as Chicago and St. Louis. In the New York/Brooklyn area alone, meat packers slaughtered more than 1.5 million animals in 1886. Foul smells permeated the area around the packinghouses, and animal wastes were simply dumped on vacant lots. Slaughterhouses and related animal processing industries such as tanneries, glue factories, and fat and bone boiling companies were often located in residential areas. The tanning industry contributed directly to water pollution, since hides were washed in urban watering places.[14]

The presence of a factory in a given location most often meant the deterioration of physical surroundings. Yet factories also contributed an even more insidious, if not so obvious, form of pollution—noise. Many factories produced excessively high noise levels, attributable to machinery that was inadequately lubricated or not equipped with mufflers or noise arresters. These high noise levels not only impaired the hearing of employees but also annoyed adjacent residential communities. In time, businessmen began to realize that some loud factory noises were caused by mechanical inefficiency and they then sought technical solutions, but more often they tolerated the din since production, not conservation, was the raison d'être for their factories.[15]

The concentration of factories in or near urban areas substantially increased the polluting capability of industrial development. It stands to reason that two factories in close proximity compound the stress on the environment. A single factory may be responsible for tainting a water supply, but two or more may make the water toxic.[16] From the late nineteenth century until 1920, American industry was concentrated in the Northeast. The so-called manufacturing belt included New England, the Middle Atlantic states, and the North Central states. At least three-fourths of American manufacturing was contained within the region bounded by the Great Lakes to the north, the Mississippi River to the west, and the Ohio River and the Mason-Dixon line to the south.[17] Within this area, manufacturing was centered in the cities. As early as 1900, no less than thirty-four of the forty-four states produced more than 50 percent of their manufactured goods in urban rather than rural areas. In eighteen states more than 75 percent of products came from urban factories. The most intense concentration was in New England, where 296 cities contained more than 75 percent of the region's population and 81 percent of the manufacturing establishments. The Middle Atlantic states were not far behind.[18] What made concentration of factories a critical environmental problem, aside from their density, was the fact that neither city authorities nor businessmen did much to confine factories to industrial areas or to segregate the most offensive industries from residential communities.

Industrial specialization in certain urban communities compounded the problems created by factory operations and concentration. Industrial specialization implies specialization of function and location—that is, special types of industry clustered in a single geographic location. Especially after 1870, there was a growing tendency for certain industries to congregate in or near specific urban centers for the sake of efficiency. Although this arrangement was economically sound, it often had disastrous environmental effects, especially if the industry was a blatant polluter. The Pennsylvania cities of McKeesport, Johnstown, and Pittsburgh, which produced large quantities of iron and steel, were inundated with environmental pollution. For instance, Pittsburgh in 1904 produced 63.8 percent of the national total of pig iron and 53.5 percent of the nation's steel.[19] Little wonder that Pittsburgh had the reputation of being "the smoky city." As the chamber of commerce explained during debate over a 1906 anti-smoke ordinance, "With the palls of smoke which darken our sky continually and the almost continuous deposits of soot, our dirty streets and grimy buildings are simply evidences of the difficulty under which we labor in any endeavor to present Pittsburgh as an ideal home city."[20] Slaughtering and meat packing, another industry notorious for pollution, was also highly concentrated in such cities as Chicago, St. Louis, and Kansas City. Chicago alone was responsible for 35.6 percent of the national market. Even in cities that did not produce the largest national percentage of a given product, the specialized industry located there might generate a high percentage of that city's total industrial output. For instance, South Omaha, Nebraska, produced only 9.7 percent of the nation's output in slaughtering and meat packing, but that industry represented 96.3 percent of South Omaha's total industry. Youngstown, Ohio, produced only 3.5 percent of the nation's iron and steel, but that was 81 percent of the city's industry.[21]

Human concentration in the cities matched industrial concentration as a major cause of pollution. The phenomenal increase in the American population in general and the urban population in particular during the nineteenth century is well known. It is staggering to consider that, between 1850 and 1920, the world population increased only 55 percent, while the population of the United States grew 357 percent. In 1850, the total population of the United States was approximately 23 million; by 1920 it was 106 million. As the population continued to enlarge, it concentrated increasingly in the cities, as demonstrated by table 1.1. Also by 1920, the number of urban areas rose from 392 to 2,722, and the number of cities with a population of 50,000 or more increased from 16 to 144.[22]

Table 1.1 *Urban Population in the United States*

Year	Urban Population [a]	Percentage of Total Population
1800	322,371	6
1860	6,216,518	20
1920	54,157,973	51

[a] Those living in cities with 2,500 or more population.

The amazing growth of the population was due primarily to spectacular increases in immigration and rural-to-urban migration. During these years almost 32 million people came to the United States, largely from southern and eastern Europe. By 1910, 41 percent of all urbanites in the nation were foreign-born, and approximately 80 percent of the new immigrants settled in the Northeast. Migration from countryside to city was also impressive; a conservative estimate is 15 million between 1880 and 1920. During those years, the proportion of the population living in rural America fell from 71.4 percent to 48.6 percent.[23]

One of the most obvious reasons for the urbanization of the American population was the dramatic shift of the labor force from agricultural to non-agricultural jobs. Between 1860 and 1900 the number of workers employed in manufacturing and construction quadrupled, while population increased less than two and a half times. In 1820, about 70 percent of the labor force was engaged in agricultural occupations, but by 1920 that proportion had dwindled to about 27 percent.[24]

With the urban population steadily on the rise and the bulk of the working force being attracted to industrial jobs, the cities underwent an incredible physical strain. None suffered the repercussions of the environmental crisis more than the working class. Overcrowding was the worst of the problems. Forced to live close to their places of employment, many workers found themselves crammed into the burgeoning slums in the central city. Housing was at a premium; few could afford to buy single-unit dwellings, so they rented what they could. In his classic expose of tenement conditions in New York, *How the Other Half Lives*, Jacob Riis recounted:

> Thousands were living in cellars. There were three hundred underground lodginghouses in the city when the Health Department was organized. Some fifteen years before that [about 1852] the old Baptist Church in Mulberry Street, just off Chatham Street, had been sold, and the rear half of the frame structure had been converted into tenements that with their swarming population became the scandal even of that reckless age.[25]

In a seller's market, landlords did little to upgrade the deteriorating tenements and converted buildings that many workers were forced to use as residences. Often families would share quarters with other individuals or groups. David Brody describes living conditions of Slavic steelworkers in Pennsylvania:

> The inadequate dwellings were greatly overcrowded. The boarding boss and his family slept in one downstairs room in the standard four-room farm house. The kitchen was set aside for eating and living purposes, although it, too, often served as a bedroom. Upstairs the boss crammed double beds which were in use night and day when the mill was running full. Investigators came upon many cases of extreme crowding. Thirty-three Serbians and their boarding boss lived in a five-room house in Steelton. In Sharpsburg, Pennsylvania, an Italian family and nine boarders existed without running water or toilet in four rooms on the third floor of a ramshackle tenement.

Brody went on to state, according to an Immigration Commission report, that the number per sleeping room in immigrant households averaged about three, with quite a few having four or as many as six or more per sleeping room.[26]

Not only were individual dwellings overcrowded, but neighborhood densities were staggering. The average block density in lower Manhattan increased from 157.5 persons in 1820 to 272.5 persons in 1850. New York City's Sanitary District "A" averaged 986.4 people to the acre for thirty-two acres in 1894—or approximately 30,000 people in a space of five or six blocks. In comparison, Bombay, India—the next most crowded area in the world—had 759.7 people per acre, and Prague, the European city with the worst slum conditions, had only 485.4 people per acre.[27]

Such crowded conditions and such limited city services provided fertile ground for health and sanitation problems. Many workers had little choice but to live in the least desirable sections of the city, usually close to the smoke-belching factories where they worked or near marshy bogs and stagnant pools, which speculators could not develop into prime residential communities. City services, especially sewage and refuse collection, failed to keep up with the demand. Smoke from wood-burning and coal-burning stoves and fireplaces fouled the air of the inner city, and the noise level in some areas reached a roar. Contemporary accounts of slum life were filled with horror stories of unsanitary living conditions. Jane Addams, in *Twenty Years at Hull House*, recalled the shock of English visitors over living conditions in Chicago:

> The most obvious faults [of the city] were those connected with
> the congested housing of the immigrant population, nine/tenths
> of them from the country, who carried on all sorts of traditional
> activities in the crowded tenements. That a group of Greeks
> should be permitted to slaughter sheep in a basement, that Italian
> women should be allowed to sort over rags collected from the
> city dumps, not only within the city limits but in a court swarm-
> ing with little children, that immigrant bakers should continue
> unmolested to bake bread for their neighbors in unspeakably
> filthy spaces under the pavement, appeared incredible to visitors
> accustomed to careful city regulations.[28]

In another episode, Jacob Riis told how a family with boarders in New York City's Cedar Street fed hogs in their cellar, which "contained eight or ten loads of manure."[29]

These impressions of living conditions were only the most dramatic recountings of life in the slums. The statistics on health problems, disease, and high mortality rates were even more sobering. In one of the most widely publicized epidemics of its day, Memphis lost almost 10 percent of its population in 1873 to yellow fever, which ostensibly originated in its slums. In New Orleans, typhoid was spread throughout the city by sewage that oozed from the unpaved streets. In "Murder Bay," not far from the White House in Washington, D.C., black families picked their dinners out of garbage cans and dumps. Mortality figures for the area were consistently twice as high as in white neighborhoods; infant mortality in 1900 ranged as high as 317 per thousand. By 1870, the infant mortality rate in New York was 65 percent higher than in 1810.[30] The enumeration of statistics could go on and on; the sad fact is that the personal tragedies of families in the crowded slums of the major cities were part of massive health, sanitation, and pollution problems that could not be corrected without the total commitment of the community. As industrial development continued to push westward, the environmental crisis of the Northeast spread with it, creating regionwide as well as citywide environmental problems.

Industrial expansion alone does not explain the severity and complexity of the environmental crisis of the cities. To suggest that an exploitative producing class intentionally devastated the urban environment for the sake of economic gain and at the expense of the working class is too simplistic an answer. Certainly the compulsion for limitless economic growth and prosperity, which underlay industrial expansion, blinded the so-called robber barons and their supporters to the deterioration of the environment which that development produced. The primacy of economic gain over the maintenance of a tolerable physical environment was, however, an idea not restricted to producers. Furthermore, the defilement of the environment was not a conscious choice between two well-defined alternatives. Numerous factors, other than the impact of industrial development, threatened the preservation of a palatable urban quality of life, none more significantly than the physical form that the industrial cities took and their distinctive patterns of growth.

The industrial city, characterized by urban sprawl, rapidly multiplying suburbs, an ever-rising skyline, and a congested downtown area, contrasted sharply with the "walking city" of the previous era. After the 1870s, the intimacy and homogeneity of the walking city virtually disappeared. Preindustrial urban areas were small enough that citizens could walk or ride in carriages or omnibuses to most places, but in the industrial city vast growth made mass transit the only viable means of travel. The relatively spacious neighborhoods in the walking city had allowed for at least some casual contact among social classes. Rigid segregation of residences was avoided, and people, both rich and poor, tended to live close to where they worked. In the industrial city, rapid growth constantly shifted residential neighborhoods and economic districts, eventually producing more rigid class delineations. With the extension of effi-

cient transit lines into surrounding districts, relatively affluent urbanites moved
out of the walking city into the more spacious suburbs. This tendency quickly
produced well-defined residential subdivisions, divided primarily along income
lines. Those who lacked the economic means to move to suburbia were rele-
gated to the central city residential areas, which often degenerated into slums.
The wealthiest citizens frequently moved to the farthest reaches of the city's
environs and took up lavish estates. Middle-income groups inhabited the more
diversified series of suburbs between the inner city and the country estates.
As a result, the downtown area of the walking city, which had once been distinguished by warehouses, small financial establishments, and shops, was transformed into a congested business district, where retailing became the major
function. Store owners conducted much of their retail business for the middle-
and upper-income commuters who came downtown to shop. Many of the larger
manufacturers relocated away from the downtown area along intercity transportation routes. This movement of sites often led to the creation of satellite
communities, which the metropolitan area would later absorb. In his pioneering study of the process of urban growth, *Streetcar Suburbs*, Sam Bass Warner,
Jr., concludes, "With the new metropolis and all its changes the ancient problems of the large cities once more came to life: the individual members of
urban society became isolated within a physical and social network which had
passed their comprehension and control."[31]

Since the industrial city grew skyward at its core as well as expanding outward into the surrounding districts, not one but two distinct processes of expansion contributed to its environmental degradation. In the central city, the
concentration of people, businesses, and transportation facilities, plus the
rising skyline, produced one pattern; rapid suburban development produced
the other. Together, the pollution problems of the city's core and its suburbs
contributed to a complex matrix of environmental degradation.

The pollution problems of the central city were much more obvious, and
initially more serious, than those of the suburbs. The growth of the local consumer market and technological innovations in transportation, communication,
and construction made possible the high concentration of retail stores and
service-oriented firms in the central business district. The industrial city re-
versed the previous wide dispersal of retail establishments that had characterized the walking city. According to Howard P. Chudacoff,

> Chicago's Loop represented the ultimate central business district.
> As one official described it in 1910: "Within an area of less than
> a square mile there are found the railway terminals and business
> offices, the big retail stores, the wholesale and jobbing businesses,

the financial centers, the main offices of the chief firms of the city,
a considerable proportion of the medical and dental professions,
the legal profession, the city and county governments, the post
office, the courts, the leading social and political clubs, the hotels,
theaters, Art Institute, principal libraries, labor headquarters, and
a great number of lesser factors of city life."[32]

The high density of retail outlets and other attractions in a central location
made them accessible to a wider cross-section of the community, especially to
commuters. Not until the 1920s, when the automobile began to dominate urban transportation, did specialty stores and sprawling shopping centers and
malls situated in the suburbs begin to wrest shoppers away from the central
business districts.

City governments were ill-prepared to provide adequate sanitation services
in the central city. Garbage and rubbish accumulated in the streets faster than
it could be collected. Street cleaning crews in Manhattan collected as much as
1,100 tons of garbage a day during the summer months and approximately
612 tons during the winter. Nonetheless, much of the refuse, especially away
from the major thoroughfares, was not picked up at all. In almost all the major cities, collection and disposal methods were haphazard and technologically
primitive. New York street teams carelessly collected the garbage, loaded it on
barges, and dumped it at sea. In Philadelphia, inefficient contractors disposed
of the city's wastes. In St. Louis, Boston, Baltimore, and Chicago, much of
the refuse was simply carted to open dumps near centers of population. And,
in Cleveland, no public provision was made for gathering household garbage
until the late 1880s.[33]

Similar problems existed with waterborne wastes. Joel A. Tarr coined the
phrase "presewer period" to refer to the years between 1800 and 1880 in the
United States. During that time a relatively primitive system of wastewater
removal was in effect. Human waste was deposited in privy vaults and cesspools, which municipal or private scavengers cleaned periodically. For most
of this period, no sewers for human waste removal existed; the only sewers
were those used for the removal of storm or surface water. After 1880, many
cities installed elaborate sewer systems, which helped alleviate immediate health
problems. These systems, however, did not service all portions of the community and often polluted rivers and streams where the raw sewage was deposited.[34] In the industrial cities of the period an "out of sight, out of mind"
mentality prevailed: as long as someone removed wastes from the immediate
range of the senses, the problem was solved. Unfortunately, cities were not
even capable of getting their wastes "out of sight." Citizens and city officials

paid little attention to the hazards created by flushing raw sewage into the ocean, lakes, or rivers, open burning of rubbish, or indiscriminate dumping of uncovered garbage on vacant lots.

The technological advances that made possible the physical development of the central business districts also contributed to pollution problems. The balloon frame, the steel girder, and the elevator facilitated the construction of multistory buildings, thus making land use more economical. Yet these innovations encouraged high-density building, which further strained meager city services and added to congestion problems. Advances in transportation—the horsecar, trolley, and electric streetcar—exacerbated congestion and sometimes contributed directly to pollution. Horsecars had several drawbacks, the most serious being disposal of manure. A single horse discharged gallons of urine and nearly twenty pounds of fecal matter into the streets daily, which not only posed a health hazard but also deteriorated streetcar rails. Many horsecar firms maintained manure pits as income supplements, but storing this offensive fertilizer angered the local residents. The environmental problems posed by horsecars were considerable and widespread, since more than 100,000 horses and mules were pulling 18,000 horsecars on 3,500 miles of track throughout the nation by the mid-1880s.[35]

Phasing out the horsecar did not end pollution problems stemming from inner-city transportation. Steam-driven commuter trains produced dense smoke and encountered substantial public opposition. Engineers and inventors had little success in finding solutions to emissions problems or harnessing adequate alternative power sources until electricity was introduced into the traction business. And, even though the electric streetcar alleviated some of the air pollution problems in the streets (coal-generated power produced other sources), it was not free of difficulties. For a time, the public was quite fearful of electricity, and this fear was aggravated by several fatal electrical accidents. Even when most of the electrical problems were resolved, noise pollution remained. Increased transportation in the inner city substantially raised the general noise level, adding screeching brakes, grinding gears, whining motors, and clanging bells to the din.[36] As traffic congestion became more serious, cities had to construct new and wider streets and alleys. And, while improved surfaces reduced mud and dust, they also contributed to greater noise and added more surface area for street crews to keep clean.

Needless to say, contemporaries had little inkling of the long-term effects of high-density building on the urban ecology. The wholesale uprooting and destruction of plants and trees to make way for stores, terminals, houses, and streets reduced oxygen generation in the city's core. Also, wildlife in the area lost its natural protection and habitat. The park movement, which began in

New York City in the 1850s with the authorization for Central Park, helped somewhat in reducing the wanton destruction of natural life in urban areas. The great landscape architect, Frederick Law Olmsted, was one of a few Americans who emphasized that parks were a "palliative" for urban ills. Believing that the movement of people "townward" was a permanent phenomenon, Olmsted became concerned with the debilitating effects of the city upon the health and well-being of its citizenry. He was convinced that the air in the cities "carrie[d] into the lungs highly corrupt and irritating matters, the action of which tends strongly to vitiate all our sources of vigor." Parks and parkways were a major way to reclaim the urban atmosphere from the effects of the noxious elements poured into it,[37] but even Olmsted's exhortations and the success of the park movement throughout the United States could not repair the damage already done or to be done in the future.

Outward expansion of the industrial cities, in the form of suburbs, produced a variant to the environmental problems of the inner cities. The greatest cliché about suburban development in the nineteenth century is that middle- and upper-income people, who wished to escape the inner cities, fled to pristine suburbs where the urban blight could not engulf them. In reality, suburban development was not so simplistic or uniform as the cliché suggests. Suburbs of varying types cropped up around the cities—working-class suburbs, ethnic communities, white-collar suburbs.[38] And, from a broad environmental perspective, these outgrowths rarely escaped for long many of the pollution problems of the inner city. Early on, suburbs suffered from their distance from the major cities that supplied needed services. Eventually, suburbs suffered from their proximity to the cities, being engulfed by many of the problems they had tried to avoid.

The initial detachment from the central city, which suburbanites prized, sometimes worked as a disadvantage. The need to extend services to the suburbs was crucial. Sometimes the building of sewer lines, like good transportation lines, was a precondition of suburban expansion, but sometimes it was not. In pre-1870 Boston, such services were haphazard for the new home builders, and little effort was made to coordinate the development of city services with the building of new dwellings.[39] Finding adequate water supplies was a related problem, which was intensified by the competition between suburbs and industrial cities. Many waterways became overtaxed from being required to absorb wastes from the inner city as well as from nearby suburbs; they were often lost as water supplies to both. Sometimes demands on a given waterway for pure water were too great, and suburbs had to seek distant sources. One solution, which became an inevitability for some suburbs, was annexation to the city in order to get adequate services. For example, the suburbs of Morrisania and West Farms, finding it difficult to locate a source of high-quality water on their own, voted to join New York City in 1873. Between 1867 and 1873, Boston successfully annexed Roxbury, Dorchester, Brighton, and West Roxbury, largely because these suburbs had lower water tables and were being choked on their own sewage, which was dumped into the tidal estuaries.[40]

Eventually, many of the newer suburbs were able to overcome some of the vulnerabilities that had plagued the earlier ones and establish decent city services. But the continual growth in number and size of suburbs insured that many would ultimately suffer the same congestion and density problems of the inner cities. It should be remembered that the transit lines, which had helped produce the nineteenth-century suburbs, tended to cluster people rather than to scatter them along the commuter routes. Often the result was a series of densely populated smaller communities strewn along the periphery of the urban core. For instance, the Boston suburbs of Roxbury, West Roxbury, and Dorchester grew dramatically. In 1870, after about fifteen years of the horse-car lines, the population of the three towns was 60,000; by 1900, it was 227,000. If these suburbs had been combined into a single city, it would have rivaled Minneapolis, Louisville, and Jersey City in size.[41]

The habitual practice of annexation, implemented by most large cities, provided only another means for suburbs to become engulfed by central city pollution problems. Many of the annexations were incredibly expansive. In 1899, Chicago swallowed up Hyde Park township, quadrupling the city's land area and raising the population to nearly a million. In what amounted to the most important boundary adjustment in American urban history, New York City absorbed Brooklyn, Queens, Staten Island, and part of the Bronx in 1898. The size of the city thus increased from 40 to 300 square miles and the population jumped by well over a million.[42] Before 1880, many suburbs regarded annexation as a way to tap the superior services and resources of the major cities. However, the heavy demand for extension of services, sometimes over many miles, severely taxed the abilities of the major cities. The process of deterioration that had inundated central cities often spread to suburbs.

By the late nineteenth century, the saturation of cities and suburbs with air, water, refuse, and noise pollution finally produced an environmental consciousness among the complacent citizenry. Until this time, almost everyone had ignored questions of environmental quality. Their desire for economic prosperity had cut across class lines, and most individuals had resigned themselves to pollution as an inconvenience to be endured. However, it soon became evident that industrial expansion, which made urban centers advantageous places to work, also made them unbearable places to live. Predictably, frustration over the quality of life in the cities was greatest for those who did not have the means of separating their working environment from their residential environment. However, even those who fled the inner city for the suburbs could not be assured of escaping pollution. Although suburbs provided relief from some environmental problems, commuters still had to contend with the deteriorating central city at least part of the time in their capacities as workers and consumers. Early protests against pollution, therefore, tended to be responses to the obvious irritations, such as bad-tasting water, eye-smarting smoke, stench-ridden garbage, or noisy machinery. The concept of pollution as "nuisance" dominated these early complaints. Indeed, "nuisance" was a popular contemporary term, which urbanites applied indiscriminately to any more serious environmental problems. Contemporary observers often referred to all manner of ills in this way: "the noise nuisance," "hooting nuisance," "the garbage nuisance," "the smoke nuisance." As the noted sanitarian, John S. Billings, stated,

> The great majority of the dwellers in our cities have not, heretofore, taken any active personal interest in the sanitary condition of their respective towns. They may grumble occasionally when some nuisance is forced on their notice, but, as a rule, they look on the city as a sort of hotel, with the details of the management of which they have no desire to become acquainted.[43]

Their ignorance, as well as their acceptance of unrestrained industrial growth as a positive good, produced the urbanites' initial mild response to pollution. Few city dwellers possessed a broad ecological perspective about pollution problems because such an outlook did not exist at the time, even within the scientific community. The biological revolution of the 1880s helped demonstrate that germs, rather than noxious smells or miasmas, were responsible for many diseases, but not until the twentieth century did the scientific community begin to acquire sophisticated notions about the relationship between pollutants and health problems.[44] Needless to say, social scientists had yet to analyze the complex interrelationships between urban/industrial growth and environmental degradation. No wonder most Americans were unprepared to confront urban pollution—no one had a total grasp of the problem.

By the turn of the century, however, sporadic protests against the irritations of a dirty city led to individual and group efforts to deal with smoke, sewage, garbage, and noise. Demands for cleansing the environment grew out of citizens' complaints for the most part, but reformers occasionally pursued substantive changes in nuisance laws, industrial operations, municipal services, and even public behavior and conduct. Sometimes reform came from within municipal health and public works departments. Environmental reform never took the shape of a permanent or comprehensive movement during the period. Instead, it was an outgrowth of protests against specific problems, usually on the local level, but occasionally state-, region-, or nationwide.

Initially, environmental reform was a response to obvious health hazards. Thus, public awareness focused a step beyond the nuisance stage, especially if the health hazard was cholera, yellow fever, typhoid fever, or dysentary. In time, the concept of "health hazard" expanded to include such afflictions as lung disease or emotional disorders associated with high noise levels. The lack of medical sophistication sometimes produced unwarranted fears of foul smells, miasmas, and water discoloration. Speaking about the apparent dangers of "sewer gas," sanitary engineer Colonel George E. Waring, Jr., stated:

> It is in the decomposition of [household wastes] in soil-pipes and in sewers, alone, that we are to find the seat of the enemy of which we hear so much under the name of "sewer gas." This much decried and insidious sewer-gas is probably entitled to most of the blame it receives for its own direct action, and to as much more from the fact that it so often acts as a vehicle for the germs, or causative particle of specific diseases.[45]

The environmental reformers perhaps faulted in the direction of exaggerating a potential threat, but that was certainly preferable to a lack of caution.

By the 1890s, the concern for health expanded into a broader environmental perspective, indicating that reformers were beginning to see pollution not simply as an irritant but as an unwanted by-product of industrialization. However, pollution was linked with wastefulness and inefficiency in such a way as to avoid the conclusion that industrial activity was intrinsically responsible for despoiling the environment. Smoke abatement advocates, for example, often charged that air pollution not only produced a health hazard but graphically demonstrated the squandering of natural resources. One observer, extolling the virtues of technical improvements made to a furnace of the Power Building in Cincinnati, stated: "The large Power Building at Eighth and Sycamore for the past year has been a standing monument of what a good appliance and careful firing will do. The stack has been and is absolutely smokeless, and the saving in coal bills has been over twenty-five percent."[46] Anti-noise advocates also drew ammunition from the link between pollution and inefficiency. They often argued that excessive noise in factories worked against high productivity by employees. As Raymond Smilor suggests, "Noise was a liability in business; it cost money. Although it failed to appear on the balance sheet, noise showed in the profit-and-loss statement as an unrealized economy."[47]

Critics of environmental degradation were not always so pragmatic. To some, pollution was a sign of barbarity. E. L. Godkin asserted that excessive noise "invades the house like a troop of savages on a raid, and respects neither age nor sex." "Indeed," another observer suggested, "there is no more significant distinction between ancient and modern cities than their respective attitudes towards the evils of [the garbage problem] ."[48] To many reformers, the curtailing of pollution was one measure of civilization. The "White City" of the 1893 Chicago World's Fair and "Hygeia," the mythical Victorian city of health, were standards toward which to strive. After all, the city was supposed to put in order what was chaotic in nature. Citizens who littered the streets or defiled their physical surroundings were classified with cavemen or even animals. The interest in the City Aesthetic, best expressed in the City Beautiful movement of the 1890s, was a very subjective indictment of pollution. Many people continued to equate pollutants, such as factory smoke, with material progress. But advocacy of the aesthetic elevated concern about the environment from the purely utilitarian realm.

What gave environmental reform a broader appeal and national attention was its almost inevitable association with progressivism in the 1890s and beyond. Since progressive reform was rooted in the industrial city, environmental protesters had little trouble associating themselves with the larger movement. Despite the diversity of the Progressives, they shared several common beliefs and values that environmental reformers could readily accept. Progressives were trying to bring order out of the chaos caused by the transition of the United States from a rural/agrarian to an urban/industrial society. They had faith in the inherent good of humankind and believed progress was possible by eliminating evils produced by the physical and social environment. They placed great confidence in the ability to measure problems scientifically and to resolve them through the efforts of an expert elite. Of course, the Progressives' limitations were as unbounded as their optimism. They couched their reforms in moralism, often declaring a monopoly on determining what was right and what was wrong. Their faith in simplistic solutions to complex problems was naive at best, and, although they decried poverty, injustice, and corruption, they were paternalistic and even hostile to those who fell outside their societal norms.[49]

Yet the conviction of Progressives that the environment in which humans lived could be improved and their adherence to scientific solutions gave substantial support to the protest against urban degradation. Several leading Progressives, especially those with strong interests in urban affairs, were important advocates of environmental reform. Among these were Theodore Roosevelt; Albert Shaw, editor of *Review of Reviews*; Hazen Pingree, mayor of Detroit and governor of Michigan; "Golden Rule" Jones, mayor of Toledo; and Tom Johnson, mayor of Cleveland. Likewise, environmental reformers often became strong adherents to various progressive reforms. The link to progressivism is clear in the following statement by municipal engineer William Mayo Venable:

> The reason why the problem of refuse disposal is receiving an ever-increasing amount of attention from engineers, municipal authorities, and from the American public does not lie in the newness of the problem, but rather in an intellectual awakening of the people. The same spirit that leads men to realize the corruption of politics and business, and to attempt to remedy those conditions by adopting new methods of administration and new laws, also leads to a realization of the primitiveness of the methods of waste disposal still employed by many communities, and to a consequent desire for improvement.[50]

By the early twentieth century, environmental protest had undergone some important changes. The appeal for reform had broadened substantially from the earliest complaints about nuisances. Major cities began to grapple with the problems of sewage and garbage collection and disposal. Civic and professional organizations, including smoke and noise abatement committees, were putting pressure on city government for change. And the association of environmental reform with progressivism had brought some national attention to several urban problems. Yet environmental reform had serious limitations during this period, which kept it from exerting the kind of influence necessary to achieve adequate solutions. The most severe restriction was the lack of what might be called "environmental perspective." Pollution problems were most often approached as isolated cases. The smoke problem was considered independent of the noise problem and the noise problem independent of the sewage problem. Rarely did environmental protest groups confront pollution comprehensively, as part of an overall urban crisis. In fact, other than civic reform groups, which developed interests in many phases of urban life, there were no organizations that were broadly concerned with environmental quality. Urban reformers had yet to consider pollution in terms of its root causes—the processes of urbanization and industrialization; instead, they concentrated on the results and consequences of pollution. As commendable as their efforts were, the reformers, as the well-worn cliché states, "could not see the forest for the trees."

The order in which urban reformers confronted specific pollution problems indicates the crisis orientation of environmental protest in this period. Almost simultaneously with the advent of industrial cities came demands for the distribution of pure water and improvements in sewerage. Because urban centers were so dependent on good water supplies and basic sanitation requirements, municipal governments required little persuasion to provide adequate service and to eliminate the grossest defects. However, the public regarded refuse simply as a nuisance rather than as a serious threat until the 1890s, when mounds of waste were so high and so plentiful that the citizens could not avoid them any longer. Demands for smoke abatement arose as the use of coal rapidly increased during the late 1880s and early 1890s. Not surprisingly, noise was the last of the major pollution problems of the era to gain public attention, largely because it was a much more elusive form of pollution. Noise abatement efforts did not begin until the mid-1890s.

Rallying to combat the most flagrant pollution problems, protesters and reformers rarely found it easy to agree on solutions. As stated above, environmental reformers shared many of the characteristics of the middle-class reformers of the period. Various factors, especially occupation, influenced the environmental goals of the reformers and often limited collective action. Sanitarians and public health officials, who played a central role in many reform efforts, tended to give priority to high standards of health as a goal of pollution control. Many engineers who became involved in environmental reform placed great stock in finding technological solutions to pollution, not simply for the sake of health but also for the efficient use of machinery and energy resources. Civic reform groups, especially those dominated by women, represented the nonspecialist's interest in the health question; they generally accepted the efficacy of a technical solution to pollution and placed substantial emphasis upon aesthetic benefits of improving the urban environment. The societal role played by women as housewives and mothers also tended to dictate their perspective. Similarly, the occupational interests of other groups dictated their behavior. For instance, political leaders had to consider environmental issues that would appease their constituencies, and businessmen sought to protect their special interests. Efforts at compromise were always difficult. Overlapping interests made clear environmental goals almost impossible to achieve.[51]

Of all those involved with environmental problems, city planners seemed the most likely group to combine the myriad interests of reformers and devise a plan of action. But even this group contributed little to a comprehensive solution to environmental problems between 1870 and 1920. City planning did not become a profession until about 1909, when the National Conference on City Planning was founded. Consequently, planners as a group did not exert much influence over the environmental reform efforts of the late nineteenth and early twentieth centuries. Pioneers in planning, such as Frederick

Law Olmsted, were influential, but the tendency was for environmental issues to influence the development of planning rather than vice versa. Such movements as conservation, housing reform, the City Beautiful movement, and the Garden City movement actually shaped the planning profession.[52] In a provocative paper delivered at the 1976 meeting of the Organization of American Historians, Jon A. Peterson argued persuasively that the sanitary reform movement, which influenced, among other things, demands for improved sewerage, "led to urban planning—or to something like it."[53] Even after city planning was established as a profession, it played only a limited role in resolving existing pollution problems. Planners, of course, were deeply involved in housing reform, land-use controls, and social manipulation in the form of zoning regulations, but not as chief architects of a comprehensive anti-pollution plan. After 1920, the profession was gradually transforming the planners' role from that of reformer to that of technician. As Roy Lubove argues:

> Increasingly . . . the professional planner evolved into a technician
> who minimized normative goals—structural or institutional inno-
> vation—and became the prophet of the "City Scientific" or "City
> Efficient." Technical matters relating to zoning, law, finance,
> capital expenditure, and transportation became his province. He
> did not seek fundamental changes in urban form and structure,
> but projected existing demographic and institutional trends into
> the future as a basis for planning.[54]

If environmental reformers were fortunate enough to overcome competing occupational interests, to compromise rival goals, and to work out a potential solution to an existing pollution threat, they still faced the task of convincing the city fathers to accept their plan. Reform was worthless without implementation, and implementation was difficult at a time when the line between individual and municipal responsibility was still unclear. Few government officials could make a distinction between environmental degradation as a citywide problem requiring community action and as a problem of personal discomfort requiring private action. Between 1870 and 1920, many cities were just attempting to establish home rule in basic areas of governance. In the 1850s, rural-dominated state legislatures began to exercise extensive control over the major cities in their states, especially by creating independent departments and boards as a means of decentralizing authority. The industrial cities were not very successful in restoring home rule and often were vulnerable to control by political machines that simply overlooked the directives of the legislatures. Machine—or boss—rule was based upon personal loyalties. Bosses actually sustained themselves through the disorder of the industrial cities and used political power as a marketable commodity, with patronage going to the highest bidder.[55] In this kind of system, large-scale environmental reform, based on notions of community responsibility, was virtually impossible. Even with the establishment of so-called reform governments, a solution to environmental problems was no easy task. Commission and city manager systems of government, for instance, which were intended to allow efficient execution of municipal responsibilities, often swapped the working-class constituency of the boss for a middle- or upper-class constituency. If middle-class reformers applied pressure for environmental reform in a city dominated by middle-class leaders, change was more likely. If the protests came from the working class, the results might be quite different. The special interests that influenced most municipal governments of the period played a large part in determining municipal priorities and could work against communitywide solutions to problems, especially environmental problems that depended upon comprehensive action.[56]

As the following selections will illustrate, most cities responded fairly rapidly and effectively in those areas where solutions had to be found in order to avoid rampant health hazards. This was especially true with respect to the search for pure water supplies and improved sewerage systems. However, water pollution per se was not eliminated; industrial wastes and raw household sewage continued to pour into waterways without proper treatment or filtration. Numerous cities adopted new methods of collection and disposal of refuse, but these methods did nothing to reduce ever-growing quantities of solid waste and often created alternate forms of pollution, such as smoke from incineration of rubbish. Some cities effectively reduced smoke pollution through better regulation of coal-burning practices, but smoke did not disappear entirely and ultimately even more toxic forms of air pollution were added from other sources, especially automobiles. Anti-noise ordinances and new technological devices challenged the problem of noise but did not eliminate it. The successes of environmental reform efforts, therefore, were often ephemeral or incomplete. A comprehensive solution to environmental blight in the cities was still a dream. Yet it would be unfair to overlook the major accomplishment of environmental protests of the era—a heightened environmental awareness or consciousness that made urbanites take notice of many of the threats posed by this first environmental crisis in the cities.

Both the environmental problems in the wake of accelerating industrialization and the nascent environmental consciousness of urbanites were legacies for the cities of the post–World War I decades. After 1920, urban growth changed more in degree than in form. Growth for many industrial cities in this period meant not only expansion of their primary industries but industrial diversification as well. These "metropolises," in the words of Allen M. Wakstein, served as "centers for a hinterland." Their economic, political, and social importance had to be measured in regional terms.[57]

Metropolitan growth perpetuated many of the environmental problems of the 1850-1920 period and also created some new ones. The automobile, more than any other technological innovation, changed the face of the American city. In 1903 there were fewer than 10,000 automobiles in the United States; by the end of the 1920s there were approximately 26 million. The automobile in the metropolis was not an expensive toy but an integral part of life. As the automobile became a vital component of American society, demands for more and better roads increased, and federal, state, and local governments made a massive commitment to road building. The Highway Aid Act of 1956 was the foremost expression of the national commitment to the primacy of automobile transportation. It created the National Systems Interstate and Defense Highway, to be financed 90 percent by federal revenues (in some cases 95 percent). The 41,000-mile system was to include routes that would connect nearly all American cities with a population of 50,000 or more. The act also created the Highway Trust Fund, financed by federal taxes on lubricating oils and gasoline as well as excise taxes on buses and trucks. Thus a self-perpetuating construction financing system was created. The $100-billion-plus commitment to highway development helped insure the dependence of the United States on a one-dimensional transportation system that virtually eliminated mass transit in many communities.[58]

The decline of mass transit and the rise of the automobile did not diminish suburban growth; on the contrary, these two developments transformed it. Boulevards, and later expressways, accelerated the movement of urbanites and rural dwellers to the suburbs, thus enhancing urban sprawl. Although the Great Depression in the 1930s slowed suburban growth, the coming of peace in 1945 following World War II brought with it a new suburban scourge. Increased road construction and a housing boom hurried the process. Between 1946 and 1955 more than twice as many new houses were constructed as in the previous fifteen years. In the peak year, 1950, over one million single-family dwellings were begun. Shopping areas, new office buildings, and chain restaurants followed the mass of people into the suburbs, while retail businesses in the central city declined. The heyday of the great downtown stores such as Marshall Field in Chicago, Rich's in Atlanta, Jordan Marsh in Boston, Gimbel's and Macy's in New York, and John Wanamaker's in Philadelphia was coming to an end in 1930 as companies like Sears, Roebuck, and Company were embracing the concept of "America on wheels." The new suburbs were designed for the automobile; no conveniences were within walking distance anymore. Soon two cars would become a virtual necessity for middle-class families who wanted to exploit what the new surroundings had to offer.[59]

The automobile and suburban growth added new dimensions to urban environmental problems. Suburban expansion sapped the central city of its economic life and contributed to its physical degeneration. Despite the flight of middle-class America to suburbia, the central city remained congested, as expanded freeway systems brought more automobiles into and through town. The more freeways that were built in order to move traffic through cities quickly, the more traffic there was. The Los Angeles Harbor Freeway (opened in 1954), designed to carry a maximum of 100,000 cars a day, was averaging 168,000 cars a day by 1956. As the freeways brought more people into the central business districts, the pressure on existing parking spaces increased. To alleviate the strain, cities erected high-rise parking garages after clearing many older buildings. By the late 1960s, at least a third of the land area of each major city had gone for parking space in downtown sections. Road building and parking-space development also played a major role in reducing the amount of low-cost housing available to the poor, thus intensifying inner-city social dislocations.[60]

The automobile has contributed its own unique forms of pollution. Those who touted its arrival as a blessing for the street cleaner could not have imagined what a poor trade that was. Americans are only beginning to become aware of the monumental problem posed by junked cars strewn about the landscape. And then there is smog. The toxic fumes of the automobile have overwhelmed the metropolises and extended the bands of air pollution many miles away from the urban centers, even into the countryside. Smaller communities, which prided themselves on absence of industrial air pollution, are subjected to ubiquitous gasoline fumes that have drifted miles away from their place of origin. The approximately 110 million automobiles in this country emit into the atmosphere carbon monoxide, oxides of nitrogen, lead, hydrocarbons, and waste heat in high concentrations. In small amounts, these pollutants can cause headaches, nausea, dizziness, ringing in the ears, and breathing difficulties. In large doses they can cause pulmonary fibrosis and emphysema, which may result in death or serious illness. Recent federal legislation, such as the 1967 Air Quality Act, has been implemented to reduce health and atmospheric threats from smog and other air pollutants, but the problems are far from solved. In the early 1970s, air pollution in the cities stemmed from motor fuel consumption, electrical power production, and industrial activity of various kinds. Since World War II, total power production has increased 662 percent, motor fuel consumption 100 percent, and electrical power production 276 percent.[61]

Other creations of modern technology have been responsible for new sources of pollution. Public air transportion, especially jetliners, has contributed new, disruptive sources of air and noise pollution. The proliferation of nuclear reactors for generating electricity has unleashed ominous potential environmental threats. Despite the assurances of experts that nuclear reactors are safe, many individuals and some groups remain skeptical. Visions of the destructive power of the atomic bomb and the resulting fallout are not easily dispelled.[62] Furthermore, experimentation with new chemicals, pesticides, and synthetic materials provides additional sources of air and water pollution. Joseph M. Petulla has pointed out that "synthetic industries grew exponentially between 1946 and 1970 in parallel proportions with electricity and oil consumption. During the same period air and water pollution in the United States increased from 200% to 1,000% depending on the source and region."[63] The advent of the plastic age and the widespread acceptance of packaged and canned products have led not only to substantially more waste but also to less easily disposable waste. Nonbiodegradable packaging produces serious problems for those engaged in refuse disposal.

Since the 1920s, public awareness of environmental problems has also undergone some important adjustments. Certainly the acceptance of pollution as a partner of economic gain is still apparent. The energy crisis of 1973 made that quite evident. The fear of economic stagnation or regression led many citizens and leaders to rationalize putting aside high environmental standards, at least temporarily, as a means of encouraging industries to increase the production of goods and services. In his first environmental policy message, President Gerald R. Ford said on 15 August 1974 (six days after his inauguration) that the "zero economic growth" approach to conserving natural resources "flies in the face of human nature." Ford went on to say that the previous winter's energy crisis demonstrated the need for more coal mining, nuclear power plant construction, offshore oil exploration, and oil shale development. He further rejected the zero-growth argument that economic expansion and a clean environment were inconsistent. But he concluded that full energy production would entail "environmental costs or risks of one kind or another."[64]

If the energy crisis produced a setback in immediate efforts to provide a cleaner environment, some long-term changes at least brighten prospects for the future. First, scientific knowledge has increased markedly in the last few decades. Ecologists have encouraged a more sophisticated understanding of the world we live in and the important interrelationships among its parts. However, much environmental research remains to be done and a substantial portion of what has been accomplished has yet to filter down to the popular level. Second, the mechanisms for dealing with environmental problems have been

28   *The Context*

institutionalized, to some degree, at the national level. The establishment of
the Environmental Protection Agency in 1970 was the first attempt to codify
many of the federal programs dealing with the environment. Although that
agency has not been consistently effective, it nevertheless represents a great
advance over the time when local protest was the only means for dealing with
environmental degradation. And, finally, the advent of the ecology movement
in the 1960s provided a forum for discussing a variety of environmental issues
that are facing the country. The strength of the ecology movement has been
its ability to publicize the interrelationships among environmental problems
—a perception of the totality of those problems. For the first time, urban pollution has been placed in a national, societal, and even international context
along with problems related to conservation, natural resources, and energy development.

Notes

1. Sam Bass Warner, Jr., *The Urban Wilderness: A History of the American City* (New
York, 1972), p. 86.

2. See Maury Klein and Harvey A. Kantor, *Prisoners of Progress: American Industrial
Cities, 1850-1920* (New York, 1976), pp. 68-108; Warner, *Urban Wilderness*, pp. 55-112.

3. Lewis Mumford, *The City in History: Its Origins, Its Transformations, and Its
Prospects* (New York, 1961), p. 446.

4. Robert R. Russel, *A History of the American Economic System* (New York, 1964),
pp. 186-99; Klein and Kantor, *Prisoners of Progress*, pp. 4-6.

5. Russel, *American Economic System*, p. 338; Warner, *Urban Wilderness*, pp. 98 ff.;
Carl N. Degler, *The Age of the Economic Revolution, 1876-1900* (Glenview, Ill., 1967),
pp. 31, 42-43.

6. Sam H. Schurr and Bruce C. Netschert, *Energy in the American Economy, 1850-1975*
(Baltimore, 1960), pp. 57-83; Joseph M. Petulla, *American Environmental History* (San
Francisco, 1977), pp. 149-51.

7. See R. Dale Grinder, "The Anti-Smoke Crusades: Early Attempts to Reform the
Urban Environment, 1893-1918" (Ph.D. diss., University of Missouri-Columbia, 1973);
Richard H. K. Vietor, "Environmental Politics and the Coal Industry" (Ph.D. diss., Uni-
versity of Pittsburgh, 1975); Petulla, *American Environmental History*, pp. 189-91.

8. John Duffy, *A History of Public Health in New York City, 1866-1966* (New York,
1974), pp. 524-25.

9. Edward C. Kirkland, *Industry Comes of Age: Business, Labor and Public Policy,
1860-1897* (Chicago, 1967; orig. pub. 1961), p. 171; Klein and Kantor, *Prisoners of
Progress*, p. 12; U.S. Department of Commerce, Bureau of the Census, *Historical Statistics of the United States . . . to 1970*, 2 vols. (Washington, D.C., 1975), pp. 693-94.

10. Blake McKelvey, *The Urbanization of America, 1800-1915* (New Brunswick, N.J.,
1963), p. 45.

11. American Public Works Association, *History of Public Works in the United States,*

1776-1976, ed. Ellis C. Armstrong, Michael Robinson, and Suellen Hoy (Chicago, 1976), p. 410 [author hereafter cited as APWA].

12. Stuart Galishoff, *Safeguarding the Public Health: Newark, 1895-1918* (Westport, Conn., 1975), pp. 54-55.

13. Mumford, *The City in History*, p. 459.

14. Russel, *American Economic System*, p. 183; Stuart Galishoff, "Sanitation in Nineteenth and Early Twentieth Century Urban America: An Overview" (unpublished paper), pp. 4-5.

15. Raymond W. Smilor, "Cacophony at 34th and 6th: The Noise Problem in America, 1900-1930," *American Studies* 28 (Spring 1977): 28-29.

16. See Mumford, *The City in History*, pp. 460-61.

17. Harold U. Faulkner, *The Decline of Laissez Faire, 1897-1917* (New York, 1951), p. 135; Russel, *American Economic System*, pp. 195 ff., 370 ff.

18. Klein and Kantor, *Prisoners of Progress*, pp. 101-2.

19. Faulkner, *Decline of Laissez Faire*, p. 146.

20. Pittsburgh Chamber of Commerce, "Report of the Committee on Municipal Affairs, October 29, 1906," cited in Roy Lubove, *Twentieth-Century Pittsburgh: Government, Business and Environmental Change* (New York, 1969), p. 47. See also R. Dale Grinder, "The Smoke Abatement Campaign in Pittsburgh before World War I: From Insurgency to Efficiency" (unpublished paper), p. 3.

21. Klein and Kantor, *Prisoners of Progress*, pp. 102-4.

22. Ibid., pp. 69-71. See also Russel, *American Economic System*, pp. 293-95.

23. Leonard Dinnerstein and David M. Reimers, *Ethnic Americans: A History of Immigration and Assimilation* (New York, 1975), pp. 36-40; Klein and Kantor, *Prisoners of Progress*, pp. 70-71; Russel, *American Economic System*, pp. 295-97, 305-6.

24. Degler, *Age of the Economic Revolution*, p. 31; Klein and Kantor, *Prisoners of Progress*, p. 72.

25. Jacob A. Riis, *How the Other Half Lives* (New York, 1957; orig. pub. 1890), pp. 9-10.

26. David Brody, "Slavic Immigrants in the Steel Mills," in *The Private Side of American History*, ed. Thomas R. Frazier (New York, 1975), p. 133.

27. Thomas C. Cochran and William Miller, *The Age of Enterprise: A Social History of Industrial America*, rev. ed. (New York, 1961), p. 264. See also Ronald H. Bayor, "The Darker Side of Urban Life: Slums in the City," in *Cities in Transition: From the Ancient World to Urban America*, ed. Frank J. Coppa and Philip C. Dolce (Chicago, 1974), p. 130.

28. Jane Addams, *Twenty Years at Hull House* (New York, 1961; orig. pub. 1910), pp. 207-9.

29. Riis, *How the Other Half Lives*, p. 8.

30. Cochran and Miller, *Age of Enterprise*, p. 262; Klein and Kantor, *Prisoners of Progress*, pp. 314 ff.; Lubove, *Twentieth-Century Pittsburgh*, p. 18.

31. Sam Bass Warner, Jr., *Streetcar Suburbs: The Process of Growth in Boston, 1870-1900* (New York, 1973; orig. pub. 1962), p. 3.

32. Howard P. Chudacoff, *The Evolution of American Urban Society* (Englewood Cliffs, N.J., 1975), pp. 80-81. See also Zane L. Miller, *The Urbanization of Modern America: Brief History* (New York, 1973), pp. 76-79.

33. Martin V. Melosi, "'Out of Sight, Out of Mind': The Environment and the Disposal of Municipal Refuse, 1860-1920," *The Historian* 35 (August 1973): 622-24.

34. Joel A. Tarr and Francis Clay McMichael, "Decisions about Wastewater Technol-

ogy, 1850-1932," *Journal of the Water Resources Planning and Management Division*, ASCE 103 (May 1977): 47-61.

35. APWA, *History of Public Works*, p. 164.

36. Ibid., pp. 165-71. See also Smilor, "Cacophony at 34th and 6th," pp. 26 ff.

37. Frederick Law Olmsted, "On Parks and Parkways as a Palliative for Urban Ills: 1870," in Bayrd Still, *Urban America: A History with Documents* (Boston, 1974), pp. 192-93.

38. For example, see Joel Schwartz, "Evolution of the Suburbs," in *Suburbia: The American Dream and Dilemma*, ed. Philip C. Dolce (New York, 1976), pp. 6-7.

39. Warner, *Streetcar Suburbs*, pp. 29-31.

40. Schwartz, "Evolution of the Suburbs," p. 8.

41. Charles N. Glaab and A. Theodore Brown, *A History of Urban America* (New York, 1967), pp. 155-56; APWA, *History of Public Works*, pp. 170-71.

42. Kenneth T. Jackson, "The Crabgrass Frontier: 150 Years of Suburban Growth in America," in *The Urban Experience: Themes in American History*, ed. Raymond A. Mohl and James F. Richardson (Belmont, Calif., 1973), pp. 206-7; Schwartz, "Evolution of the Suburbs," p. 8.

43. John S. Billings, "Municipal Sanitation: Defects in American Cities," *The Forum* 15 (May 1893): 304-5.

44. Duffy, *Public Health in New York City*, pp. 91 ff.

45. George E. Waring, Jr., "Suggestions for the Sanitary Drainage of Washington City," *Smithsonian Miscellaneous Collections* 26 (Washington, D.C., 1883): 12. See also Duffy, *Public Health in New York City*, pp. 112 ff.

46. Matthew Nelson, "Smoke Abatement in Cincinnati" (1910), in *Industrial America: The Environment and Social Problems, 1865-1920*, ed. H. Wayne Morgan (Chicago, 1974), p. 74.

47. Smilor, "Cacophony at 34th and 6th," p. 28.

48. Ibid., p. 26; Melosi, "'Out of Sight, Out of Mind,'" p. 623.

49. For good bibliographic treatments of progressivism, see David M. Kennedy, ed., *Progressivism: The Critical Issues* (Boston, 1971); Lewis L. Gould, ed., *The Progressive Era* (Syracuse, 1974); Michael H. Ebner and Eugene M. Tobin, eds., *The Age of Urban Reform: New Perspectives on the Progressive Era* (Port Washington, N.Y., 1977).

50. Melosi, "'Out of Sight, Out of Mind,'" pp. 632-33.

51. Several of the other selections in this volume will deal with these themes.

52. Roy Lubove, "The Roots of Urban Planning," in *The Urbanization of America: An Historical Anthology*, ed. Allen M. Wakstein (Boston, 1970), pp. 315 ff.

53. Jon A. Peterson, "The Impact of Sanitary Reform upon American Urban Planning, 1840-1890" (unpublished paper, 1976), p. 1.

54. Lubove, "Roots of Urban Planning," p. 324.

55. For good bibliographic treatments of boss rule, see Blaine A. Brownell and Warren E. Stickle, eds., *Bosses and Reformers* (Boston, 1973); Bruce M. Stave, ed., *Urban Bosses, Machines, and Progressive Reformers* (Lexington, Mass., 1972).

56. See nn. 49 and 55 for bibliographic references about governmental reform in the cities.

57. Wakstein, *Urbanization of America*, p. 341.

58. Richard O. Davies, *The Age of Asphalt: The Automobile, the Freeway, and the Condition of Metropolitan America* (Philadelphia, 1975), pp. 3 ff.

59. Jackson, "Crabgrass Frontier," pp. 215 ff.

60. Davies, *Age of Asphalt*, pp. 30-31.

61. Petulla, *American Environmental History*, pp. 368-69.

62. See David Howard Davis, *Energy Politics* (New York, 1974); Frank G. Dawson, *Nuclear Power: Development and Management of a Technology* (Seattle, 1976); Norman Metzger, *Energy: The Continuing Crisis* (New York, 1977); and H. Stephen Stoker, Spencer L. Seager, and Robert L. Capener, *Energy: From Source to Use* (Glenview, Ill., 1975).

63. Petulla, *American Environmental History*, p. 367.

64. Lester A. Sobel, ed., *Energy Crisis, 1974-1975*, 3 vols. (New York, 1974-77), 2: 96-97.

Specific Pollution Problems and Reform

2. Triumph and Failure: The American Response to the Urban Water Supply Problem, 1860–1923

By Stuart Galishoff

By the Civil War, American cities had outgrown the cisterns, wells, and springs that furnished most of the nation's drinking water. As domestic water sources dried up or became polluted, cities were compelled to develop public water supplies by bringing in water by gravity from mountain streams or, more commonly, by pumping it from nearby rivers and lakes. In the years 1860 to 1896, the number of public water supplies increased from 136 to 3,196; a little more than half, including nearly all of the largest ones, were municipally owned. Tragically, population growth and industrialization led to such increased pollution of surface waters that most communities drank their own sewage or that of their neighbors upstream. Typhoid fever and dysentery became endemic, and urban mortality rates were shockingly high. In the following decades, effective methods of water purification were discovered that prevented most waterborne diseases, and cities rushed to take advantage of them. By the mid-1920s, nearly all urban water supplies were being filtered or chlorinated.[1]

The urban quest for pure and abundant water supplies is as old as American cities themselves. The townsite for Boston was selected largely on the basis of the area's springs. Newark residents received much of their water from two streams that came together to form a small triangular pond, which the city fathers set aside for common use. As the need arose, fire cisterns were placed beneath the streets and public pumps were built throughout the community for the convenience of residents. For over a century, Newark's requirements for water were met in this manner, supplemented by private wells and springs.[2]

By 1800, rusticity had become a luxury that the nation's leading cities could ill afford. As cities grew, streams within the community were filled in or were converted into sewage outlets. The water collected from roof gutters was flecked with the soot of nearby chimneys. The older wells, when they worked, provided a diminished supply of heavily mineralized and often polluted water. Volunteer fire companies were formed to combat the growing menace of fire in the congested cities, but, armed only with buckets and primitive hand pump engines, the fire fighters were virtually powerless.[3]

Cities turned first to private aqueduct companies to satisfy their water needs, but with disappointing results. Building a modern municipal waterworks required a large initial outlay of capital and heavy subsequent expenditures for maintaining and extending the system. Few aqueduct companies became rich selling water, and they balked at providing water for important civic purposes such as flushing gutters and drains and installing fire hydrants. They were also reluctant to service remote districts or to furnish water to high elevations because of the extra expense involved. Most distressing was the companies' unwillingness to abandon polluted water supplies in which they had made a large investment or to enlarge their waterworks in anticipation of future population growth.[4]

Fires and epidemics brought to a head the growing public dissatisfaction with private ownership of urban water supplies and led to demands for municipal control. In 1801, Philadelphia began pumping water from the Schuylkill River. The Schuylkill waterworks was significant for two reasons: it was the first large municipally owned waterworks, and it marked the first use of steam engines for municipal water conveyance. Steam engines provided a constant supply of power for operating water pumps and also greatly enhanced the ability of engineers to raise water from low-lying rivers and lakes.[5]

In 1835 New York City undertook the most ambitious municipal waterworks so far. Work began on the construction of a dam on the Croton River 40 miles north of New York, from which the water was to be taken by gravity in masonry aqueducts to the city. To maintain a uniform grade, the aqueducts had to be tunneled through hills and carried over deep ravines and across numerous streams. Boston and Baltimore also developed upland water sources, although in the latter city fiscal conservatism prevailed and a small nearby stream was tapped.[6]

During the years 1850-1920, water was a vital concern of American cities, second in importance only to transportation improvements. The specter of pestilence hung over a city without a pure water supply, deterring persons and businesses from settling there. Urban destinies were inextricably tied to local health conditions. For example, New Orleans, which suffered grievously from attacks of cholera and yellow fever, began to lose its control over western commerce to its healthier rivals to the north, St. Louis and Chicago. One local physician calculated that from January 1846 to May 1850 the economic cost of preventable sickness and premature death to New Orleans was over $45 million. Similarly, epidemics in Memphis in the 1870s nearly destroyed its economy, and it was not until the following decade, when major sanitary reforms including the introduction of sewerage and a new water supply were made, that the city's fortunes began to recover. In northern cities the principal threat came from typhoid fever. A high typhoid fever death rate not only caused economic losses; it also damaged a city's reputation for salubrity and sanitary enlightenment, which, as the Newark Board of Trade noted, could be more harmful than the disease itself.[7]

One city's misfortunes of health were often another's gain. Atlanta had long remained free from major epidemics (which local leaders attributed to its mild climate) and enjoyed the reputation of being one of the few healthy cities in the South. When a massive yellow fever epidemic struck Louisiana in 1905, Atlanta welcomed persons fleeing the pestilence. The local chamber of commerce boasted that over 4,000 refugees were sheltered in Atlanta without a single case of sickness. To emphasize the city's alleged immunity from yellow fever, the Atlanta Board of Health defied a state quarantine imposed on persons coming from the area of the epidemic. Despite the testimony of the city bacteriologist that the *aëdes aegypti* mosquito was present in Atlanta, the mayor encouraged the board in its actions.[8] The general council supported them both with a resolution stating,

> the demand of the state board is uncalled for . . . and tends to put
> Atlanta in a false light. . . . This city has built up a reputation based
> upon its history as well as its natural advantages, which is of vast
> advantage and importance to itself and its citizens.[9]

Ultimately, however, the city had to acquiesce to the state's supremacy in matters of quarantine.

In this discussion of the development of urban water supplies in the late nineteenth and early twentieth centuries, three cities—Atlanta, Chicago, and Newark—will be emphasized to provide a cross-section of the national experience. Atlanta was chosen because it was the South's leading city and the speaker of the "New South" that emerged after the Civil War. Chicago was the urban phenomenon of the period, for in just seventy years it had developed from a desolate army post into the leading commercial and industrial center of the Midwest, with a population of over a million, second only to New York City. Furthermore, its vitality and rawness best symbolized the nation's surging urban development. Newark was selected to represent the Northeast and the smaller industrial cities of the era.

Throughout the first half of the nineteenth century the dangers of drinking impure water were misunderstood. Water was usually judged by its physical qualities; hence water that was clear, odorless, and tasteless was considered pure and safe. Some physicians believed that drinking hard water or water contaminated with vegetable and animal matter was bad for the kidneys and was responsible for many stomach and digestive disorders. But it was not until Dr. John Snow's work with cholera in the 1850s that the link between polluted water and epidemic diseases was firmly established.[10]

Snow, a distinguished London physician, wrote a pamphlet in 1849 wherein he argued that cholera was caused by an organic poison that attacked the intestines and was discharged in the feces. If the infected feces should find their way into public water supply, he maintained, an epidemic would ensue. In 1854 Snow had an opportunity to test his hypothesis. Investigating a cholera epidemic near Broad Street in London, in which five hundred persons had died, Snow was able to trace its origin to a polluted well. A workshop in the same area, which had its own well, reported no cases among its seventy employees. Simply by breaking the pump handle to the polluted well, Snow ended the epidemic.[11]

Within a short time after the publication of Snow's work, cholera was brought under control in most parts of the Western world. The cholera vibrio is a frail organism that dies upon exposure to light or when deprived of moisture and thus is relatively easy to control. Cholera usually occurs only in communities where wretched living conditions prevail and where little or no attention is paid to personal hygiene. The last serious outbreak of cholera in the United States took place in 1873.[12]

Snow's studies of waterborne transmission of disease were replicated by Dr. William Budd in his investigations of typhoid fever. Through the use of field studies and statistical investigation, Budd showed that typhoid fever also was spread through fecally contaminated water supplies. The typhoid bacillus, however, is a hardier specimen than the cholera vibrio, better able to withstand heat and cold or the actions of various disinfectants. Close scrutiny of watersheds and water supplies was essential in preventing typhoid fever epidemics. The problem was compounded by the widespread distribution of the disease. In addition to sewage-contaminated water, typhoid fever may be transmitted by milk produced under unsanitary conditions, by raw fruits and vegetables fertilized with night soil, by oysters and other shellfish harvested in polluted waters, and by flies that gain access to privies and kitchens. It may also be spread by convalescents and carriers, such as the well-known "Typhoid Mary," a New York City cook who, before her arrest, left a trail of at least twenty-eight sick persons in the homes where she worked.[13]

As typhoid invariably accompanied the distribution of sewage-contaminated water into the homes of urban residents, the typhoid fever death rate was commonly used as a measure of the purity of the local water supply. In 1908, George C. Whipple, one of the nation's leading public health authorities, maintained that a typhoid fever death rate greater than 15 to 20 per 100,000 population was a sign that the water supply was being polluted. A death rate lower than that figure he attributed to "residual," or nonwaterborne, typhoid.[14]

The knowledge that polluted water harbored deadly diseases posed a crisis for American cities, a majority of which obtained their potable water from nearby rivers and lakes that were being increasingly fouled by sewage and industrial wastes. The inhabitants of these cities were drinking extremely polluted water, with disastrous consequences. A few examples will illustrate the problems confronting American cities as they sought to satisfy the demands placed on their water supplies by rapid growth and industrialization.

By the end of the Civil War, the local wells and springs that supplied Newark with water had become inadequate, and the city turned to the Passaic River for relief. Fearing a return of cholera, which had three times ravaged the community, the Newark Aqueduct Board carefully considered the safety of the new water supply. A chemist engaged by the board for this purpose determined that the water of the Passaic River was as pure as that of the famed Croton, quite suitable for drinking and other domestic purposes. Confidence was expressed in the "law of purification," which stated that a stream would purify itself by oxidation after a few miles of flow. To be on the safe side, infiltration basins were set on the alluvial sand and gravel banks of the river to cleanse the water.[15]

The precautions taken by the Newark Aqueduct Board were to no avail. As cities and industries developed along the Passaic River and its tributaries, the river became hopelessly polluted. In 1872 complaints about the quality of the water supply led to an investigation by the *Newark Daily Advertiser*, which disclosed that the river was being polluted with sewage, animal carcasses, dead human bodies, and industrial poisons. Professor Albert R. Leeds of the Stevens Institute in a report to the Board of Public Works of Jersey City, which also drew its water from the Passaic River, stated that chemical tests had revealed "a shocking degree of contamination by organic matter."[16]

Other cities located along the banks of rivers that washed heavily industrial areas suffered grievously from waterborne diseases. During 1890-91, Lowell and Lawrence, Massachusetts, experienced a severe typhoid fever epidemic. Both cities obtained their water from the Merrimac River, a large stream draining an industrial area in New Hampshire and northern Massachusetts. The source of the epidemic was traced to several outhouses overhanging the banks of a small tributary of the Merrimac River a little upstream from Lowell. The privies were owned by local businesses, and a number of workers had used them while ill with typhoid fever. The epidemic began in Lowell, where it claimed 132 lives in a population of 78,000. From Lowell it spread downstream about a month later to Lawrence, population 47,000, where 74 persons died.[17]

Pittsburgh received its water from the Allegheny and Monongahela rivers. Both rivers were contaminated by the sewage and industrial wastes of large communities located within a few miles of Pittsburgh. The water was not filtered and was sometimes muddy and tasted bad. In 1894-1906, Pittsburgh's typhoid fever death rate never fell below 100 per 100,000 population. More than 5,000 cases occurred each year. Nearby Allegheny drew its water solely from the Allegheny River and suffered even more from typhoid than its neighbor.[18]

The cities along the Great Lakes were blessed with large supplies of fresh water at their doorsteps and were thus spared the expense incurred by the great eastern metropolises in bringing in water from distant highlands. But the lakes were also used as sewage receptacles, with predictable results. Moreover, the typhoid fever epidemics of the lake cities were likely to be of long duration since, as the epidemic intensified, the sewage of the city became more saturated with typhoid bacilli, which in turn increased the pollution of the water supply.[19]

Chicago's first waterworks, established in 1842, was operated by the privately owned Chicago Hydraulic Company. The company's primitive pump and distribution system served only a small number of Chicagoans and in 1852, during a severe cholera epidemic, the city assumed management of the waterworks. In 1854 the waterworks was enlarged to provide lake water for all who wanted it. To avoid shoreline pollution and to escape the ill effects of the Chicago River, which carried off the city's wastes, the intake of the waterworks was located some 600 feet out in Lake Michigan.[20] As the pollution of the Chicago River grew worse, it became necessary to move the intake deeper and deeper into the lake.

City officials attempted to improve the water supply by reversing the flow of the Chicago River so that it emptied into the Mississippi River system instead of Lake Michigan. This rerouting was possible because Chicago was situated at a very low point on the divide separating the Lake Michigan and Mississippi River watersheds.[21] With the building of the Illinois and Michigan Canal in 1848, the Chicago River had become linked to the Mississippi by means of the Des Plaines and Illinois rivers. In 1862 a pumping station was built on the Chicago River to redirect its current. However, the Illinois and Michigan Canal, which had been opened as a barge canal, was not deep enough to handle the city's increasing waste, much of which still found its way into Lake Michigan. The canal was deepened in the late 1860s but without success. Hence Chicago continued to suffer from typhoid fever, dysentery, and other waterborne diseases.[22]

The Civil War left much of the South prostrate, but Atlanta recovered quickly and rose from the ashes to become the state's leading transportation and commercial center, with a population in 1870 of nearly 20,000. It was first proposed to let private interests furnish the city with water. But, when two aqueduct companies organized for this purpose failed to act, the city decided to build its own waterworks. The South River, which flows below downtown Atlanta, was chosen as the source of the new supply. The waterworks, completed in September 1876 at a cost of $226,000, had a daily capacity of two million gallons. A single sixteen-inch main conveyed water from the pumping station over a distance of approximately five miles into the city, and from there three additional miles of smaller mains fanned out to serve the business district.[23]

The waterworks' major purpose was to provide an increased volume of water for business and industrial needs and fire protection; it seems to have been no part of the plan to furnish citizens with a potable supply for drinking and household uses. The South River reservoir was fed by rain washings from the city's natural drainage courses, which by the 1870s had become open sewers. The initial proposals for waterworks in the 1860s had emphasized the value of water for sanitary purposes, but the limited capacity of the waterworks was wholly inadequate for flushing the crude rock sewers built after 1873. Even for the main purposes it proposed to serve, the waterworks was inadequate the day it went into operation. The chances for obtaining sufficient pressure to combat fires were best at night when industrial use was minimal, but the pumping machinery often had to be repaired in the evenings because of the daily overload that was placed on it.[24]

In the absence of a dependable municipal water supply, some well-to-do residents purchased drinking water delivered from Ponce de Leon and outlying springs, but the great majority of citizens continued to drink from public and private wells. The results of a study published in the *Atlanta Medical Register* in 1883 indicated that many wells were badly contaminated. The main sufferers were Negroes, whose relation to the city's topography corresponded to their social status; their lots and wells received the drainage from the premises above, since the extension of sewer outfalls invariably stopped in black neighborhoods. The lack of pure, wholesome water combined with poor drainage in the hollows of the city led to increased sickness among the poor. The lower sections of the city were literally drained on from above by the downtown business area and the homes of the wealthy that occupied the higher elevations.[25] Commenting on the fact that the death rate among Atlanta's Negroes in 1885 was two and a half times greater than that for whites, Mayor George Hillyer said, "I believe that if good clear water were supplied to all the lower levels of the city, where so many of the colored people live, and their contaminated wells were all filled up and obliterated, a very marked change for the better would immediately appear."[26]

In the great northeastern seaports that had developed upland water supplies the problem was more one of quantity than quality. Both the land area and the population of cities were growing enormously, adding new burdens to municipal water systems. In 1854-98, Philadelphia, Boston, and New York annexed much of the surrounding countryside. Philadelphia's annexation of Spring Garden, Kensington, and West Philadelphia in 1854 more than doubled its size, and the incorporation of Brooklyn, Queens, Richmond, and sections of the Bronx in 1898 placed an additional 1.5 million water consumers within the city limits of New York. Most of these suburban districts either did not have public water supplies or had inadequate waterworks that would have to be expanded.[27]

A rising standard of living for the urban middle class also exacerbated the water supply problem. Before the Civil War few persons enjoyed the comforts of indoor plumbing. Philadelphia, which had a reputation among travelers as the cleanest American city, had only 3,521 baths in 1849. New York in 1856 had 1,361 baths and 10,384 water closets in a population of over 630,000. By the late nineteenth century, private bathroom fixtures such as bathtubs, shower baths, and water closets were becoming standard items in new home construction and a necessity for the middle-class market, thus placing new strains on municipal water supplies.[28]

Population growth, annexation of suburban areas, industrial demands, a rising standard of living, and wasteful water practices—all combined to render obsolete the expensive water supply systems of the eastern metropolises within a few years after their completion. Boston, New York, and Baltimore responded by enlarging the existing waterworks and by impounding new water supplies from relatively distant mountain watersheds. Municipal self-congratulations following the completion of this expansion were short-lived, however, because water consumption was growing faster than anyone had predicted and would soon threaten to exceed even the increased capacity of the waterworks. Cities had a seemingly insatiable thirst that could be quenched only by the tapping of still larger and more distant watersheds.

Within ten years after completing the Croton Reservoir system, New York City was confronted with the first of many water shortages that would occur intermittently for the next hundred years. In the early 1860s the capacity of the waterworks was increased from 42 million gallons a day to 72 million gallons, and a billion-gallon reservoir was constructed in Central Park. These extensions, however, were not sufficient, as became apparent in 1870 and

1880 when the city suffered severe droughts that sharply decreased the availability of water from the Croton River. During the hot summer months public water was available only on the first stories in tenement buildings. Many persons were forced to resort to wells. Consequently, in both years the typhoid fever death rate in New York City climbed sharply to more than 40 per 100,000 population. In 1885 construction began on the New Croton Aqueduct. Completed in 1893, it had a capacity of 300 million gallons a day, which together with the old Croton waterworks and other improvements gave the city a daily supply of 425 million gallons. Since the average daily consumption was only 183 million gallons, there appeared to be ample margin for future population growth. But city leaders had not counted on the expansion of the city's boundaries in 1898, nor could they foresee the enormous tide of immigrants that would inundate New York from 1885 to 1914. In a characteristically bold decision, New York in the early 1900s decided to tap the Catskill Mountains watershed 100 miles to the north. Even when that project was completed, the city still had to search for new water sources.[29]

In Philadelphia city officials made an unwise decision to enlarge the Schuylkill waterworks despite that waterway's growing pollution. Proposals that water from upland streams some twenty-five to thirty miles away be impounded and brought to the city by an aqueduct were rejected because of the expense involved. As a result, Philadelphia suffered the notoriety of having one of the highest typhoid fever death rates in the country.[30]

Even good water supplies could become accidentally polluted, as was demonstrated by the typhoid fever epidemic that struck the small mining community of Plymouth, Pennsylvania, in 1885. The epidemic was notable for its severity and for its influence in awakening Americans to the need for treatment of public water supplies. The river that supplied Plymouth's water ran through a mountain wilderness and was known for its purity. However, a man who occupied one of the few houses in the watershed area had contracted typhoid fever while in Philadelphia for the Christmas holidays. He returned home on 2 January 1885 and remained ill with the disease until the middle of April. During the course of his illness his excreta were cast without disinfection upon the snow and frozen ground within a few feet of the edge of a bank overlooking the river. Throughout January and February the excreta remained trapped on the frozen earth. But during the first week of spring there was a thaw, and on 4 April the temperature climbed to seventy degrees. As the snow and ice melted, accumulated excreta from many weeks were washed into the river, carrying with them the still potent typhoid bacilli. The first case of typhoid fever in Plymouth occurred on 9 April. Within a week, from 50 to 100 cases were appearing daily in all parts of town and among all classes of people. By

the time the epidemic had run its course, 1,104 of the town's 8,000 residents
had been stricken, 114 of them fatally.[31]

Plymouth's tragic experience stimulated American interest in new methods
of water purification. Some water supplies were already undergoing treatment
in slow sand filters, in which water was percolated through a bed of sand and
gravel to remove suspended matter. During the 1860s the city of St. Louis,
searching for a means of making its water supply less turbid, had sent James F.
Kirkwood to Europe to investigate the latest methods for clarifying river
water. His classic *Report on the Filtration of River Water* appeared in 1869.
Although St. Louis rejected Kirkwood's proposal for building a filtration plant
on the Mississippi River, several other cities went ahead with the construction
of slow sand filters based on his designs. The first slow sand filter plant was
built in Poughkeepsie, New York, in 1872. The plant's primary purpose was
aesthetic—to improve the water's clarity, taste, and odor.[32]

It had long been suspected on the basis of statistical investigation that polluted water was responsible for the transmission of cholera, typhoid fever, and
other waterborne diseases, but conclusive evidence was lacking until the development of bacteriology and the germ theory of disease. No one had ever
even looked through a microscope at the microorganisms responsible for these
diseases, much less demonstrated that the tiny organisms were the sole cause
of the illnesses. Finally, in the 1880s Robert Koch provided the long-awaited
laboratory proof that microorganisms were responsible for many of these most
fearful diseases. The cholera vibrio and the typhoid bacillus were soon discovered and were shown to be transmitted through any medium that provided
a circuit between an infected excreta and a healthy intestine. Studies made in
the United States in 1883 by William Ripley Nichols of the Massachusetts
Institute of Technology and Dr. Morton Prince of Boston similarly pointed to
the dangers of fecal contamination and the value of filtration in cleansing
water.[33]

By the 1880s several American cities were involved in some form of research
on filtration. The Lawrence (Massachusetts State Board of Health) Experiment
Station was the leading research center in water purification and the one that
placed the practice on a sound scientific footing. The station housed a brilliant
staff of sanitary engineers, chemists, and biologists who pioneered the inter-
disciplinary approach to the study of water purification and sewage treatment.
One of the important discoveries made at this laboratory was that improved
slow sand filters could remove typhoid germs in river water supplies. In 1893
the experiment station built a slow sand plant for the city of Lawrence, which
had suffered unmercifully in the past from typhoid fever. The effectiveness of
the plant was immediately apparent. The typhoid fever mortality rate in

Lawrence dropped from an average of about 120 per 100,000 population in the years 1887-92 to an annual rate of between 20 and 30. By 1900 about twenty cities had constructed slow sand filters.[34]

Within a few years rapid sand or mechanical filters replaced slow sand filters in the United States. Experiments revealed that the mechanical filters were better suited for removing dirt and clay and the bacteria that adhered to them. This feature was especially important in the Midwest, where the rivers were highly turbid. In addition, mechanical filters were easier and less expensive to clean. Slow sand filters required frequent scraping and washing, whereas the mechanical filters could be cleaned by reverse flow, eliminating an important labor cost. In 1902 Little Falls, New Jersey, installed the first large municipal mechanical filter.[35]

In the first two decades of the twentieth century several significant advances were made in water treatment. Water plants added sedimentation and coagulation basins to remove suspended matter from the water before it was sent to the filters. The annoying problem of algae in stored water, which caused water to have a "fishy" taste, was overcome by the addition of copper sulfate. Most important, chlorine was found to be effective against pathogenic microorganisms. In 1908 the privately owned Jersey City Water Company at Boonton Reservoir began the first continuous chlorination of an urban water supply to disinfect the suspect water of the Rockaway River.[36]

The development of scientific methods of filtration and disinfection increased the water options available to cities. Some cities abandoned their polluted water supplies for clear mountain streams. A few fortunate communities, notably Memphis, discovered that they were located on huge aquifers that could supply pure water at little expense. Most cities, however, did not have alternative water sources available to them and had to rely on filtration and disinfection to make their water supplies safe.

It was usually futile for cities to attempt to prevent the pollution of commercial waterways, as will be seen in the case of Newark. A few cities, such as Milwaukee, that were drinking water contaminated by their own sewage built sewage-treatment plants, but this approach was usually rejected because of the high cost. Cities that invested a great deal in impounding mountain streams were compelled to protect their purity, most often by instituting sanitary patrols of the watershed and by removing leaking privies and other nuisances from the area. Of course, Chicago's solution, to rid Lake Michigan of pollution by reversing the flow of the Chicago River, was unique.

Local conditions, such as the topography of the city and its drainage system, its size and financial condition, and the water sources it could tap, determined how each city responded to the water crisis. In Newark there was strong financial incentive for maintaining the existing waterworks. The Passaic River plant had been built at a cost of more than $1 million, which was about the amount of Newark's total tax appropriations for 1880. The cost of a new water supply was estimated at between $2 million and $4 million. Rather than undertake such an expensive project, Newark and Jersey City adopted a plan for cleansing the Passaic River and making it safe for drinking once again.[37]

The plan had its genesis in a water scare that struck Newark in 1880. Complaints were received from all sections of the city that the water smelled like creosote, tasted bad, and was discolored. Upon investigation, inspectors discovered that carbolic acid from the Kingsland Paper Mill on the Third River, some two miles above the Newark intake, was contaminating the water. An indictment was brought against the mill for creating a public nuisance, and the company was forced to stop discharging its wastes into the river. Encouraged by this success, Newark and Jersey City joined forces to prevent further pollution of the Passaic. On 27 October 1861, the Board of Inspection of the Pollution of the Passaic River and Its Tributaries, composed of members of the water departments of Newark and Jersey City, was organized. The board established a sanitary patrol to achieve its goals,[38] undertaking its task with much fanfare and great promise. The chief engineer of Jersey City confidently predicted that in a few years the water would return to its original state of purity and both Jersey City and Newark would "have the best, purest and most abundant source of water supply of any city within 500 miles."[39] The board's accomplishments during its first years of operation gave grounds for the optimism of its supporters. In 1884 the board reported that

> the rigid inspection of the stream has succeeded in keeping it free
> from [the] carcasses of dead animals, from its being used as a
> dumping place for night soil, offal and refuse of all description.
> It has caused the removal of closets and drains which formerly
> carried the excreta of thousands of [mill and factory] operatives
> [and river bank inhabitants] directly into the Passaic or some of
> its tributaries. It has caused the smaller communities located on
> Second and Third rivers to give up the project of converting
> these streams into sewers, and instead to resort to systems of
> sewage utilization. . . . It has caused so large a community as that
> of the town of Passaic to seriously consider the problem of dis-
> posing of its sewage by a method which should return the effluent
> waters in a purified condition to the Passaic.[40]

Yet the board's efforts in combatting the contamination of the Passaic River were largely unsuccessful. In 1880, the population of the lower Passaic

River Valley was 250,000; by 1918 it was 800,000. Communities such as Passaic and Belleville, which the board hoped would use other methods of sewage disposal, found it easier to empty their wastes into the nearby Passaic River or its tributaries. Cities that had always used the Passaic for this purpose, such as Paterson and Newark, contributed ever-increasing amounts of waste.[41]

After some initial successes, the board was unable to prevent factory owners from polluting the river. "Legal notices and warnings are unheeded by them," reported Thomas W. Leeds, river inspector for the board of pollution, "and it will be a useless task for me to try to stop them until legal action is instituted against them."[42] Civil proceedings were slow, and when the board threatened to bring criminal action against polluters, the owners banded together, "determined to sustain one another in the event of criminal action being instituted against any of them."[43]

While city officials tried to determine a course of action, the citizens of Newark coped as best they could with the situation. Many physicians advised their patients to filter and boil public water before using it, and thousands of Newarkers never drank Passaic River water under any circumstances. In its place they drank well water (which usually was polluted), spring water, distilled water, mineral water, aerated beverages, and beer. One popular beverage, Poland Spring Water, sold for the exorbitant price of eight dollars for forty gallons. Citizens spent about $250,000 annually for water substitutes, enough to pay the interest on the debt that would be incurred in obtaining a new water supply.[44]

The fortunes of Newark's largest water consumers, its extensive industrial establishments, were inexorably bound up with the water crisis. Newark's sizable lager beer industry, in particular, was threatened by lack of suitable water for brewing. In 1885 the president of the Board of Trade warned that Newark could never attain commercial eminence while the threat of pestilence cast a shadow over it. In 1889, largely because of pressure from the business community, Newark gave up on the Passaic River and contracted with a private aqueduct company to deliver water from the Pequannock River, an upland tributary of the Passaic.[45]

The abandonment of the Passaic brought a marked improvement in Newark's health. The death rate from typhoid fever in 1891, the last year Passaic River water was used exclusively, was nearly 80 per 100,000 population. In 1893, the first year that Newark relied solely upon Pequannock River water, the rate dropped to 30 per 100,000 population. Similarly, the typhoid mortality rate in Jersey City was cut by two-thirds after its adoption of a new water supply in 1898.[46]

Chicago, which had a reputation for audacity, attempted to solve its water supply problem by sending its wastes to the Mississippi River. Following a water scare in the summer of 1879 in which sewage was discharged into Lake Michigan for thirty consecutive days, the Citizens' Association of Chicago, an organization of prominent businessmen, appointed a Main Drainage Committee to find a permanent solution to the water problem. The association echoed the attitude of civic boosters everywhere—what was good for their city was good for business. A dependable water supply would improve Chicago's business climate and thus insure the prosperity of their members. In December 1880 the committee recommended the construction of a new and larger drainage channel paralleling and replacing the Illinois and Michigan Canal to increase the current in the stagnant Chicago River.

The proposed drainage canal was widely supported. City and state public health officials endorsed it, as did sanitary engineers. Leading Chicago social and business groups lobbied for the canal before the Illinois legislature, and the newspapers kept the subject constantly before the public. The Chicago medical profession was almost the only group with an interest in the canal who did not actively support it. At the time, physicians were not esteemed by the general public because they were unable to treat most illnesses and they were too preoccupied with trying to proscribe the practice of sectarian medicine to take much of a role in public health issues. Physicians were more interested in treating illnesses than in preventing them.[47]

In 1889 the Illinois legislature established the Chicago Sanitary District and created a public authority to finance, build, and maintain the canal. The authority was given sanitary jurisdiction over all of Chicago north of Eighty-seventh Street and some forty-three square miles of Cook County outside the city limits.[48] In a combined referendum and election of sanitary district trustees held shortly thereafter, Chicagoans demonstrated their nearly unanimous support for the canal by a vote of 70,958 to 242.

Lawsuits, political fights, and administrative tangles delayed work on the canal until 1892. In the meantime, Chicago experienced the worst typhoid fever epidemic in its history. In 1890-92, the disease killed 4,494 persons. During the twelve-month period from April 1891 to April 1892, it accounted for 2,400 fatalities and probably at least 25,000 illnesses. Chicago's typhoid fever death rate in 1891 climbed to 159 per 100,000 population, second highest in the nation.[49]

To guard against pollution while work on the canal proceeded, a new water crib was built four miles from the Lake Michigan shoreline in 1894. Finally, on 17 January 1900 the Chicago Sanitary and Ship Canal was opened. Twenty-eight miles long, twenty-four feet deep, and built at a cost of $45 million, the canal markedly improved the quality of Chicago water. But some of the city's sewers along the lakefront continued to drain into Lake Michigan, and bacteriological examination of water specimens revealed that even a four-mile water intake did not provide complete protection. In 1902 Chicago experienced another epidemic of typhoid fever, which claimed the lives of 801 persons.[50]

Chicago's vulnerability to typhoid epidemics in the early 1900s made it clear that the building of the sanitary and ship canal had not ended the pollution of the city's water supply. In 1910 an intercepting sewer was built along the shoreline to reroute the area's sewage. In 1912 Chicago began experimenting with chlorination and four years later chlorinated its entire water supply. At long last the city had solved its water supply problem. The typhoid fever mortality rate, which had averaged 67 per 100,000 in the 1890s was reduced by 80 percent over the next twenty years as pollution of Lake Michigan abated; the death rate fell to 1 per 100,000 in 1919 after chlorination came into use.[51]

In 1889 a committee of businessmen and public officials asked the noted sanitary engineer, Rudolph Hering, to study Atlanta's water needs. Hering's report recommended that Atlanta abandon the polluted South River for a copious supply of pure mountain water to be drawn from the Chattahoochee River. In 1891 the city purchased a 100-acre site for a pumping station on the Chattahoochee River above the mouth of Peachtree Creek and another site for a 176-million-gallon reservoir and relay station at an elevated point 3.5 miles from the city. On 29 September 1893, the new system went into operation and furnished a capacity of 20 million gallons per day.[52]

The opening of the Chattahoochee plant did not end the city's water crisis. When the water came into the reservoir it was badly discolored by red clay particles. While the Chattahoochee River was relatively free of fecal contamination and other harmful wastes, it was filled with sand, necessitating that its waters be treated before being piped to Atlanta residents.[53]

Even worse than dirty water was no water at all. Throughout the years 1900 to 1910, the building of water mains and sewer lines failed to keep pace with the city's rapid growth. In 1908, one-third of the city's area and 40 percent of the population did not have water mains or sewers, a condition that the chamber of commerce described as being "worthy of the plague-stricken cities of the middle ages." Moreover, it was the richer, less populous areas that enjoyed modern sanitary facilities. Streets without water averaged 132 houses to the mile, whereas those with water had 104 per mile. In the absence of sewerage and running water, large numbers of Atlantans were forced to rely upon surface privies and wells, most of which were polluted. In addition, Atlanta had no sewage-treatment facilities. Trunk sewers took the bodily wastes of 80,000 persons to or near the city limits, where the untreated sewage was dumped into streams. Because of these unsanitary conditions, the city continued to suffer greatly from waterborne diseases. From 1906 to 1910, Atlanta had an annual typhoid fever death rate of 62.1 per 100,000 population, second highest in the nation of any city of over 100,000 population.[54]

Atlanta's new reputation as an unhealthy city led the chamber of commerce to lobby for major improvements in the city's water supply and sewerage. Commenting on the importance of public health to a city's economic welfare, the chamber noted that

> it is only within the recent past that the interest of the community,
> in a financial or commercial sense, in the health of the individuals
> composing it has been aroused. Formerly the health question
> was viewed from the selfish standpoint of the individual or the
> family . . . But now municipal governments have come to realize
> that to them the general health is quite as important and profitable
> as to the individual. With communities, as with individuals, it has
> developed that it is impossible to prosper without health, as it
> is to build a house without a foundation.[55]

In 1910 city officials proposed a $3 million bond issue, of which they earmarked $900,000 for the waterworks and $1,350,000 for sewage-disposal plants. In the months preceeding the referendum, the chamber of commerce, with the blessings of Mayor Robert Maddox, waged an all-out fight for the bond issue. To spearhead the campaign, the chamber appointed a special bond committee with a war chest of $3,500. The chief efforts of the committee were directed toward registering voters and getting them to the polls on election day. The chamber of commerce was responsible for registering voters among the commercial classes. The Atlanta Federation of Trades was assigned the workingmen, and the Federation of Women's Clubs did the door-to-door canvassing. Every person in Atlanta was listed according to occupation and assigned to an organization for registration. The chamber of commerce alone had thirty-two committees at work canvassing business houses and boasted that "no campaign in Atlanta's history was ever more systematically made. Each ward is divided into districts and every street is polled by committees." The chamber's efforts paid off handsomely. On 1 February, by the lopsided talley of 8,409 to 66, voters approved the bond issue.[56]

The new waterworks and sewerage facilities built with the bond money resulted in a dramatic improvement in the city's public health. As city water and sewerage became available, citizens abandoned wells and surface closets (although 4,000 surface closets were still in use in 1917). From 1911 to 1916, the typhoid fever death rate fell from 56 to 17 per 100,000 population, a 70 percent reduction.[57]

Thus during the years 1860-1920 American cities succeeded in developing waterworks that provided safe and plentiful water for nearly all their inhabitants. The United States Public Health Service estimated that in 1923 nearly 31.5 million persons, or about 97 percent of the residents of the nation's hundred largest cities, used public water supplies; the remaining 3 percent were largely dependent upon private wells. A little over two-thirds of the cities' residents were furnished with surface water (open rivers, impounded streams, and lakes), one-fourth used mixed surface and groundwater, and less than a tenth used groundwater alone.[58]

The decline in the typhoid fever death rate attested to the progress made in safeguarding urban water supplies. During the decade of the 1880s, the forty-seven American cities with populations of 100,000 or more had an average typhoid fever death rate of 58 per 100,000. In 1923 the typhoid fever death rate for the nation's largest cities was 3.6, reflecting substantial advancement not only in the quality of public water supplies but also in general sanitation.[59]

As indicated in figure 2.1, all but thirteen of the one hundred cities surveyed by the United States government adopted their existing water supplies after 1859, a majority of them in the years 1860-99. Purification of water supplies came largely in the period 1900-1920. In 1880 only 30,000 Americans drank filtered water. By 1923 the only water that was not undergoing some form of purification was the groundwater found in deep artesian wells, which, because of its natural purification while in the ground, was safe to drink raw. Filtration was the primary method of treatment, while chlorine was used for disinfection.[60]

Businessmen spearheaded the fight for improved urban water supplies, a commitment prompted by both economic necessity and civic pride. They realized that, without a copious supply of clear water, industry would be threatened. There would be insufficient water for cooling, for producing steam, and for washing away filth. The threat of conflagration would grow, increasing the cost of obtaining fire insurance. The industrialists of each city, moreover, saw themselves bound together in competition with businessmen in other communities and were anxious that their city project an image of progress and modernity. A city with dirty streets and unflushed sewers was aesthetically offensive, a reproach to city boosters, and a poor advertisement.

Public health authorities vigorously supported the adoption of better water supplies, especially after the 1880s when the link between impure water and high urban death rates was firmly established. Initially some health officials

Figure 2.1. Summary for one hundred cities, 1923, giving date of installation of present source of water supplies, treatment plants, and disinfection apparatus

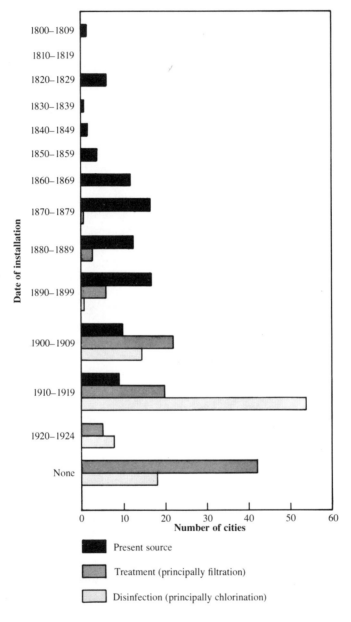

SOURCE: U.S. Public Health Service, *Public Health Bulletin No. 164, Municipal Health Department Practice for the Year 1923* (Washington, D.C., 1926), p. 469.

had been reluctant to condemn the use of polluted water supplies because of the widely held belief that running water purified itself by oxidation after a few miles of flow. Furthermore, the discovery that diseases were caused by living organisms cast doubt on the value of chemical analysis in determining the safety of water supplies. Chemical examination of a water supply reveals the presence of organic matter or its constituents and thus is useful in detecting fecal contamination, but it will not reveal the presence of harmful microorganisms. The development of bacteriological methods of testing water and the accumulation of both statistical and laboratory evidence of the waterborne transmission of some major diseases gave public health officials greater confidence in calling for the abandonment of polluted water supplies. Finally, the general public overwhelmingly approved new water supplies in special referendums because they began to understand that pure water, in addition to its importance for health, was essential for cooking, washing, bathing, and other daily activities.

By impounding mountain streams, by bringing up water from beneath the ground, and by treating and disinfecting surface waters, Americans had secured safe, dependable water supplies for their cities. They did so, however, at the expense of nearby streams and lakes, which received ever-increasing loads of sewage and industrial wastes. For example, after Newark abandoned the Passaic River for its drinking water, the river's condition grew worse, since the incentive for protecting its purity had been removed. By 1894 the Passaic River had all the characteristics of an open sewer.[61]

Whipple believed that the loss of rivers for public use and the damage done riverfront property interests would inspire cities and industries to begin purifying their wastes. In a statement remarkable for its prescience he warned that

> unquestionably many American streams are being rapidly spoiled,
> and before it is too late much energetic work ought to be done to
> prevent this. Stream pollution is the result of the prosperity of
> our cities, but if by increasing our capital in the form of mills and
> factories, we decrease it in the form of natural water resources,
> we are not, as a nation, growing rich as rapidly as we think.[62]

Although a few persons voiced concern that society would suffer an incalculable loss if the recreational uses of its waterways were destroyed by pollution and although research was conducted on the treatment of effluents, little was done to prevent stream pollution. As long as environmental quality was regarded as a free resource, people would use the atmosphere and the waterways as receptacles for waste products. Efforts to protect rivers and lakes from despoilment were doomed to failure by the widely held belief that the waterways should be utilized in the ways that best served their immediate economic interests. Moreover, the lack of a national uniform standard of stream pollution placed states with tough pollution laws at a competitive disadvantage alongside states with few restrictions in attracting industry. Because stream pollution was a state responsibility and because industries were mobile, officials refrained from prosecuting polluters for fear that they would move to another state. Even those states that boasted sewage-research facilities and regulatory agencies for protecting the purity of streams either tacitly or openly permitted defilement of their great waterways.[63]

In the years 1850 to 1930, American cities scored one of their greatest triumphs in making available pure and abundant water to millions of urban residents. Few individuals, however, thought beyond the current health and business needs of society and, as a consequence, the pollution of the nation's waterways was allowed to go unchecked. Perhaps now, in view of mounting concern about the harm being done to the environment by uncontrolled growth, we will recognize our duty to posterity to pass on in an unspoiled condition the natural wonders that are our rivers, lakes, and oceans.

Notes

I would like to thank Clifford L. Lord, director of the New Jersey Historical Society, and Craig Donegan, editor of *The Maryland Historian*, respectively, for permission to quote brief passages from my "The Passaic Valley Trunk Sewer," *New Jersey History* 88 (Winter 1970): 199–203; and "Atlanta's Water Supply, 1865–1918," *The Maryland Historian* 8 (Spring 1977): 7–8, 10, 16–18.

1. Nelson Manfred Blake, *Water for the Cities: A History of the Urban Water Supply Problem in the United States* (Syracuse, 1956), p. 267; Charles V. Chapin, *Municipal Sanitation in the United States* (Providence, R.I., 1901), p. 263; John Shaw Billings, "Sewage Disposal in Cities," *Harper's New Monthly Magazine* 71 (September 1885): 582; Charles-Edward Amory Winslow, *The Evolution and Significance of the Modern Public Health Campaign* (New Haven, Conn., 1923), p. 38; United States Public Health Service, *Public Health Bulletin No. 164, Municipal Health Department Practice for the Year 1923 Based upon Surveys of the 100 Largest Cities in the United States* (Washington, D.C., 1926), pp. 474–75 (hereafter referred to as USPHS, *Municipal Health*).

2. American Public Works Association, *History of Public Works in the United States, 1776–1976*, ed. Ellis C. Armstrong, Michael Robinson, and Suellen Hoy (Chicago, 1976), p. 219, Newark Department of Public Works, *Annual Report of the Division of Water, 1941, Early History of Newark's Water Supply System*, p. 7.

3. Blake, *Water for the Cities*, pp. 5, 177.

4. Ibid., pp. 76–77.

5. Ibid., p. 26; APWA, *History of Public Works*, p. 218.

6. Blake, *Water for the Cities*, pp. 142–44, 169, 231.

7. John H. Ellis, "Businessmen and Public Health in the Urban South during the Nineteenth Century: New Orleans, Memphis, and Atlanta," *Bulletin of the History of Medicine* 44 (May–June 1970): 203–7; *Newark Evening News*, 10 January 1884.

8. Atlanta Chamber of Commerce, *Annual Report for 1905*, p. 8; *Atlanta Constitution*, 5 and 8 September 1905.

9. *Atlanta Constitution*, 19 September 1905.

10. Blake, *Water for the Cities*, pp. 248–54.

11. Charles-Edward Amory Winslow, *Man and Epidemics* (Princeton, 1952), pp. 271-76; Charles E. Rosenberg, *The Cholera Years: The United States in 1832, 1849, and 1866* (Chicago, 1962), pp. 193–94.

12. James A. Doull, "Cholera," in Kenneth F. Maxcy and Milton J. Rosenau, *Preventative Medicine and Public Health*, ed. Philip E. Sartwell, 9th ed., rev. and enl. (New York, 1965), pp. 243, 246–47.

13. George Rosen, *A History of Public Health* (New York, 1958), pp. 285–88; George C. Whipple, *Typhoid Fever, Its Causation, Transmission, and Prevention* (New York, 1908), pp. 20–23, 132.

14. Whipple, *Typhoid Fever*, pp. 132, 228–30.

15. George H. Bailey, *Report to the Newark Aqueduct Board upon the Subject of a Supply of Water for the City of Newark* (Newark, 1861), pp. 23–24, 43; George H. Bailey, *Report of the Newark Aqueduct Board* (Newark, 1871), pp. 4–5.

16. Albert R. Leeds, *Shall We Continue to Use the Sewage Polluted Passaic; or Shall We Get Pure Water?* (Jersey City, 1887), pp. 13–14.

17. Whipple, *Typhoid Fever*, pp. 149–52.

18. Ibid., pp. 158–61.

19. Ibid., p. 163.

20. James C. O'Connell, "Chicago's Quest for Pure Water," *Essays in Public Works History*, no. 1 (Washington, D.C., 1976), pp. 1–3.

21. Louis P. Cain, "Unfouling the Public's Nest: Chicago's Sanitary Diversion of Lake Michigan Water," *Technology and Culture* 15 (October 1974): 594–95.

22. O'Connell, "Chicago's Quest for Pure Water," p. 4–5.

23. John R. Hornady, *Atlanta Yesterday, Today, and Tomorrow* (n.p., 1922), pp. 105-6; Franklin M. Garrett, *Atlanta and Environs: A Chronicle of Its People and Events*, 3 vols. (New York, 1954), 1:914–18; *Atlanta Constitution*, 4 February 1885.

24. Garrett, *Atlanta and Environs*, 2:260; United States Department of Commerce, Bureau of the Census, *Tenth Census of the United States, 1880* (Washington, D.C., 1886–87), 14:160; *Atlanta Constitution*, 6 and 21 June 1879, 9 July 1881.

25. *Atlanta Constitution*, 5 September 1883, 30 January 1885; "Annual Report of the Committee on Wells, Pumps, and Cisterns for the Year 1878," in Minutes of the City Council of Atlanta, City Hall, Atlanta, Georgia, vol. 9, n.d.

26. *Annual Report of the Officer of the City of Atlanta for the Year Ending December 31, 1885, Showing the Condition of Municipal Affairs* (Atlanta, 1886), p. 22 (hereafter cited as *Atlanta Annual Reports*).

27. Blake, *Water for the Cities*, pp. 272–76.

28. Edgar W. Martin, *The Standard of Living in 1860* (Chicago, 1942), pp. 111–12; *Annual Report of the [Newark] Board of Health, 1894*, p. 20; Stuart Galishoff, *Safeguarding the Public Health: Newark, 1895-1918* (Westport, Conn., 1975), p. 44.

29. Blake, *Water for the Cities*, pp. 276–82; Whipple, *Typhoid Fever*, p. 276; APWA,

History of Public Works, pp. 222-24.

30. Blake, *Water for the Cities*, p. 275; Whipple, *Typhoid Fever*, pp. 246-47.

31. Whipple, *Typhoid Fever*, pp. 136-40.

32. APWA, *History of Public Works*, pp. 236-37.

33. Rosen, *History of Public Health*, pp. 311-14; Moses N. Baker, *The Quest for Pure Water: The History of Water Purification from the Earliest Records to the Twentieth Century* (New York, 1948), pp. 136-40; Blake, *Water for the Cities*, p. 261.

34. George C. Whipple, "Fifty Years of Water Purification," in *A Half Century of Public Health: Jubilee Historical Volume of the American Public Health Association*, ed. Mazyck Porcher Ravenel (New York, 1921), p. 164; APWA, *History of Public Works*, p. 237.

35. APWA, *History of Public Works*, pp. 237-38. Allen Hazen, *Clear Water and How to Get It* (New York, 1907), pp. 77-79; Baker, *Quest for Pure Water*, p. 227.

36. APWA, *History of Public Works*, pp. 238-39.

37. Newark Aqueduct Board, *Pollution of the Passaic River: Embracing the Report of the Special Committee Appointed to Represent the Newark Aqueduct Board in the Board of Inspection of the Passaic River and its Tributaries* (Newark, 1882), pp. 8-9 (hereafter cited as Newark Aqueduct Board, *Report of the Special Committee*).

38. *Newark Sunday Call*, 25 April 1880; Newark Aqueduct Board, *Report of the Special Committee*, pp. 3-6, 12-19; *Newark Evening News*, 12 June 1886.

39. Ezra M. Hunt, "The Passaic River as Related to Water Supply and Death Rates," in New Jersey, Board of Health, *Annual Report for 1887*, p. 335.

40. *Annual Report of the Newark Aqueduct Board, 1884*, pp. 131-32.

41. Leeds, *Sewage Polluted Passaic*, pp. 10-13; New Jersey, Passaic Valley Sewerage Commissioners, *Brief Description of Passaic Valley Sewerage Commission* [by William Gavin Taylor] (n.p., 1916), p. 3.

42. *Newark Evening News*, 2 September 1887.

43. Ibid.

44. *Newark Sunday Call*, 26 June 1887, 10 February 1889; *Newark Evening News*, 4 June 1887.

45. Samuel Harry Popper, "Newark, N.J., 1870-1910; Chapters in the Evolution of an American Metropolis" (Ph.D. diss., New York University, 1952), p. 279; *Annual Report of the [Newark] Board of Trade, 1885*, p. 12.

46. *Annual Report of the [Newark] Board of Health, 1899*, pp. 7, 106, and *1900*, p. 71.

47. O'Connell, "Chicago's Quest for Pure Water," pp. 5-14.

48. F. Garvin Davenport, "The Sanitation Revolution in Illinois, 1870-1900," *Journal of the Illinois State Historical Society* 66 (Autumn 1973): 313.

49. Whipple, *Typhoid Fever*, pp. 162-63.

50. Ibid., pp. 164-65.

51. O'Connell, "Chicago's Quest for Pure Water," p. 18.

52. *Atlanta Annual Reports, 1889, Mayor John T. Glenn's Address*, pp. 14-15; Rudolph Hering, "Report on Water Supply for Atlanta," in ibid., pp. 254-72; *Atlanta Constitution*, 16 December 1888, 3 September 1889, 3 December 1891, 30 September 1893.

53. *Points of Information of the Atlanta Water Works* (Atlanta, 1913), pp. 6-7; Baker, *Quest for Pure Water*, p. 194.

54. Atlanta Chamber of Commerce, *Urgent Needs of Atlanta* (Atlanta, 1908), pp. 7-8; United States Department of Commerce, Bureau of the Census, *Mortality Statistics*,

1910, pp. 15-18; *Progress* [Journal of the Atlanta Chamber of Commerce] 1 (May 1909): 5.

55. *Progress* 1 (October 1909): 3.

56. Garrett, *Atlanta and Environs*, 2:559; *Progress* 1 (February 1910): 13-14; 3 (January 1912): 4.

57. Hugh M. Willett, *Public Health in Atlanta* (Atlanta, 1917), p. 7.

58. USPHS, *Municipal Health*, pp. 471, 489, 501.

59. Blake, *Water for the Cities*, pp. 263-64; USPHS, *Municipal Health*, p. 141.

60. USPHS, *Municipal Health*, pp. 467-69, 474-77.

61. *Newark Evening News*, 23 May 1884; [Anonymous], *History of Passaic Valley District Sewerage and Drainage Commission* (n.p., n.d.); Frank John Urquhart, *A History of the City of Newark, New Jersey*, 3 vols. (New York, 1913), 2:672; *Newark Star Ledger*, 20 July 1946.

62. Whipple, *Typhoid Fever*, p. 266.

63. Ibid.; Earle B. Phelps, "Stream Pollution by Industrial Wastes and Its Control," in *A Half Century of Public Health*, ed. Ravenel, pp. 206-8; H. Wayne Morgan, "America's First Environmental Challenge, 1865-1920," in *Essays on the Gilded Age*, ed. Margaret Francine Morris (Austin, 1973), pp. 87-90.

3. The Development and Impact of Urban Wastewater Technology: Changing Concepts of Water Quality Control, 1850–1930

By Joel A. Tarr, James McCurley, and Terry F. Yosie

Introduction

Throughout its history, urban America has confronted the task of supplying potable water to its citizens and disposing of their wastes in a manner that would not contaminate the environment in which they lived. Although these two problems are not necessarily related, they became increasingly so over time, not because of any inherent characteristics of the wastes themselves but because of conscious choices made about the type of technology utilized for removal. The form of technology that cities adopted and implemented in the late nineteenth century (the sewerage or water-carriage system) solved immediate local problems but produced pollution difficulties for other communities. The study of the development of sewerage systems, therefore, reflects a classic case of a technology that benefited its users but imposed its costs on others in the society.

The period from 1850 to 1930 was marked both by the widespread adoption of water-carriage systems by urban America and by attempts to deal with the unexpected and negative impacts of this technology. This essay focuses upon the reasons for the adoption of the technology, its impacts upon the public health, and the various attempts made by government to deal with its negative consequences through regulatory policy.

The Water Supply and Wastewater Collection System, 1800–1860

Until well into the second half of the nineteenth century, most American urbanites depended upon local sources for water supply. A characteristic feature of the early-nineteenth-century city was public wells and pumps that utilized local groundwater supplies; householders also dug their own private wells or used water from neighborhood ponds and streams. In cities such as New Orleans, where the poor quality of the groundwater prevented dependence on wells, cisterns were used to catch and preserve rainwater. Water consumption per capita under these supply conditions probably averaged between three and five gallons a day, with higher consumption by those who could afford to purchase larger supplies from water peddlers.[1]

Wastewater was disposed of in the most convenient manner possible, sometimes merely by casting it on the ground or in a dry well or leaching cesspool (a hole lined with broken stone). Human wastes were occasionally deposited in cesspools but more often in privy vaults close to or in the cellars of houses. Usually the vaults were not watertight, and their contents leaked into the surrounding ground. A few cities experimented with covered removable tubs as an alternative to the privy vault, but they were never widely adopted.[2]

Privy vaults had limited capacities and had to be replaced or emptied periodically to prevent overflow. In some cities, filled vaults were covered over with dirt and new ones dug. Most large cities tried to institute periodic emptying by private scavengers under city contract or by city employees. However, the cleaning process was inefficient and the workmen were often careless, creating both aesthetic and health problems.[3] Nauseating odors arose from the opened vaults and the removal carts invariably left a trail of wastes behind them. In most cities ordinances required that privies be emptied only at night.[4]

The wastes were disposed of in nearby watercourses, dumped on land beyond the city's boundaries, recycled on nearby farmland, or sold to reprocessing plants to be made into fertilizer. In 1880, the wastes of 103 of 222 United States cities were used on the land. In a few of the cities wastes were collected by the farmers themselves rather than by scavengers. However, in the latter part of the nineteenth century, dumping or use on the land within the catchment area of the urban water supply was forbidden, and the practice of recycling waters and nutrients from human wastes was extensive.[5]

The larger cities such as New York and Boston had sewers as early as the end of the eighteenth century, but they were intended for stormwater rather than human waste removal. In fact, ordinances forbade the placing of waste in the sewers. These sewers were constructed of brick or wood, large enough to allow men to enter for cleaning. The majority of cities throughout much of the nineteenth century, however, had no underground drains. Street gutters, either on the sides or in the middle of the roadway provided for stormwater and occasionally for waste removal, although human wastes usually were placed in cesspools or privy vaults.[6]

Certain characteristics of this system of wastewater disposal sharply distinguished it from the system that followed. System maintenance was primarily an individual rather than a municipal responsibility. Even though municipalities had ordinances requiring the periodic cleaning of privies, they were enforced only when an overflow created a nuisance. Also, removal of waste was a labor-intensive rather than a capital-intensive activity. The equipment used for cleaning and removal was typically buckets, dippers, and casks, with horse-drawn carts for transport. Although this equipment did require some financial outlay, the largest expenditures went for labor.[7] Finally, the system created both nuisances and health hazards. Medical opinion was not agreed over the nature of the danger to health. Physicians were divided into contagionists and anti-contagionists, with the contagionists generally maintaining that disease was transmitted by contact with a diseased individual and the anti-contagionists arguing that "vitiated" atmosphere was the cause. As the century advanced, an increasing number of physicians came to believe that filth facilitated disease transmission, but few cities cleaned their environs unless epidemics threatened.[8]

The Breakdown of the Cesspool–Privy Vault–Scavenger System of Waste Removal

During the years between 1820 and 1880, demographic and technological factors combined to place a great strain on the cesspool–privy vault–scavenger system and to cause its eventual collapse and replacement. One of the most important reasons for this breakdown was the urban population growth of the nineteenth century and the accompanying increases in population density. Densities were highest in the original central cores of the cities; in 1880 figures of over one hundred persons per acre were common.[9] While cities did grow in area in response to population growth, spatial expansion of population was confined by a slow and rudimentary public transportation system.[10] High concentrations of people severely overloaded existing waste collection systems. Overflowing privies and cesspools filled the alleys and yards of the urban slums and often seeped into nearby wells from which the population drew its water supply.[11]

Ironically, the development of new water supply systems, which provided running water, also critically overextended the existing waste removal systems. Running water, the negative impacts of which were not anticipated, resulted in the adoption of another innovation, water closets, which became the newest means of collecting and removing human waste from the home. The advent of piped water had numerous repercussions. Cities soon had to rely more heavily on distant supplies of water because of the widespread contamination of local sources by sewage and the variety and extent of demand for water.

As the number of cities with waterworks rapidly multiplied in the late nineteenth century, household installation of water fixtures soared.[12] In 1848, for instance, Boston opened the Cochituate Aqueduct, and by 1853 there were 31,750 water fixtures in use. By 1864, the number of fixtures had increased to 86,949. Detroit opened a new waterworks in 1841 with 611 connected households; by 1859 the number had risen to 6,794 and by 1874 to 17,019.[13] The availability and convenience of a constant supply of water caused a rapid increase in per capita use. Chicago went from 33 gallons per person per day in 1856 to 144 in 1882. Cleveland's usage increased from 8 gallons per capita per day in 1857 to 55 in 1872; Detroit went from 55 gallons in 1856 to 149 in 1882.[14] (These figures include industrial and other nonhousehold uses but still represent substantial water consumption increases over a relatively short period of time.)

Despite the proliferation of waterworks in the first three-quarters of the nineteenth century, no city simultaneously constructed a sewer system to remove the water and wastes, although in some cities householders had short, private sewers constructed to avoid nuisance. In most cities with waterworks, wastewater initially was diverted into cesspools or existing stormwater sewers or street gutters. The introduction of such large volumes of water into systems designed to accommodate much smaller amounts caused flooding and serious disposal problems. Chicago introduced piped-in water in 1842 and soon had difficulties with stagnant water and damp cellars on low-lying land. Pawtucket, Rhode Island, introduced running water in 1878. Soon the town council was besieged with petitions for relief. "Water was here," said one Pawtucket report, "and had become a nuisance."[15]

While the water itself caused severe problems, the situation was exacerbated by the adoption of the water closet, a device that actually dated back centuries but was patented in England only in the late eighteenth century and in 1833 in the United States. Affluent families in cities with waterworks were quick to install the convenience. In Boston (population 178,000) in 1863, there were 14,000 water closets out of approximately 87,000 water fixtures. In Buffalo (population 118,000) in 1874, there were 5,191 dwellings supplied with water, 3,310 of which had water closets. Approximately one-quarter of urban households had water closets by 1880.[16]

The absolute increase in water usage created difficulties for cities with inadequate means of disposal, while the water closet greatly added to the problems of nuisance and sanitary hazard. Water closets were usually connected to cesspools or privy vaults. Ordinances prevented connection of water closets to the sewers in cities that had them. Soon the collectors overflowed with the increased volume of water. Soil became saturated, cellars were "flooded with stagnant and offensive fluids," cleaning became "nearly futile," and the level of nuisance was greatly increased.[17]

The spread of water polluted with fecal matter created serious health hazards and grave concern. Putrefying fecal matter was believed to be especially objectionable and productive of "dangerous gases" and "unwholesome vapors."[18] Public health officials viewed overflowing cesspools with water closet connections as a dangerous threat to a healthful environment. As late as 1894, the secretary of the Pennsylvania State Board of Health, Benjamin Lee, complained that householders persisted in installing water closets in towns without sewers and connecting them to "leaching" cesspools. Lee warned:

> Copious water supplies constitute a means of distributing fecal pollution over immense areas and no water closet should ever be allowed to be constructed until provision has been made for the disposition of its effluent in such a manner that it shall not constitute a nuisance prejudicial to the public health.[19]

The health and nuisance problems caused by running water and the consequent adoption of water closets and other water-using fixtures led to a search for devices to make the wastewater disposal system more efficient. These innovations were intended to modify the existing system rather than replace it entirely. Three methods were widely adopted: the pail system, the earth closet, and the odorless excavator—all of which had distinct limitations. The pail system and the earth closet both required regular removal to avoid sanitary nuisance, and such service was difficult to achieve, given the inefficiency of municipal scavengers in the United States in the nineteenth century.[20] The so-called odorless excavator—a steam-powered vacuum pump used to empty cesspools and privy vaults—was adopted in a number of American cities. This device, often plagued by maintenance difficulties, solved the collection problem but not the problem of transportation.[21]

As use of water closets increased and cesspool and privy nuisance grew, citizens demanded that they be permitted to connect their water closets to existing stormwater sewers. In 1844 in New York, the Common Council and the press recommended the repeal of statutes forbidding such connections.[22] Although such repeal occurred in New York as well as other cities, the wooden or brick storm sewers were ill-suited to be carriers of human wastes. Water flow was insufficient to remove deposits and the mechanism of the "self-cleaning" sewer had not yet been perfected. Sewers became "elongated cesspools" filled with putrescent material that supposedly generated dangerous sewer gases and spread "zymotic" or infectious diseases.[23] Increasingly, sanitarians and citizens demanded that cities construct a wastewater removal system that would safely remove water closet wastes and eliminate the alleged disease-producing sewer gas.

The Shift to a New Technology—
the Water-Carriage System of Removal

The modern concept of a water-carriage system designed for the removal of human excreta originated in England in the 1840s, although versions of this technology had existed for centuries. In the 1850s, English authorities decided to construct a system of brick sewers, called the combined system, that would carry both household wastes and stormwater.[24] The water-carriage system of waste removal had a number of characteristics that sharply differentiated it from the cesspool–privy vault–scavenger system. First of all, it was capital-intensive rather than labor-intensive and required the construction of large public works. Second, the new system employed batch, rather than individual, collection. It also removed waste automatically through the plumbing, which eliminated the need for humans to remove the wastes from the immediate premises. The third critical characteristic was that the system depended on municipal maintenance and responsibility, not upon individual action.

Arguments over adoption of the water-carriage system focused on economic considerations, health factors, and questions of comparative urban advantage. Water-carriage systems—along with water supply systems—represented the most expensive capital projects undertaken by nineteenth-century municipalities. However, the advocates of the water-carriage system argued that costs were less and benefits greater compared to annual charges for collection under the cesspool–privy vault–scavenger system. In New York City in the 1850s, the department responsible for sewers noted that it cost $18 a year to clean a single privy but only $10 for a sewer connection, a one-time charge.[25] In 1883, sanitary engineer Rudolph Hering conducted a survey of the sewerage needs of Wilmington, Delaware, and estimated the cost of a system at $300,000. He observed that, since the annual cost of cleaning privy vaults was approximately $15,000 (the interest at 5 percent on $300,000), building a sewerage system would represent a long-term savings and would allow increased cleanliness. In Baltimore, health authorities argued that, while a water-carriage system would cost each household between $2.00 and $2.90 more per year than the cesspool-privy vault-scavenger system, "the enjoyment of a thorough and clean system of sewerage" would fully justify the excess costs.[26]

Advocates of water-carriage systems also maintained that the new technology would lower morbidity and mortality rates. They predicted that improved health and sanitation would justify the expenditures necessary for construction. Speaking in 1899, Dr. William Osler of the Johns Hopkins Medical School confidently forecast that, "with the completion of a good sewerage system, the present typhoid death rate of Baltimore, about 40 per 100,000, [would] fall to that of from 4 to 8 per 100,000." Many Americans cited the health improvements of sewered European cities as evidence for their optimism (see table 3.1).[27]

A number of leading sanitary experts and engineers attempted to assign a specific dollar value to the costs of sickness and death and calculated the benefits that would accrue from improved sanitation. In 1875 the Massachusetts Board of Health published an article entitled "The Value of Health to the State," the authors of which maintained that "the prosperity of a town, city, state, or country stands in immediate relation with is sanitary condition" and calculated the annual cost of wages lost through morbidity and mortality to the Massachusetts working population. They argued that sanitary facilities such as sewers could reduce the death rate from 19 to 15 per 1,000 population and that the savings thus accomplished could be used to finance additional improvements.[28]

Several prominent sanitary engineers quantified health benefits in this fashion in urging the construction of sewerage systems. In his book *The Sanitary Drainage of Houses and Towns* (1876), George E. Waring, Jr., argued that the financial savings accomplished through health improvements, rather than compassion for the sick, should persuade municipalities to invest in sewerage systems.[29] Waring, as well as others who asserted that sanitary improvements would save money, often cited the writings of British sanitarian Sir Edwin Chadwick, British sanitary engineer Baldwin Latham, and German public health authority Max von Pettenkofer to support their position. Baldwin, for instance, made hypothetical calculations of the costs of funerals, sickness, and days lost through illness or premature death to British cities if they had not constructed sewerage systems and concluded that this sum exceeded by 25 percent the total expenditures on the works. Sanitary advocates promised equivalent savings to American cities that replaced their cesspool–privy vault–scavenger systems with water-carriage technology.[30]

Advocates of sewerage often cited the benefits that would accrue to a city in terms of comparative urban advantage if they constructed water-carriage systems. Sanitary engineer M. N. Baker noted that "a village or town without water-works and sewers is at a great disadvantage as compared with communities having these conveniences and safeguards. Industries and population are not so quickly attracted to it." With a system of sewerage, however, as the engineer for New London, Connecticut, observed, "the general good name" of the city appreciated, "thus attracting population and business, thereby in-

Table 3.1 *Sewer Construction and Typhoid Fever Mortality Rate (Deaths per 100,000 Population) in Fifteen American Cities Located on Streams and Lakes, 1880–1905*

	1880		1890	
	Miles of Sewers	Mortality Rate	Miles of Sewers	Mortality Rate
Atlanta	—.	66.8	24	72
Chicago	337	33.9	525	72.2
Louisville	41	65.7	52	75.7
Nashville	—	133.7	24	64
Newark	47	52.7	87	99.5
Philadelphia	200	58.7	376	73.6
Pittsburgh	22.5	134.9	87	127.4
Richmond	—	61.3	35	61
Rochester	—	23.4	138	39.6
Salt Lake City	0	—	5	—
San Francisco	126	35.4	193	55.5
Spokane	—	—	3	—
Toledo	—	35.9	61	36
Trenton	0	17.1	4	16
Washington	169	53.4	266	86.8

SOURCES: U.S. Department of Commerce and Labor, Bureau of the Census, *Statistics of Cities Having a Population of Over 30,000: 1905* (Washington, D.C., 1907), pp. 104–5; U.S. Department of Commerce, Bureau of the Census, *General Statistics of Cities: 1915* (Washington, D.C., 1916), pp. 152–53.

creasing the value of real estate."[31] Civic leaders in the South, where urban growth had been limited by high morbidity and mortality rates from infectious diseases, stressed the importance of waterworks and sewerage for stimulating prosperity. Southern urban businessmen and industrialists took the lead in the movement for sanitary improvements. According to the historian of the movement, they "thought of public works on sewerage and water supply as business investments in the projection of a favorable urban image."[32]

While in most cities the benefits of the water-carriage system were emphasized, there was also some discussion of possible costs. Concern tended to concentrate in three areas: waste of resources, possible health dangers, and costs. Opposition to the system based on the first two factors arose from physicians,

1900		1905		Date of Filtration of Water (F),
Miles of Sewers	Mortality Rate	Miles of Sewers	Mortality Rate	Change in Supply or Disposal Site (C)
–	74.6	122	70.1	1892, 1904, 1910 (F)
1,453	21.1	1,633	16.5	1900 (C)
97	64.0	122	49.4	1910 (F)
–	49.5	79	71.2	1908, 1909 (F)
180	21.1	232	14.1	1889 (C), 1903 (F)
887	37.2	1,041	51.1	1902, 1913 (F)
275	144.3	365	107.9	1908 (F)
–	104.6	85	44.9	1909 (F)
–	17.2	241	11.5	–
–	39.2	56	101.8	–
307	30.3	332	23.9	–
–	45.9	23	86.1	–
156	41.0	191	45.7	1910 (F)
–	32.7	65	24.9	1911, 1914 (F)
405	79.7	484	48.2	1906 (F)

chemists, and agriculturists, while politicians and citizens stressed the last factor. In addition, one special interest group—scavengers and odorless-excavator companies—opposed sewerage systems because of the direct threat posed to their own economic welfare.[33]

The concern over the waste of resources by water carriages was based upon the calculation that excreta contained valuable fertilizing materials. Chemists in 1873 estimated that the annual voidings of an individual were worth between $1.64 and $2.01 and were valuable for crops that required a large amount of nitrogen or ammonia.[34] Those concerned with the loss of the fertilizing materials in excreta argued that the odorless excavator or the earth closet should be substituted for the water closet and the water-carriage system. "Is it then wise, is it true economy," asked a Baltimore physician, "to allow these sources of wealth to flow through our drains and sewers into the bays and rivers, to be forever lost," when they could be utilized "for the benefit of agriculture?"[35] In Baltimore, where no sewerage system was built until 1912, the answer was clearly no.

Opponents also cited the health hazards of the water-carriage system: contamination of the subsoil by leakage from faulty sewer joints, pollution of waterways with an accompanying threat to drinking water and shellfish, and disease-carrying sewer gas. As early as 1869, *Scientific American* editorially quoted a chemist who warned about these hazards:

> The present water closet system, with all its boasted advantages
> is the worst that can be generally adopted, briefly because it is
> a most extravagant method of converting a mole-hill into a moun-
> tain. It merely removes the bulk of our excreta from our houses,
> to choke our rivers with foul deposits and rot at our neighbors'
> door. It introduces into our houses, a most deadly enemy, in
> the shape of sewer gases.[36]

Forecasts such as these warning about the potential health dangers of sewerage, however, were far less common than promises of health benefits.

Another reason for the opposition to sewerage systems was cost, since these systems involved large capital outlays. Unlike water supply systems, sewerage yielded no income aside from a connection fee, for no adequate metering devices had yet been developed. Three methods of financing were available to cities that wished to install sewerage: bonds, special assessments on individual property owners, or payment out of a general tax fund. There was opposition by citizens to each of these types of financing.[37]

The perceived benefits of sewerage in fact so clearly outweighed the costs that the nation's cities undertook a great wave of sewer-building activity in the late nineteenth and early twentiety centuries, beginning in the 1870s. The first year for which aggregate figures are available is 1890, when the U.S. Census recorded 8,199 miles of all types of sewers (data for cities with more than 10,000 population); by 1909, the mileage had increased to 24,972 (data for cities with more than 30,000 population), a near threefold increase in mileage or from 1,795 persons per mile of sewer to 825 persons per mile.[38]

An important question in sewerage implementation was the design of the sewers. During the 1880s and 1890s, engineers and public health officials debated over whether cities should build combined or separate sewers. The separate system employed two sets of pipes—one set for household wastes, called sanitary sewers, and another set for stormwater only, and the combined system used one large pipe for both kinds of wastewater. Some sanitarians, led by Colonel George E. Waring, Jr., argued that separate sewers had superior health benefits compared to the combined, but by 1900 engineers agreed that the two systems had similar health effects. Choices between them, they maintained, should be based on the financial capabilities of the city and its needs for economical underground removal of stormwater.[39]

From 1880 to 1909, large cities constructed mainly combined sewers that accommodated both stormwater and household wastes. In 1909, for instance, in cities with populations of over 100,000, there were 14,240 miles of combined sewers, 2,194 miles of sanitary sewers, and 634 miles of storm sewers. Smaller cities, on the other hand, often constructed separate sanitary sewers, leaving stormwater to flow along surface channels. In 1909, cities with between 30,000 and 50,000 population had 1,313 miles of sanitary sewers, 327 miles of storm sewers, and 1,507 miles of combined sewers. Exact data for cities under 30,000 are not available, but the usual rule was that the smaller the city the more likely it was to install sanitary sewers only.[40]

Large cities constructed combined sewers because high densities and heavy traffic required provision for stormwater and the collection of both types of wastewater in a single pipe was more economical than building separate systems. The use of combined rather than separate systems, given the available treatment technology in the late nineteenth and early twentieth centuries, made both wastewater treatment and resource recovery difficult. Because of the greater volumes of water in combined sewers, it was more expensive to treat their output than that of separate sewers. Most urban policymakers and their consulting engineers, who still accepted the concept of the self-purifying nature of running water, assumed that dumping raw sewage into streams was adequate treatment.[41]

Health Impacts of the Adoption of the Water–Carriage System of Wastewater Removal

Although the adoption of the water-carriage system had widespread political, social, and aesthetic consequences, only its health impacts will be considered here.

Those espousing the adoption of water-carriage technology often predicted that it would substantially lower urban death rates from typhoid fever and other infectious diseases. This hypothesis was confirmed by the experience of a number of cities. Between 1880 and 1900, for example, St. Louis increased its sewer system from 202 to 496 miles, and its typhoid death rate declined from 39.6 to 32.5 per 100,000 population; Providence increased its sewer mileage from 43 to 168 miles during the same period, and the typhoid death rate declined from 53.4 to 40.1 per 100,000; and Omaha built 125 miles of sewers from 1880 to 1900 and its typhoid death rate went from 85.1 to 23.4.[42]

Purer water also substantially influenced typhoid rates, but the evidence seems clear that sewers had positive health effects if other elements were constant.

Health benefits, however, were often less impressive than anticipated. In Baltimore, where it had been predicted that a "good sewerage system" would reduce typhoid death rates from 40 to between 4 and 8 per 100,000 population, the decline was actually only from 24.9 to 20.7.[43] What had not been predicted, except by a few solitary voices, was the rise in typhoid death rates for cities that drew their water supplies from streams or lakes into which other cities discharged their raw sewage. Of course, this effect applied whether or not a city had a sewerage system.

Water-carriage technology had been implemented because of expectations of health benefits, but it was now found to produce serious repercussions for downstream or neighboring cities. Typhoid death rates in these cities soared, as upstream or lake cities constructed sewerage systems and discharged their raw sewage into the streams or lakes from which downstream cities drew their water supplies. Some of the more striking examples were Atlanta, Pittsburgh, Trenton, and Toledo, all of whom had constructed sewerage systems in the last twenty years of the nineteenth century but also had experienced rises in typhoid death rates during the same years. Mortality rates in these cities reached levels as high as 100 to 144 per 100,000.[44] Engineers and city officials traditionally viewed waterways as the natural vehicles for wastes under the old assumption that running water purified itself and that the dilution would eliminate hazard. The adverse health effects in downstream cities clearly exposed the limitations of this theory. In addition to the negative health effects, the use of waterways for disposal of raw sewage created nuisances, restricted water use for manufacturing purposes, and reduced recreational possibilities.

One logical source of relief for municipalities and individuals suffering from the health and nuisance effects of sewage-polluted waterways was the courts. In the absence of any specific legislative statutes governing water pollution, the common-law doctrine of nuisance prevailed, used by the courts to restrain any "unreasonable" use of property that damaged others. In regard to water quality, nuisance law emphasized the rights of lower riparian owners to water "with quality unimpaired and quantity undiminished." In actual practice, however, courts usually maintained that lower riparian owners could not expect water of absolute purity since such a doctrine would prohibit all upstream use.[45] While the law theoretically had potential for reducing water pollution, it was most slow and cumbersome, hedged around with difficulties in the judicial process and vagaries in interpretation.[46]

Some relief was, however, secured through the courts. In a number of cases decided between 1899 and 1905, state courts held that discharge of sewage into a river by an upper riparian user, if it constituted a nuisance and thereby violated the rights of a lower riparian user, entitled the latter to recover damages. In an 1899 case involving sewage pollution of the York, Pennsylvania, water supply, for instance, the Pennsylvania Supreme Court held, "No prescription or usage can justify the pollution of a stream by the discharge of sewage in such a manner as to be injurious to the public health . . . to deposit [sewage] in a natural water course, in close proximity to a source of supply from which the water is used for domestic purposes . . . is a public nuisance."[47] In a Connecticut case of 1900, the state supreme court noted that the "right to pour into rivers surface drainage does not include the right to mix with that drainage noxious substances in such quantities that the river cannot dilute them, nor safely carry them off without injury to the property of another."[48] In a few cases, the awarding by courts of damage against municipalities because of the creation of downstream nuisances or property damage resulted in the construction of municipal sewage-treatment plants.[49]

On the other hand, in a critical exception, given the difficulty in identifying the exact sources of waterborne disease, the courts refused to take the position that upper riparian users were responsible for damages to the health of lower users in regard to waterborne disease.[50] In many ways, the courts were not administratively capable of deciding cases involving complex scientific and medical information. They were most important in cases involving damage to property or the creation of nuisances and relatively unimportant in cases involving hazards to health through waterborne disease.[51]

Society, however, had another option—that of statutory regulation of water quality through the police power. In a legal sense the police power was the key to protecting the lives and health of citizens; for much of the nineteenth century, municipalities exercised control under its authority and that of the nuisance law to maintain sanitary conditions.[52] In addition, state legislatures realized that health problems required special attention and permitted municipalities to create boards of health. By the late nineteenth century most major cities had boards of health with some enforcement powers, while in New York City and Boston, in recognition of the extra-local nature of sanitary hazards, the state had allowed the creation of metropolitan authorities to regulate conditions. The need in many cases, however, was for statewide or interstate regulation of stream pollution. Beginning with Massachusetts in 1867 and increasingly through the late nineteenth century, a number of states created state boards of health.[53] Except in Massachusetts, however, these boards usually had only advisory and investigatory powers and could do little to halt sewage pollution of waterways.

As typhoid death rates rose and a number of cities experienced epidemics, public health officials and other professional groups demanded more power-ful legislation. By 1905, of the forty-four states with some law regarding stream pollution, eight states had regulations with enforcement capabilities. In several cases state legislatures had passed this legislation only after a typhoid epidem-ic. Those states with the more stringent legislation were Connecticut, Massa-chusetts, Minnesota, New Jersey, Ohio, and Pennsylvania.[54]

The Pennsylvania law indicated the difficulty of restricting the use of a capital technology installed for the benefit of one city but to the detri-ment of another. While the law forbade the placing of raw sewage into state waters, it did not extend to municipalities already following this disposal practice or to industrial wastes from coal mines or tanneries. Its restrictions were aimed at cities installing new sewerage systems or extending already existing facilities.[55] The lack of retroactive capabilities, future orientation, and focus on human wastes were typical of the strongest legislation concerning water pollution enacted in the first generation of the twentieth century.

Water Quality Policy, 1900–1930

During 1905–14, a major conflict over water quality policy developed between activist public health officials on state boards of health and leading sanitary engineers in such states as New York, Pennsylvania, and Minnesota. The dispute essentially involved questions about the most efficient and economical means to protect the public against waterborne disease and the extent to which water-ways should be utilized to dispose of sewage. Public health officials in the above-mentioned states argued that untreated sewage should not be discharged into streams that were used as sources of drinking water. The strongest ad-vocates of this position were physicians imbued with the ethos of the "New Public Health," such as Samuel Dixon in Pennsylvania or H. H. Hill in Minne-sota. The New Public Health that emerged in the twentieth century stressed the necessity of identifying and combatting the routes of infection in order to prevent disease, especially typhoid fever.[56]

This policy received full elaboration in the report of the Committee on the Pollution of Streams at the 1908 Conference of State and Provincial Boards of Health. The committee observed that there was a "very widespread errone-ous idea" that sewage disposal was a proper use of streams. In no case, it ar-gued, should rivers be used for sewage disposal if they also served as a source of water supply. In addition, the committee maintained that sewage disposal in waterways should be curtailed because the practice restricted their use for recreation.[57]

Most leading sanitary engineers, in league with the municipalities that they served as consultants, took a much more lenient attitude toward the use of waterways for sewage disposal. In November 1912, the committee on standards of purity for rivers and waterways of the National Association for Preventing the Pollution of Rivers and Waterways, a group dominated by sanitary engineers, issued a report supporting disposal of sewage by dilution. It was impossible, the committee noted, to maintain or restore rivers and waterways to "their original and natural condition of purity," and therefore the "discharge of raw sewage into our streams and waterways should not be universally prohibited by law." The committee did maintain that "conditions prejudicial to the public health and comfort and damage to property be kept at a minimum" and that the "safety of public water supplies" be protected.[58]

Sanitary engineers generally held that sewage treatment should be used primarily to prevent nuisance, while the purity of water supplies should be protected by water filtration. Water filtration technology, which had proved effective against waterborne disease in a series of experiments in the 1890s, was rapidly adopted by municipalities after 1900; by 1910 28 percent of the urban population was drinking filtered water. In his influential book, *Clean Water and How to Get It* (1907), sanitary engineer Allen Hazen argued that it was "clearly and unmistakably better to purify the water supplies taken from the rivers than to purify the sewage before it is discharged into them." This approach was preferable, said Hazen, because of its relatively low cost and its effectiveness in disease control, since one dollar spent in purifying water "would do as much as ten dollars spent in sewage purification."[59]

By the beginning of World War I, the perspective of sanitary engineers on the question of the disposal of raw sewage in streams had triumphed over that of "sentimentalists and medical authorities" (as one sanitary engineer characterized them) who opposed the concept of treatment by dilution.[60] The engineers' view was that the dilution power of streams should be utilized to its fullest extent as long as this practice did not create a nuisance or pose a danger to the public health or to property rights. In addition, sanitary engineers successfully asserted that "local problems of sewage disposal must be solved . . . by adjustment to a wide range of local factors and conditions. The problems differ so widely that the idea of a general solution applicable to a great many problems is no longer satisfactory."[61]

During the 1920s, the conflict over water quality policy that had marked the previous generation was largely muted. Gone were the protests of activist public health figures of the earlier years of the century, such as Samuel Dixon of Pennsylvania or H. H. Hill of Minnesota, who had called for the end of sewage disposal in streams. In their stead, sanitary engineers worked in coop-

Table 3.2   *Total United States Population, Urban Population, Water Treat-ment, Sewers, and Sewage Treatment, 1880–1930*

Time	Total Population	Urban Population
1880	50,155,783	14,129,735
1890	62,947,714	22,106,265
1900	75,994,575	30,159,921
1910	91,972,266	41,998,932
1920	105,710,620	54,157,973
1930	122,775,046	68,954,823

SOURCES: Charles G. Hyde, "A Review of Progress in Sewage Treatment during the Past Fifty Years in the United States," in *Modern Sewage Disposal*, ed. Langdon Pearse (New York, 1938), p. 13. United States National Resources Committee, *Water Pollution in the United States: Third Report of the Special Advisory Committee on Water Pollution*, House Document no. 155, 76th Cong., 1st sess. (Washington, D.C., 1939).

eration with a moderate group of public health officials to produce a gradual-ist, "realistic," and cost-effective approach to state water quality policy that emphasized the reasonable use of streams for waste assimilation and protected drinking water quality through filtration and chlorination.[62]

Continued urbanization, population growth, and increased industrial pro-duction resulted in growing miles of overloaded streams—often precluding their use for any purposes other than waste disposal or as the source of water supplies requiring purification. Some of the worst problems occurred in highly urbanized and industrialized river basins in interstate regions, stimulating new initiatives toward interstate pollution controls. In 1922 New Jersey and Penn-sylvania (joined by New York in 1925) initiated the first such agreement with regard to the Delaware River Basin. In 1928 nine states along the Ohio River formed the Board of Public Health Engineers of the Ohio River Basin for pol-lution control and a similar body was organized by states located on the Great Lakes.[63]

Simultaneously, chemical impacts on water quality focused attention on the problems of industrial wastewater disposal. In 1923 the Pennsylvania Sanitary Water Board adopted a unique system to classify the state's streams according to their present water quality and allowed continued pollution in low-quality waters. High-quality water resources were protected, and administrative ef-forts to secure abatement focused on streams designated by the middle classi-fication.[64] The board's scheme established an early precedent for the later use of water quality standards by the federal government.

Other organizations led the way in the 1920s for more effective administra-

Water Treatment	Sewers	Sewer Treatment
30,000	9,500,000	5,000
310,000	16,100,000	100,000
1,860,000	24,500,000	1,000,000
13,264,140	34,700,000	4,455,117
—	47,500,000	9,500,000
46,059,000[a]	60,000,000	18,000,000

[a]1932 data.

tive control over water pollution. Important here was the Conference of State Sanitary Engineers, formed in 1920 and composed of the chief sanitary engineers from state boards of health. This was followed in 1928 by the formation of the Federation of Sewage Works Associations, an organization that coordinated the efforts of sanitary engineers and technicians working in the field. Initiated largely by the work of sanitary engineers George W. Fuller and Harrison P. Eddy, the federation collected and disseminated valuable scientific and technical information concerning sewage and industrial waste treatment.[65]

Prior to the administration of Franklin D. Roosevelt, the federal government assumed little authority with respect to water pollution control. In the nineteenth century a National Board of Health was created but survived for only a short time. The 1899 Rivers and Harbors Act banned refuse disposal in navigable waters but exempted sewage discharges and street runoff.[66] And the Oil Pollution Act of 1924, designed to protect aquatic life and limit fire hazards, applied only to coastal waters.[67] The most important federal body dealing with water pollution in these years was the Public Health Service, which had been empowered to investigate waterborne disease by the Public Health Service Act of 1912. The service conducted scientific studies of water pollution, water purification, and sewage treatment, thereby greatly advancing basic knowledge in these areas. The function of the service was purely an advisory one; it tended to warn about the future consequences of growth rather than to criticize existing water pollution control programs.[68]

In essence, relatively little change in sewage and wastewater disposal policies took place in the 1920s. Few states required construction of treatment facilities, seemingly content with the protection of water supplies afforded by filtration or chlorination. Industries continued to discharge untreated wastes into waterways except when it proved profitable to recover the wastes. Be-

Figure 3.1. Urban population, water treatment, and sewage treatment, 1880–1940

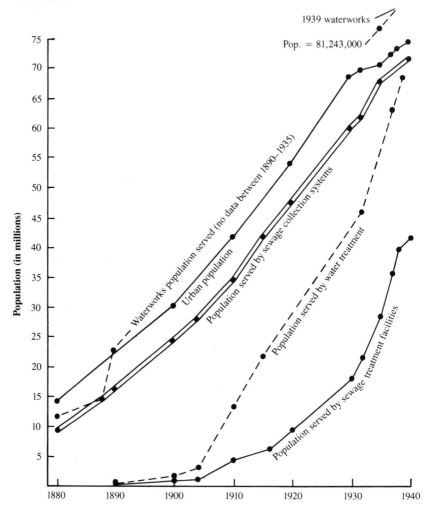

tween 1920 and 1930, while the population served by sewage treatment increased from about 4.5 to 18 million, the population served by sewers increased from about 35 to 60 million. Simultaneously, those served by water treatment increased from about 13 to 46 million, reflecting the emphasis on protecting potable water supplies.[69] In the absence of uniform state laws and administration, as well as monetary aid to municipalities for sewage-treatment facilities, the nation's waterways reached a high degree of contamination by the end of the decade.

Conclusions

The material presented in this chapter suggests a number of conclusions about the interaction of technology and the environment and the resulting formation of public policy, which apply not only to the past but also to contemporary water quality problems.

The water-carriage or sewerage system of wastewater collection and removal developed out of the failure of the previous cesspool-privy vault-scavenger system. The latter failed primarily because of the pressures of urbanization and as a result of the unanticipated impacts of water supply technology and water closet adoption. While the old system was labor-intensive and private, the new system was capital-intensive and public and appeared to promise benefits in terms of health, financial economies, and efficiencies of collection and transportation. Sewerage systems did deliver some of the promised benefits, but they also had the effect of transferring the problem of pollution from the immediate locale to downstream cities. The main unexpected impact of sewerage, therefore, was its negative effect upon the drinking water quality of cities downstream from or neighboring those that discharged untreated sewage into adjacent waterways. In addition, the practice of using streams for the disposal of both municipal and industrial wastewaters reduced their potential for recreational, industrial, and other uses.

The negative health impacts were eventually dealt with by another "technological fix," which emphasized treating drinking water rather than sewage. Municipalities constructed sewage-treatment facilities, mainly for the purpose of preventing nuisance rather than protecting drinking water supplies. In 1930, while 87 percent of America's urbanites lived in sewered places and 66 percent drank filtered and/or chlorinated water, only 26 percent had their sewage treated (see table 3.2 and fig. 3.1).[70] Most states passed some legislation dealing with water pollution, but the growing magnitude of the problem and the fact that the worst instances of pollution involved interstate basins determined the minimal effect of public policy. Thus by 1930 American cities had widely adopted a capital-intensive system of wastewater removal that used waterways as the place of final disposal. The negative impacts of this system were partially met by a policy of "retrofit," which focused on health costs but largely ignored the other uses of streams. The many thousands of miles of sewers constructed from about 1865 to 1930, discharging their untreated wastes into waterways constituted a heritage to future policymakers seeking to deal with problems of water pollution.

Notes

This work was partially supported by a grant from the National Science Foundation-RANN ERP75-08870. Any opinions, findings, and conclusions or recommendations expressed in this publication are those of the authors and do not necessarily reflect the views of the National Science Foundation.

The authors wish to express their thanks to Francis Clay McMichael for his aid in the preparation of this manuscript.

1. Nelson M. Blake, *Water for the Cities: A History of the Urban Water Supply Problem in the United States* (Syracuse, 1956), pp. 12–13; Constance M. Green, *Washington: Village and Capital, 1800-1878* (Princeton, 1962), p. 95. The estimates on water usage are based on figures reported for cities without waterworks in John D. Bell, "Report on the Importance and Economy of Sanitary Measures to Cities," *Proceedings and Debates of the Third National Quarantine and Sanitary Convention* (New York, 1859), pp. 576–77.

2. B. A. Segur, "Privy-Vaults and Cesspools," *Papers and Reports of the American Public Health Association* [hereafter cited as *APHA*] 3 (1876): 185–87; Mansfield Merriman, *Elements of Sanitary Engineering*, 3d ed. (New York, 1906), pp. 139–42.

3. There is information on the "municipal cleansing" practices of over 100 cities in George E. Waring, Jr., comp. *Report on the Social Statistics of Cities, Tenth Census of the United States, 1880*, 2 vols. (Washington, D.C., 1887); "Report of Committee on Disposal of Waste and Garbage," *APHA* 17 (1891): 90–119.

4. Joel A. Tarr, "From City to Farm: Urban Wastes and the American Farmer," *Agricultural History* 49 (October 1975): 601–2.

5. Ibid., pp. 600–6.

6. See, for instance, descriptions in [Julius W. Adams] , *Report of the Engineers to the Commissioners of Drainage*, 10 September 1857 (Brooklyn, 1857); Henry L. Bowditch, *Public Hygiene in America* (Boston, 1877), pp. 103–9; Leonard Metcalf and Harrison P. Eddy, *American Sewerage Practice*, 2d ed., 3 vols. (New York, 1928), 1: 15–19.

7. J. W. Magruder, "The House Awakening," *Survey* 26 (21 September 1911): 809–14; John Duffy, *A History of Public Health in New York City, 1625-1866* (New York, 1968), pp. 182–83.

8. Bell, "Sanitary Measures," pp. 479–575; Charles E. Rosenberg, *The Cholera Years: The United States in 1832, 1849, and 1866* (Chicago, 1962), pp. 75–81, 117, 202.

9. United States Department of Commerce, Bureau of the Census, *Historical Statistics of the United States . . . to 1970*, 2 vols. (Washington, D.C., 1975), 1:11–12.

10. Joel A. Tarr, "From City to Suburb: The 'Moral' Influence of Transportation Technology," in *American Urban History*, ed. Alexander B. Callow, Jr., rev. ed. (New York, 1973), pp. 202–12.

11. George E. Waring, Jr., "The Sanitary Drainage of Houses and Towns, II," *Atlantic Monthly* 36 (October 1875): 434.

12. See Blake, *Water for the Cities*. In 1860, the sixteen largest cities in the nation had waterworks and there were a total of 136 systems in the country; by 1880 the number had increased to 598.

13. City of Boston, Cochituate Water Board, *Annual Reports, 1855-1864* (Boston, 1855–65); City of Detroit, Board of Water Commissioners, *Annual Reports, 1841-1874* (Detroit, 1842–75).

14. J. T. Fanning, *A Practical Treatise on Hydraulic and Water-Supply Engineering* (New York, 1886), p. 625.

15. Town of Pawtucket, Committee on Sewers, *Report, 1885* (Pawtucket, 1885), p. 15; E. S. Chesbrough, "The Drainage and Sewerage of Chicago," *APHA* 4 (1878): 18–19; Town Improvement Society of East Orange, *The Sewerage of East Orange* (East Orange, 1884).

16. City of Boston, Cochituate Water Board, *Annual Report, 1863* (Boston, 1864), p. 43; City of Buffalo, *Sixth Annual Report of the City Water Works, 1874* (Buffalo, 1875), p. 47. The estimate for 1880 is based upon information in Waring, comp., *Social Statistics of Cities*.

17. William H. Bent, George H. Rhodes, and William Tinkham, *Report of Special Committee on Sewerage for City of Tauton* (Tauton, 1878), pp. 25-26; E. S. Chesbrough, *Report on Plan of Sewerage for the City of Newport* (Newport, 1880), pp. 5-6; Rudolph Hering, *Report on a System of Sewerage for the City of Wilmington, Delaware* (Wilmington, 1883), pp. 5-6; "The Sanitation of Cities and Towns and the Agricultural Utilization of Excremental Matter," *Annual Report, 1887*, Maryland State Board of Health (Baltimore, 1887), pp. 229-30.

18. Charles V. Chapin, "The End of the Filth Theory of Disease," *Popular Science Monthly* 60 (January 1902): 234–39; George E. Waring, Jr., "The Sanitary Drainage of Houses and Towns," *Atlantic Monthly* 36 (November 1875): 535-51.

19. Benjamin Lee, "The Cart before the Horse," *APHA* 20 (1895): 34-36.

20. Henry Robinson, "The Pail System," *Sanitary Engineer* 4 (15 March 1881): 179; George E. Waring, Jr., *Earth Closets* (New York, 1868), and "The Sanitary Drainage of Houses and Towns," *Atlantic Monthly* 36 (September 1875): 354-55; Rudolph Hering, "Report of the Results of an Examination Made in 1880 of Several Sewerage Works in Europe," National Board of Health, *Annual Report* (1881), p. 102.

21. Azel Ames, "The Removal and Utilization of Domestic Excreta," *APHA* 4 (1877): 70-75; R. Baumeister, *The Cleaning and Sewerage of Cities* (New York, n.d.), pp. 272-74; Tarr, "City to Farm," pp. 601-2.

22. Duffy, *Public Health in New York City*, pp. 409-11; Eliot C. Clarke, *Main Drainage Works of Boston* (Boston, 1885), p. 10; Green, *Washington*, p. 212. Boston permitted fecal matter in the sewers in 1833, St. Louis in 1842, and Washington in 1858.

23. Bowditch, *Public Hygiene*, p. 105; J. S. Billings, "Sewage Disposal in Cities," *Harper's New Monthly Magazine* 71 (September 1885): 579-80; George E. Waring, Jr., "Sanitary Drainage of Houses and Towns," *Atlantic Monthly* 36 (November 1875): 537-53.

24. Francis Sheppard, *London 1808-1870: The Infernal Wen* (Berkeley, 1971),

pp. 253–58.

25. Duffy, *Public Health in New York City*, p. 415; Hering, *System of Sewerage for Wilmington*, p. 6.

26. Baltimore, Sewerage Commission, *Second Report* (Baltimore, 1899), p. 30.

27. Ibid., p. 14; George E. Waring, Jr., *Drainage for Health and Draining for Profit* (New York, 1867), pp. 222–23; Billings, "Sewage Disposal in Cities," p. 580; Bell, "Sanitary Measures," pp. 478–83; F. H. Hamilton, "A Plea for Sanitary Engineering," *APHA* 2 (1876): 368–73; Town of Marlborough, Sewage Committee, *Report* (Marlborough, 1885), pp. 7–8.

28. "The Value of Health to the State," Massachusetts Board of Health, *Annual Report, 1875*, pp. 57–75; "Political Economy of Health," ibid., *1874*, pp. 335–90.

29. George E. Waring, Jr., *Sanitary Drainage of Houses and Towns*, 6th rev. ed. (Boston, 1885), pp. 16–23.

30. Baldwin Latham, *Sanitary Engineering* (London, 1873), pp. 10–14; Henry E. Sigerist, ed., "The Value of Health to a City: Two Lectures, Delivered in 1873, by Max Von Pettenkofer," *Bulletin of the History of Medicine* 10 (October 1941): 473–508, 593–613; Samuel M. Gray, *Proposed Plan for a Sewerage System for Providence* (Providence, 1884), pp. 8–11.

31. M. N. Baker, *Sewerage and Sewage Purification* (New York, 1896), p. 11; New London Board of Sewer Commissioners, *First Annual Report* (New London, 1887), p. 4.

32. John H. Ellis, "Businessmen and Public Health in the Urban South during the Nineteenth Century: New Orleans, Memphis, and Atlanta," *Bulletin of the History of Medicine* 44 (August 1970): 386.

33. Hering, "Examination of Sewerage Works in Europe," p. 100; Terry Yosie, "Baltimore and the Problems of Waste Disposal: A Case Study in Municipal Delay of Sanitary Improvements" (unpublished paper, Carnegie-Mellon University, 1977).

34. Tarr, "City to Farm," pp. 601–6.

35. C. A. Leas, "A Report upon the Sanitary Care and Utilization of the Refuse of Cities," *APHA* 1 (1875): 456.

36. "The Sewage Question," *Scientific American* 21 (24 July 1899), p. 57.

37. Estelle F. Feinstein, *Stamford in the Gilded Age* (Stamford, 1973), p. 169; Ernest S. Griffith, *The Conspicuous Failure: A History of American City Government 1870-1900* (New York, 1974), p. 20.

38. United States Bureau of the Census, "Sewers," *Report on the Social Statistics of Cities, Eleventh Census* (Washington, D.C., 1895), pp. 29–32, and "Sewers and Sewer Service," *General Statistics of Cities: 1909* (Washington, D.C., 1913), pp. 20–23.

39. For a discussion of the separate and combined sewer question, see Joel A. Tarr and Francis Clay McMichael, eds., *Retrospective Assessment of Wastewater Technology in the United States: 1800-1972*, A Report to the National Science Foundation (Carnegie-Mellon University, 1977), chap. 2. For an appreciation of the role of Colonel Waring, see Martin V. Melosi, "Pragmatic Environmentalist: Sanitary Engineer, George E. Waring, Jr.," *Essays in Public Works History*, 4 (Washington, D.C., 1977).

40. Bureau of the Census, *Statistics of Cities: 1909*, pp. 20–23.

41. Moses N. Baker, "Sewerage and Sewage Disposal," Department of Commerce and Labor, Bureau of the Census, *Statistics of Cities Having a Population over 30,000: 1905* (Washington, D.C., 1907), pp. 103–6. For a discussion of the concept of the self-purifying nature of streams, see William T. Sedgwick, *Principles of Sanitary Science and the Public Health* (New York, 1918), pp. 231–37; and Jay Slater, "The Self-Purification of Rivers

and Streams," *Synthesis* 2 (Autumn 1974): 41–45.

42. For a typhoid death rate figure, see United States Department of the Interior, Census Office, *Report of the Mortality and Vital Statistics of the U.S., Tenth Census*, pt. 2 (Washington, D.C., 1886), p. xxvi; United States Department of Commerce, Bureau of the Census, *Mortality Statistics 1910, Thirteenth Census* (Washington, D.C., 1913), pp. 26–27.

43. City of Baltimore, Sewerage Commission, *Second Report* (Baltimore, 1899), p. 14; Bureau of the Census, *Mortality Statistics, 1910*, pp. 26–27.

44. George C. Whipple, *Typhoid Fever, Its Causation, Transmission, and Prevention* (New York, 1908).

45. Horace G. Wood, *A Practical Treatise on the Law of Nuisances in Their Various Forms; Including Remedies Therefor at Law and in Equity* (Albany, N.Y., 1875).

46. Clay McShane, "Water Quality Law in the United States, 1865-1920," in Tarr and McMichael, *Retrospective Assessment of Wastewater Technology*, 2:7-10.

47. *Engineering News* 42 (3 August 1899): 72.

48. "A Judicial Review of American Stream Pollution Decisions," *Engineering Record* 55 (29 June 1907): 765-67.

49. "Sewage Purification and Water Pollution in the United States," *Engineering News* 49 (3 April 1902): 276.

50. "Sewage Pollution of Water Supplies," *Engineering Record* 28 (1 August 1903): 117. After 1910, the courts awarded damages against municipalities in cases where negligence in the operation of public waterworks resulted in individuals contracting typhoid fever. See James A. Tobey, *Public Health Law*, 2d ed. (New York, 1939), pp. 277–80.

51. Earl Finbar Murphy, *Water Purity: A Study in Legal Control of Natural Resources* (Madison, 1961), pp. 66–70.

52. McShane, "Water Quality Law," p. 16.

53. Charles V. Chapin, "History of State and Municipal Control of Disease," in *A Half Century of Public Health: Jubilee Historical Volume of the American Public Health Association*, ed. Mazyck Porches Ravenel (New York, 1921), pp. 155–60.

54. "Pollution of Streams," *Municipal Journal and Engineer* 21 (3 October 1906): 333; Edwin B. Goodell, *Review of Laws Forbidding Pollution of Inland Waters in the United States*, Water Supply and Irrigation Paper no. 152, U.S. Geological Survey (Washington, D.C., 1906).

55. Terry F. Yosie, "The Change in Policy Paradigms: The Public Health Movement and Stream Pollution Control in Pennsylvania, 1885-1905" (unpublished paper, Carnegie-Mellon University, 1977), pp. 54–56.

56. F. Herbert Snow, "Administration of Pennsylvania Laws Respecting Stream Pollution," *Proceedings of the Engineering Society of Western Pennsylvania* 12 (July 1907): 281; H. M. Bracken, "Sewage Pollution Made Compulsory by the Minnesota State Board of Health," *Engineering News* 51 (11 February 1904): 138, and editorial, p. 129; R. Winthrop Pratt, "The Work of the Ohio State Board of Health on Water Supply and Sewage Purification," ibid. 57 (20 June 1907): 680.

57. "The Pollution of Streams," *Engineering Record* 60 (7 August 1909): 157-59.

58. "Standards of Purity for Rivers and Waterways," *Engineering News* 68 (31 October 1912): 835-36; "Conference on Pollution of Lakes and Waterways," *Engineering Record* 66 (2 November 1912): 485-86. George C. Whipple was chairman of the committee; the president of the association was Calvin W. Hendrick.

59. Allen Hazen, *Clean Water and How to Get It* (New York, 1907), pp. 34-37.

60. George W. Fuller, "Is It Practicable to Discontinue the Emptying of Sewage into Streams?" *American City* 7 (1912): 43-45; Morris Knowles, "Keeping Boundary Waters from Pollution," *The Survey* 33 (19 December 1914): 313-14.

61. Fuller, "Relations between Sewage Disposal and Water Supply Are Changing," *Engineering News-Record* 28 (5 April 1917): 11-12.

62. Terry F. Yosie, "Changing Concepts of Stream Pollution Regulation in Pennsylvania, 1916-1937" (unpublished paper, Carnegie-Mellon University, 1977), pp. 8-9.

63. "Report of the Committee on Sewage Disposal and Stream Pollution," *Transactions of the Sixth Annual Conference of State Sanitary Engineers-1925, Public Health Bulletin*, no. 160 (Washington, D.C., 1926), p. 36-37; U.S. Public Health Service, "Stream Pollution Control Activities in the United States, 1928," unsigned report (National Archives Record Group 90, General Files 1924-1933, box 222, no. 2323-165), pp. 3-4.

64. "Discussion on Policy regarding Stream Pollution," *Transactions of the Fifth Annual Conference of State Sanitary Engineers-1924, Public Health Bulletin*, no. 154 (April 1925), p. 102.

65. C. A. Emerson, Jr., "Foreword," *Modern Sewage Disposal*, ed. Langdon Pearse (New York, 1938), pp. vi-vii.

66. Act of 3 March 1899, chap. 425; sec. 13, 30, *Statutes at Large*, 1152.

67. Act of 7 June 1924, chap. 316; sec. 3, 43, *Statutes at Large*, 605.

68. U. S. Public Health Service, "Activities of the Public Health Service with Relation to the Pollution of Streams and Coastal Waters," 1924, unsigned report (National Archives, Record Group 90, General Files 1924-1935, box 222, no. 2323); W. H. Frost, "A Review of the Work of the U. S. Public Health Service in Investigations of Stream Pollution," *Transactions* 89, American Society of Civil Engineers (New York, 1926): 1332-40; *Stream Pollution in the United States*, House Document no. 632, 69th Cong., 2d sess. (Washington, D.C., 1927), pp. 10-13, 23-27.

69. United States National Resources Committee, *Water Pollution in the United States: Third Report of the Special Advisory Committee on Water Pollution*, House Document no. 155, 76th Cong., 1st sess. (Washington, D.C., 1939), pp. 5-7; and W. D. Collins, W. L. Lamar, and E. W. Lohr, *The Industrial Utility of Public Water Supplies in the United States, 1932*, U.S. Geological Survey Water Supply Paper, no. 658 (Washington, D.C., 1934), p. 22.

70. United States National Resources Committee, *Water Pollution in the United States*, pp. 5-7.

4. The Battle for Clean Air: The Smoke Problem in Post–Civil War America

By R. Dale Grinder

Throughout the history of the United States, many key policymakers have considered economic growth essential to a healthy and well-functioning social and political system. Such high-level policymakers as Alexander Hamilton, John Marshall, Henry Clay, Roger Taney, Andrew Carnegie, and Theodore Roosevelt played a major role in encouraging rapid economic growth. In the nineteenth century, growth was often less the result of natural economic processes than the consequence of positive intervention by government on behalf of business. Perhaps the most notable expression of this policy was the legislation enacted by the Republicans who held power during the Civil War and Reconstruction. Major pieces of legislation, like the Morrill Tariff, the National Banking Act, the Homestead Act, and the Railroad Act, signaled a new era of expansion under the favoring hand of the national government. This period, known as the Gilded Age, rested largely on the railroad, and the success of the railroad in many cases was insured by subsidies from the national government and tax shelters from the states. In addition, such state laws as the New Jersey Holding Company Act abetted the flight from competition to consolidation, a phenomenon common to almost every large-scale business enterprise during that time.

Environmental degradation of the industrial cities was a major result of public policy that encouraged rapid unregulated growth. Illustrative of the trade-offs made for the sake of industrial expansion was the problem of smoke pollution in the years between the 1880s and World War I. During this time, many American metropolitan centers were plagued by what was called the "smoke nuisance" or the "smoke evil."

Industrial-based cities were seldom built for aesthetic reasons. Sites were often chosen with a single goal in mind, that of joining goods and markets. Hence, many of the cities plagued by the smoke nuisance were built along the main traffic routes, which in the nineteenth century were rivers, canals, and lakes. Pittsburgh, for example, was built at the confluence of the Allegheny and Monongahela rivers. Cincinnati was constructed near swampland in a "bandshell" along the Ohio. St. Louis emerged at the highest point near the junction of the Missouri and the Mississippi. Louisville, Chicago, Detroit, and other midwestern communities likewise were built at strategic points along important waterways. All these cities were constructed in areas susceptible to inversions, high-pressure systems that trapped the smoke and other particulate matter.

Geographic setting alone did not make a city prone to the smoke problem. It was the energy source, in this case bituminous coal, which dirtied the air during inversions. Since communities tended to utilize the fuel that was nearest them, Pittsburgh, Cincinnati, St. Louis, and the other midwestern cities located near bituminous coalfields were more likely to develop a smoke problem at this time. Other major cities—New York, Boston, and Philadelphia—relied on anthracite coal from eastern Pennsylvania. San Francisco used natural gas. By and large, those cities that did not use bituminous coal as their major energy source were free from smoke. But without fail, where high-sulfuric bituminous coal was used, there was an air pollution problem. This fact prompted Thomas Darlington, New York's health commissioner, to attempt to ban the use of bituminous coal in the city even during the anthracite coal strike of 1902. And Pittsburghers knew the consequences of the shift from natural gas back to coal in 1892. One resident observed, "We are going back to the smoke. We have had four or five years of wonderful cleanliness in Pittsburgh. . . . [When the city used gas as its primary energy source.] We all felt better. We all looked better. We all were better."[1]

By the turn of the century, the newspapers were reporting "Londoners," a combination of smoke and fog that was trapped in the city by an inversion. The accounts tell a story of darkness, of work stopped, of children sent home from school, of accidents. These "Londoners" were only an exacerbation of the problem that always existed. The editor of the *St. Louis Globe-Democrat* pointed out that "the atmosphere was so heavy that it retained the smoke poured into it. *There was no more smoke than usual,* but it hovered where it was made, and put itself into evidence not to be mistaken."[2]

At the least, smoke, like other facts of urban life, indicated that the Industrial Revolution had wrought a new order. As John C. Van Dyke stated, "There is the whir of machinery, the shriek of whistles, the clang of bells, the strident grind of trolleys, the jar of trucks and cars. And the dirt! It is not in the street and the gutter alone, but in the air and against the blue sky." And, over thirty years before Van Dyke described the city of the "money god," Rutherford B. Hayes noted in his diary: "But now succeeds the iron age, the age of petroleum, of coal, of iron, of railways, of great fortunes suddenly acquired: smoke and dust covering, concealing or destroying the lovely landscape. Coarse, hard, material things." Oscar Handlin may have captured the essence of what was happening when he described the industrialization of Pittsburgh after the War of 1812. It did not matter that "a pall of smoke was depriving its buildings of 'that clean appearance so conspicuous in most American towns.' That smoke issuing forth from a rising number of stacks, was evidence of a birth of industry."[3]

Those who longed for the economic growth that the new industrial order could provide felt that smoke was a nuisance to be endured. For many, a smoky sky was not simply a fact of urban life but a sign of progress and prosperity. As a result, much of the opposition to the crusade for clean air centered around the argument that smoke meant wealth and jobs. In describing the city where *The Turmoil* was set, Booth Tarkington caught the flavor of this theme:

> There is a midland city in the heart of fair, open country, a dirty
> and wonderful city, nestled dingily in the fog of its own smoke.
> The stranger must feel the dirt before he feels the wonder, for
> the dirt will be upon him instantly. It will be upon and within
> him since he must breathe it, and he may care for no further
> proof that wealth is here loved more than cleanliness.[4]

Despite the willingness of many policymakers and citizens to tolerate polluted air for the sake of progress and prosperity, members of civic leagues and women's organizations during the Progressive Era began to voice their concern about the possible debilitating effects of smoke. They argued that the smoke was affecting the lives of homemakers and the stores of merchants. Smoke appeared to be responsible for such varied physical problems as increases in both pulmonary disease and the number of children wearing glasses. Many doctors attested that smoke affected the psychological health and well-being of the community. And it damaged everything from viaduct supports and new church walls to marble statuary and merchandise. By the 1920s it was next to impossible to wear a clean cream-colored suit in St. Louis. The only people who seemed to prosper were the owners of laundries.[5]

The smoke nuisance was particularly debilitating to the health of those who lived in the industrial-based cities. Dr. J. B. Stoner, writing in *Military Surgeon*, asserted that statistics showed "there are more people subject to nasal, throat and bronchial troubles in a smoky city than in a clean city. There are also more fatalities from pneumonia, diphtheria and typhoid fever owing . . . to the lowering of vital forces as a result of the scarcity of sunshine, caused by heavy fogs of smoke." Dr. Charles A. L. Reed, former president of the

American Medical Association and later the driving force behind the Cincinnati Smoke Abatement League, told the members of the Anti-Tuberculosis Society of Cincinnati that "smoke must be reckoned among the demonstrated causes of consumption." The health officer of Cleveland informed the city council that all the city's residents had black lungs. "If you don't believe me, . . . just go to the City Hospital and watch some of the post-mortem examinations. Some of the lungs are so tough that the doctors have to tear them out." Herbert Wilson, who worked with the United States Geological Survey, supported these observations, arguing that physicians could tell fairly easily if someone had been a resident of a smoke-laden city. If he had resided there more than thirty days, his lungs would be black.[6]

In his article, "The Ill Effects of Smoke on Health and Comfort," Dr. Stoner seemed convinced that the smoke problem likewise affected the mental health of the citizenry. He argued that "women living in sunless, gloomy houses and attired in somber clothes [were] also prone to be irritable, to scold and whip their children and to greet their husbands with caustic speech." It was little wonder that the husband sought the "cup that cheered" and that the children were apt to become "dull, apathetic and even criminally inclined." Such psychological trauma led many to assert that the smoke nuisance caused immorality. Mrs. John B. Sherwood, president of Chicago's Women's Clubs, informed her board of directors:

> Chicago's black pall of smoke, which obscures the sun and makes
> the city dark and cheerless, is responsible for most of the low,
> sordid murders and other crimes within its limits. A dirty city is
> an immoral city, because dirt breeds immorality. Smoke and soot
> are therefore immoral.

Dr. Reed told the members of the Cincinnati Women's Clubs that "physical dirt is closely akin to moral dirt." Mrs. S. S. Merrill of Milwaukee worried, "I sometimes think [the smoke] will unchristianize the nation, and that we will have to recall our missionaries and put them to work at home."[7]

As homemakers, protectors of their families' health, and guardians of civic morals, women were particularly vexed by the "smoke evil." Edward Jerome noted this when he was superintendent of the Smoke Abatement League of Cincinnati. He wrote, "woman, the home keeper, realizes more than 'mere man' possibly can the nuisance caused by the smoke. . . . [I]nto every department of domestic life, this evil, like a cancer, steadily eats." The Wednesday Club of St. Louis expressed this from the women's perspective: "The present condition of our city . . . endangers the health of our families . . . and adds infinitely to our labors and expenses as housekeepers." In Cleveland, twenty residents petitioned the police prosecutor's office to take action against the chimney of a nearby cleaning and dyeing establishment; these residents found it impossible to dry their laundry outside, for it became polka-dotted from the dirty air. In Milwaukee, the complaints were similar: "It is impossible for me to have my laundry work done at home because of the smut that falls on the clothes while they are drying." Another resident complained, "Too much cannot be said of the smoke evil. . . . It is indescribably bad. It is bad for the furniture, for the clothing, for the health, and for the temper." As the *Yearbook* of the Civic League of St. Louis stated, "No class of dwellers receives directly the unbearable burden of this plague as do the women."[8]

However, smoke menaced more than the affairs of the gentler sex. Gardeners, painters, lawyers, and merchants were also aware of the smoke's power to devastate and degrade the cities. In a series of interviews conducted by the *Milwaukee Sentinel*, an architect observed, "The smoke evil is increasing without doubt. I have noticed it at my home. Formerly I used only to paint my home every four or five years, but I find that although I painted it only a little over a year ago, it is time again to do the work."[9]

The chief foresters in St. Louis and Cleveland saw the effects of the smoke on their trees. The St. Louis forester reported that, in the fiscal year 1905-06, the city's smoke had killed approximately one-third of the trees. In 1904, Cleveland's forester wrote that "the smoke from the factories and from the engines of the Lake Shore and Michigan Southern Railway is killing off the trees at the west side of Gordon Park. . . . [A] continuance means the entire destruction of this nice bit of woodland." Two years later he observed that "in the suburbs, where the smoke and gases from the big factories are not so prevalent, we find large, handsome trees, but downtown they are stunted by the conditions under which they exist. Without constant care and attention, Cleveland will be treeless in a few years."[10]

Indicative of the smoke's ever-present degradation of lives, health, homes, trees, and just about everything else was the following report in the *Pittsburgh Press*: "A large American flag turned black, as a result of dense smoke pouring from the tall stack of a plant on Old Avenue." The flag had been new when placed above the stack just two or three weeks earlier, "but as a result of being subjected to the dense volumes of black smoke, it now hangs like a black flag."[11]

The effects of smoke on health did not begin to be understood until the late nineteenth century, and smoke would not be regarded as an inefficient waste of resources until even later. But the roots of the smoke abatement crusade lay in yearnings for the preindustrial city. Many people could not abide these "coarse, hard, material things" associated with the new urban way of life. A rereading of Van Dyke's description of the business city in 1908 will make this point clear: "the whir of machinery, the shriek of whistles, the clang of bells, the strident grind of trolleys, the jar of trucks and cars. And the dirt! It is not in the street and the gutter alone, but in the air and against the blue sky." Every phrase used is aesthetically displeasing. One Pittsburgher of the 1890s was certain that the drive for wealth had altered his fellow citizens' sense of values, allowing aesthetic concerns to fall by the wayside. "We groped in the murky atmosphere content to gather dollars and only dollars. . . . What incentive could there be to build a fine house when we knew that in a few months it would be declared defaced or defiled." Aesthetic reasons were prime movers in getting the elite women's clubs like the Twentieth Century Club in Pittsburgh or the Wednesday Club in St. Louis to enter the fray against the smoke nuisance. Smoke's assault caused a good many women to think about the good old days, when the cities were not plutonian or filled with the soot and grime that bred immorality.[12]

From the beginning, smoke abatement attracted its most spirited support from women's clubs and other women's organizations. Many homemakers were consistently exposed to the ills of smoke pollution, and women's groups were a logical outlet for venting their concern. But since only those with leisure time could devote themselves to most reformist causes, upper-middle-class women directed the clubs' anti-smoke efforts. Leadership in the local smoke abatement campaigns included Mrs. John B. Sherwood of Chicago, Mrs. Charles P. Taft of Cincinnati, Miss Kate McKnight of Pittsburgh, and Mrs. Ernest R. Kroeger of St. Louis, all members of the upper middle class, if not of the social register. Both the Wednesday Club of St. Louis and the Twentieth Century Club of Pittsburgh, in the years prior to World War I, constructed clubhouses that indicated a membership of great wealth. Despite this tie with the social elite, these women were interested in far more than keeping their cities free of pollutants during world's fairs and expositions.[13] They were in the vanguard of the smoke abatement crusade; indeed, they more than other groups were the radicals in the movement as they sought immediate results.

In many cases, the women, even those of social prominence, did the dirty work, the tedious work, offering their services to the smoke inspectors to monitor smokestacks. In 1910, the Women's Organization of St. Louis was even assisting in the testing of smoke-consuming devices. The following year, they joined forces with Colonel James Gay Butler, again monitoring offenders and feeding the information to his central staff. Butler had put his money and material into the fray precisely because he felt the inspector was not doing enough.[14]

The same sort of activity was going on in other cities. The Ladies' Health Association of Pittsburgh helped galvanize support for a stronger smoke ordinance in 1892. The Women's Club of Cincinnati appealed to Mayor Julius Fleischmann to move to abate the smoke nuisance in that city, and the club later was a forum used by Dr. Charles Reed when he set about establishing a smoke abatement league in Cincinnati. In Chicago, Mrs. Charles Sergel was elected president of the Chicago Anti-Smoke League. In an article in 1912, Mrs. Raymond Brenner noted the activities of various women's groups arrayed against the smoke problem, not only in St. Louis, Cincinnati, and Chicago but also in Salt Lake City, Baltimore, and Youngstown, Ohio. It was only fitting that Booth Tarkington chose a group of women to petition the titan of his novel to stop the smoke.[15]

To a lesser degree, but with more profound consequences in the long run, engineers were also involved in the battle for clean air. For most of these mechanical and stationary engineers, the question of smoke abatement was largely a professional one. As they saw it, smoke was a residual effect of modern industrialization, and an unnecessary one at that. It was a problem posed by an inefficient use of resources, and they saw their job as one of cutting out this waste. As early as the 1880s, several of these engineers heard and delivered papers on the smoke problem and its remedy. The remedy was generally the installation of such technical advances as stokers and down-draft furnaces. However, the engineers did not stop with mere advocacy of technical innovation; they endorsed, and even helped draft, some of the earliest legislation passed against the smoke nuisance. In St. Louis, members of the Engineers' Club played a key role in writing the city ordinance passed in 1893. A year earlier, in response to agitation from the Ladies' Health Association of Allegheny County, the Engineers' Society of Western Pennsylvania formed a committee to investigate the smoke problem and to lobby for the passage of a stronger ordinance. When the city council considered an even tougher ordinance in 1906, engineers played a key role in securing its passage. The local chapter of the National Association of Stationary Engineers endorsed the measure unanimously. In a public meeting called to consider the ordinance, engineers representing the United States Bureau of Mines and the Civic Club of Chicago spoke in favor of smoke control.[16]

In addition to the women's clubs and the engineers, civic groups took up the smoke question. Chambers of commerce and civic leagues established committees that dealt solely with smoke abatement. In some instances, these members of the civic elite joined the anti-smoke crusade for personal and immediate reasons, as was the case with the residents of Society Hill in Kansas City. Sometimes, their participation resulted from civic pride, as in St. Louis.

Here, urban rivalry between St. Louis and Chicago, plus the prospect of the Louisiana Exposition, helped galvanize the Civic League of St. Louis to work for smoke abatement.[17]

One of the more interesting cases was that of the Pittsburgh Chamber of Commerce. In 1898, Andrew Carnegie delivered a speech to the chamber, urging it to take up the issue of smoke control. Carnegie's concern prompted the chamber to action. In the following year, the chamber created a Committee on Smoke Prevention; in its report, the committee argued that "there will always be found individuals who will insist that unless they are at liberty to make smoke at their pleasure, they will be ruined. Such protestations will have to be ignored." It recommended legislation that would not become law for another twelve years. Even so, future presidents of the chamber continued to push for smoke abatement in Pittsburgh. In 1906, Henry D. W. English helped organize support for a stronger smoke control ordinance. "The question of the abatement of the smoke nuisance," he argued, "is of as much importance as any that can come before the city for consideration. Lives of Pittsburghers are being destroyed." In 1912, William Holmes Stevenson was one of the leaders in the formation of the Smoke and Dust Abatement League of Pittsburgh, an organization that institutionalized the various anti-smoke forces in the city.[18]

Other civic groups involved in the campaign against the smoke nuisance included the Civic Club of Allegheny County, the Cleveland Chamber of Commerce, the Civic League of St. Louis, the Citizens' Smoke Abatement Association of St. Louis, the Optimists' Club of Cincinnati, the Smoke Abatement League of Hamilton County, the Civic Club of Chicago, and the Chicago Association of Commerce. The Chicago Association produced one of the most significant works on smoke abatement, a comprehensive tome titled *Smoke Abatement and the Electrification of Railway Terminals*.[19]

Comprehensive studies were results, not causes. The cause that united all these organizations, in some manner, was an attempt to make their city "a clean, sunny and efficient" place "in which to live as well as in which to work." As early as 1894, James Cox argued that the Citizens' Association was an "organization designed to aid the trade as well as the salubrity of St. Louis." And, in 1906, the Civic League complained that the smoke nuisance had cost the city $6.25 million. Both economics and civic pride were threatened by the smoke.[20]

Despite the fact that they played a key role in their cities' anti-smoke crusades, these organizations were, for the most part, not so radical as the women's groups. While the women approached the problem with a consumer consciousness, the various civic associations were producer-oriented, representing an agglomeration of interest groups (e.g., the chambers of commerce). It was these interest-group organizations that helped the various city councils formulate their smoke ordinances. They commanded the greatest power, but that influence was moderated by the fact that they were looking "to aid the trade as well as the salubrity" of their cities. While it was no surprise that the peak of their anti-pollution efforts coincided with various world's fairs and expositions, the legislation they passed was often moderate, precisely because interest-group legislation brought certain trade-offs. A good example is the accomplishments of the Manufacturers' Association of St. Louis in 1901. St. Louis residents had petitioned the state legislature to allow the city the right to pass smoke ordinances. Their ordinance of 1893 had been ruled unconstitutional as a violation of the state's police power. Only the legislature, the court ruled, had the power to call smoke a "nuisance." So the petition drive ensued. But, before the legislature passed the desired legislation, the Manufacturers' Association pushed through the following amendment: "Provided, however, . . . it shall be a good defense if the person charged with the violation shall show . . . that there is no known . . . [way] the emission or discharge of dense smoke complained of in that proceeding could have been prevented." Consequently, while the city could now pass a smoke ordinance, any inspector charged with enforcement of that ordinance would have to prove that the offenders could in fact have prevented that smoke with appliances at hand.[21]

Before the agitation for smoke abatement legislation, the courts had demonstrated a consistently soft line in dealing with polluters of the air. As late as 1906, the *Chicago Record-Herald* noted that a Justice Gibbons, who handled nearly all the smoke cases in the city, seemed to "regard the $100 fine as 'cruel and unusual punishment.' If he imposed it once or twice a year, he [thought he had been] a most stern judge." His actions helped make Chicago's mild laws "pitiably weak." But, since Gibbons was part of a legal tradition that favored big business and economic growth, he would naturally think that imposing a fine more than once or twice a year was "cruel and unusual punishment."[22]

Judges were hesitant to fine air polluters heavily because, in the nineteenth century, they did not want to hamper what J. Willard Hurst has called "the release of energy." In and out of the courts, it was almost a commonplace notion that a young, burgeoning economy could expand only if those who were injured could not sue and collect damages in full measure. New law had to be constructed and the older common-law tradition swept aside. For example, the developing law of negligence drastically limited corporate liability. The case of *Ryan* v. *The New York Central Railroad* illustrated this point most dramatically. Careless negligence of an engine caused a fire to erupt in Syracuse, New York; the ensuing conflagration consumed the plaintiff's residence, along with several other homes. Despite the fact that the railroad was at fault, the court did not hold it liable. As one scholar noted, "the railroad in *Ryan* was not held liable primarily because the harm it caused was too great."[23]

The same held true in other liability cases. Courts transformed laws that once held owners responsible for accidents on their premises into such twisted doctrines as the "fellow-servant" rule. As a result, those who chose either to live in urban areas or to work at industrial jobs found life increasingly perverse and seemingly without redress. With the law on their side, corporations found it much easier to violate rights that had heretofore been guaranteed the community, including the right to breathe clean air.

To be sure, the right to breathe unpolluted air had been guaranteed by the laws of nuisance, but the weakening of negligence and liability law during this time almost certainly affected the court's evaluation of nuisance law. Although research in this area has been sparse, it is apparent that negligence, liability, and nuisance law had similar histories. They had emerged during the evolution of Anglo-American common law, only to be changed, in some cases quite radically, by the impact of the Industrial Revolution. Because the law changed in response to industrialization, the changes began in Great Britain. Joel Franklin Brenner, who has recently investigated the impact of the Industrial Revolution on nuisance law in England, arrives at the following conclusions: (1) during the 1850s and 1860s a standard of care invaded the law of nuisance; (2) the courts applied such laws differently to factories than to private individuals; (3) the courts seldom applied nuisance law to quasi-public enterprises; and (4) the courts did not systematically prosecute public nuisances. Although the British by no means welcomed pollution, "the legislatures, the courts, and certain segments of the public [favored] industrialization, and they were not anxious to burden industry with damage actions."[24] As a result, certain manufacturers were given a "prescriptive" right to pollute the air.

This pattern of unwillingness "to burden industry with damage actions" carried over to American developments. Basically, the development was similar to the decision in *Ryan* v. *The New York Central Railroad*, except that the issue was nuisance, not negligence. When American nuisance law was hammered out in the late nineteenth century, the courts, in effect, told the people that even though their private property was "being invaded by this smoke . . . , we hold that 'public policy' is more important than private property." As a result, in smoke nuisance cases, most judges began with the premise that factories were both "legal and necessary."[25]

It was neither legal nor necessary for factories to locate where they interfered with "the rights of others to the enjoyment of their possessions." Therein lay the difficulty. The courts sought on the one hand to protect those rights and on the other hand to promote economic growth. In the process, they often expressed what would be the American equivalent to the British "standard of care." As the Minnesota Supreme Court ruled in the case of *St. Paul* v. *Gilfilian*, "The emission of dense smoke from smoke stacks is not necessarily a public nuisance: whether it is or not would have to depend on the locality and surroundings."[26]

This utilitarian notion was postulated most persuasively by Horace Gay Wood, a leading authority on late-nineteenth-century nuisance law. Wood noted that the proliferation of industrial establishments made it quite difficult to file suit against a particular firm. The problem was increasingly vivid for those who lived in large manufacturing cities at the turn of the century. Against whom does one press charges? Wood illustrated the problem with the hypothetical question: If he set up shop in a manufacturing center like Pittsburgh, and that shop were to produce quantities of smoke that would elsewhere be considered a nuisance, "can my works be restrained as a nuisance?" His answer indicated that the British "standard of care" had crossed the Atlantic. If it could be proved that his shop sufficiently increased the volume of smoke, then he should be liable. If not, "it cannot be claimed that I have infringed on the rights of others. . . . [U]nless the smoke, fumes or vapors sensibly increase, it cannot be said that anyone is injured or damaged thereby, and consequently, no right is violated."[27] Smoke was not a nuisance per se, in the eyes of the law. It violated no rights. It did not injure or damage anyone. This was the legal doctrine. The law made it virtually impossible to prosecute polluters.

The law of nuisance was not static, however. Just as the industrial revolution wrought a change in tort law in mid-century, by the end of the century, the courts began to "acknowledge the existence of social costs." Judges as well as juries began to look more sympathetically at the plaintiff. Doctrine constructed in the years just prior to the Civil War fell by the wayside. Symbolic of this change was the discrediting of the "fellow-servant" doctrine and the enactment of workers' compensation laws. Judges, as well as municipal and state legislatures, took a new look at the smoke problem. By 1912, nearly every major city had a smoke inspector, even though he may have had limited power. Little by little, the principle of regulation gained strength.[28]

Despite the various legal and legislative impediments, by 1912 the interaction of women's clubs, civic organizations, special interest groups, and engineering societies resulted in the first smoke abatement laws in nearly every major metropolitan area. In most cases, however, the ordinances were rather tame and stiff fines were uncommon. To be sure, jurists and legislators, as well as some inspectors, recognized the social costs engendered by the smoke nuisance. But they also favored the material benefits of industrialization, and, while they believed industry should be regulated, they did not want to pursue a policy that would hamper economic growth. These views were evident in the press from time to time, particularly after a slowdown in the economy. Reflecting on the depression of the 1890s, the *Chicago Inter-Ocean* commented about the efforts of those who desired to drag smoke law violators into court: "Violating the smoke ordinance is no new thing in Chicago. . . . But the great majority of us do not mind it. We are rather pleased to keep up the smoke. It was cleaner in 1893-97, but not so healthy." In the aftermath of the Panic of 1907, the *Pittsburgh Times* observed:

> This nuisance had only been too effectively abated for too long a
> time. . . . Many will be inclined to bear with [the smoke] more
> patiently henceforth, since it means so much to the community
> and to individuals—bread to the poor, education for the young,
> cheer for all! What a significant revelation of the complexity of
> our civilization that a cloud of smoke could mean so much!

This attitude was well expressed by Booth Tarkington, when he had the titan of the city, Jim Sheridan, rebuff a committee of women who sought his aid in abating the nuisance. Sheridan responded that "[s]moke's what brings your husbands' money home on Saturday nights. . . . You go home and ask your husbands what smoke put in their pockets out o' the payroll—and you'll come around here next time to get me to turn out more smoke instead o' chokin' it off."[29]

The equation of smoke with progress and the dilemma of trying to maintain a healthy physical environment while not curtailing economic growth caused many political leaders to move cautiously. Tom Johnson, the reform mayor of Cleveland, wondered whether or not to sign a smoke ordinance; while he had declared that "he would like to have the smoke nuisance abated," he "preferred to have factories with smoke than no factories at all." Mayor Julius Fleischmann of Cincinnati told the city's women's club that "to abate the smoke nuisance in Cincinnati would be to stop the manufactories."[30]

The quandary over how to reconcile smoke abatement with economic prosperity not only vexed the politicians but threatened to polarize the anti-smoke movement into two camps. Some saw smoke primarily as a threat to the physical environment, while others believed that smoke merely indicated wastefulness. Those who saw the smoke problem as a nuisance generally demanded strict enforcement of substantive ordinances. Those who equated smoke with unburned fuel generally advocated educating the offenders, coaxing them to clean their stacks. Those who favored prosecution advocated action that would clearly have gone beyond the policy that encouraged profits for economic expansion. Those who pursued a policy of education questioned the notion that smoke in and of itself meant progress, but they asserted that fuel economy, technical advances such as stokers and down-draft furnaces, and proper education of the firemen would eventually bring about economic gain. As a result, they argued, by educating the offenders, smoke inspectors and other engineers would cleanse the urban environment and at the same time help make their communities more prosperous.

The attitudes of smoke inspectors on the job clearly reflected the differences between those who advocated prosecution and those who recommended education of the polluters. One need only contrast the views of four inspectors: Frederick Upham Adams, John Schubert, E. P. Roberts, and John Henderson. In 1906 Brand Whitlock, mayor of Toledo, was searching for advice in order to frame an ordinance for his city. Adams, who had been smoke inspector of Chicago during the Carter Harrison administration, sent Whitlock the following advice: "The way to abate smoke is to abate it. I have to suggest three remedies. The first is to fine the violators. The second is to fine them again. The third is to keep on fining them until they are bankrupt or repentant." Meanwhile, John Schubert, who was smoke inspector in Chicago, observed that it had been his experience that educating the offenders accomplished little. "Leniency and the ready acceptance of excuses too often lead to procrastination and the creation of the belief that there is something weak about the ordinance and its enforcement." Roberts, on the other hand, put the issue in a different perspective: "Theoretically, [the inspector] should not act as a consulting engineer, practically [he] must. . . . Abate the smoke, but do not 'bait' the smoker." Perhaps Pittsburgh's smoke inspector, John W. Henderson, delivered the classic statement on the education-oriented philosophy. Henderson argued that the best smoke abatement was "up-to-date" smoke abatement, one in "harmony with the best spirits of the time. This is an age of education, cooperation, efficiency and economy." What this position meant in practice was that the "strong arm and the 'Big Stick' " approach should be used sparingly and only against the "ignorant, selfish, lazy and wasteful."[31]

The debate over prosecution versus education of offenders even created a rift within the smoke abatement movement itself. A major struggle occurred in St. Louis in 1911 at a meeting of all interested smoke abatement organizations called by the Million Population Club. The meeting was advertised as an attempt to "bring together delegates from the various civic associations of St. Louis, that there be a mutual meeting of minds and some concrete ideas be formed by which the smoke nuisance can be quickly and effectively abated along sane and conservative lines." After the group passed a resolution stating that "the smoke nuisance can more quickly and effectively be abated by education than by prosecution in the courts and that prosecution in the courts should only be instituted when cooperative methods fail," the Women's Organization for Smoke Abatement left in disgust. The president of that organization, Mrs. Ernest R. Kroeger, denounced both the resolution and the organization as "milk and water." As the *St. Louis Republic* observed, the Million Population Club and its allies wanted to pursue a policy of education, but the women desired to "throw good, hard stones and plenty of them" at the offending businessmen.[32]

Women's groups had been in the vanguard of the smoke abatement movement, not only in St. Louis but practically everywhere. But, by the second decade of the twentieth century, the views expressed by inspectors Roberts and Henderson and the members of the Million Population Club of St. Louis were paramount because they presented less of a threat to the desire for growth. The education forces could claim that in the long run their interest in efficiency and fuel economy would enhance economic growth, not deter it. Likewise, engineers, because of their reputation for efficiency, grew in respectability, in some cases in awe, during the first two decades of the new century. Coincidentally, progressive reformers began to advance the notion that "experts" should run the various commissions that had been established to regulate the economy. As far as smoke abatement reform was concerned, this meant that engineers tended to become smoke inspectors, since only they had expertise in fuel economy. In practice, the smoke inspectors were not unlike many of the other agents: they became spokesmen for the businesses they were regulating, and they performed their duties in such a way as to enable the polluters to delay needed plant modifications.

Although the education-oriented philosophy of smoke abatement conformed to the overall development of regulation in the Progressive era, the forces of prosecution were not routed everywhere. For example, Charles Poethke, a Milwaukee smoke inspector, strenuously pursued violators in his city. In 1907, the editor of the *Industrial World* wrote: "The noticeable absence of smoke in the districts bristling with chimneys spoke well for the effective work in smoke suppression in Milwaukee—a city only twentieth in population, yet standing seventh in industrial output." Poethke headlined his annual summary for *Industrial World* in 1914, "Anti-Smoke Prosecutions in Milwaukee." By 1915, he was the chief not of a Bureau of Smoke Inspection nor of Smoke Regulation but of a Bureau of Smoke Suppression. In fact, Poethke's department helped keep the number of smoky days in Milwaukee at a minimum until the beginning of World War I.[33]

The prosecution-oriented wing of the smoke abatement movement, far from being ineffectual, was the generating force that caused community leaders to realize the need for smoke ordinances. The Wednesday Club of St. Louis and the Ladies' Health Association of Pittsburgh played significant roles in obtaining the ordinances of 1892 and 1893. A radicalized chamber of commerce was in the forefront of the attempt to get a new ordinance into effect in Pittsburgh in 1906. The Women's Organization for Smoke Abatement helped to strengthen St. Louis' smoke law in 1911 and to turn out of office Edgar C. Parker, a man totally convinced that smoke abatement was an engineering problem, not a political one.[34]

To the more radical members of the movement smoke abatement was indeed a political issue. It was only when an aroused citizenry acted, they claimed, that positive change took place. Only when there was a massive petition drive in 1901 did the Missouri legislature enact a law enabling St. Louis to pass a constitutional smoke ordinance.[35] Even though the Manufacturers' Association softened the legislation by lobbying through a favorable amendment, the law was a step forward. In Pittsburgh, in 1906, the city council passed a smoke ordinance only after clear evidence was presented that segments of the city were in an angry mood. The mayor scolded the council:

> I don't know what their motives are and I don't care. The smoke
> in Pittsburgh undoubtedly is a nuisance, and it not only impairs
> the health but destroys property and mars the city by shutting
> out God's sunlight, to which everybody, no matter what his rank
> or condition may be, is entitled.

The *Pittsburgh Sun* demanded of the council: "You have the power, given by us, to abate the smoke nuisance that is an injury and an imposition upon us. We hereby demand that this be done." The bill that eventually passed was relatively innocuous, but it did make smoke abatement a public responsibility.[36]

Public protest could help push through anti-smoke ordinances, but constant surveillance of possible violations was difficult to sustain by citizen pressure alone. St. Louisans, for example, were genuinely aroused in 1893, 1901, 1906-07, and 1911. Pittsburghers were similarly excited in 1892, 1899, 1906, and 1912. In the meantime, smoke laws went on the books and inspectors were hired to inspect, cajole, argue, and cooperate with the offenders, to acquaint them with fuel economy. As Arthur G. Hall wrote, when he succeeded Matthew Nelson as Cincinnati's smoke inspector, "The policy of the department was immediately changed from one of prosecution to one of education."[37]

As the various departments institutionalized their inspection procedures, attempts to take the issue of smoke abatement into the public arena were less effective. Many smoke abatement crusaders confined their frustrations to an occasional outburst against the inspector himself. Newspapers like the *Chicago Record-Herald* and the *St. Louis Republic*, as well as the more prosecution-oriented groups, tried to scrutinize his every move. Citizens who bemoaned their ineffective inspectors grasped a poem by F. L. Rose, which asked, Isn't it nice to have inspected smoke? The *St. Louis Globe-Democrat* dubbed Charles H. Jones an "opera-bouffe" smoke inspector, and the Civic League went even further. The *Cleveland Tribune*, a socialist paper, accused John Krause of "patting himself on the back too much and allowing the city's air to remain smoky." St. Louis' socialists expressed just as much disapproval, arguing that the "smoke inspector was 'typically spineless,' a phenomenon common to all old party politicians" to whom "private profits are more sacred than the public welfare." Civic-minded women considered the smoke inspectors "mere figureheads rather than real officials."[38]

Such outbursts occasionally had an effect. In February 1911, the *St. Louis Republic* lashed out at the policies of inspector Edgar Parker:

> Does anyone doubt that . . . [smoke inspection by moral suasion]
> has been a failure? Let [the inspector] pick a few notable offend-
> ers and keep after them persistently and pertinaciously
> until they reform. That is the way to make it clear our Smoke
> Prevention Bureau prevents smoke.

By July, William Hoffmann had succeeded Parker, promising that he would cease writing meaningless admonitions to offenders; while eager to work with the manufacturers, he said he would "prosecute them in court" if they persisted in violating the ordinance.[39]

Although there were temporary victories, the efforts of the prosecution forces were increasingly useless. Hoffmann may have assuaged Parker's critics when he assumed his duties; however, in his official report to the mayor, he indicated that "[c]ontrary to the general impression, there has been considerable accomplished in abating the smoke nuisance without the necessity of bringing offenders to court." Similarly, after John Krause replaced C. H. Benjamin as Cleveland's inspector, he took a more education-oriented approach. Upon assuming the position in 1902, he announced that, if he came to the conclusion "that [offenders] cannot be reached I shall cause a number of them to be arrested." Six years later, he informed the Engineers' Society of Western Pennsylvania that he believed "thoroughly in education rather than coercion."[40]

Perhaps the hollow victories for the smoke abatement movement were best symbolized by two research teams combing two of the most "plutonian" municipalities—Chicago and Pittsburgh. The research groups for the Chicago Association of Commerce and the Mellon Institute of Pittsburgh, staffed by a variety of experts, submitted reports giving the impression of progress in the battle against smoke, though the results were more long-range than immediate. Both studies took about five years to complete, and as Benjamin Linsky has noted, "The major effect of a study of circumstances in Chicago, and in many communities both earlier and later, [was] that of buying time for the polluters and the hesitant politicians."[41]

Despite the pleas of press and civic groups, the newer, more "up-to-date" philosophy not only gained ground—it grew bolder. Edgar Parker wrote that "smoke abatement was a problem for the Engineer and not the Legislator." Roberts, Henderson, and Hall, not Poethke, defined the parameters of action within the smoke inspection offices. Given the temper of the times, this was probably inevitable. Nevertheless, the shift to education, by the eve of World War I, saw the fulfillment of the warnings John Schubert had pronounced a decade earlier. The campaign of education had become institutionalized, and such modernization brought with it "evasion of the law," violators "escaping punishment for several years," and the profound belief among manufacturers "that there [was] something weak about the smoke ordinance and its enforcement."[42]

Although they argued over means, both those favoring education and those favoring prosecution wanted cleaner air. Both groups were upset when World War I crippled the smoke abatement campaign. The war enabled smokestacks to emit pollutants with even greater intensity, as their owners geared up for full productivity. The results of such rapid production seemed to bolster the old notion that smoke meant prosperity. During the war, the smoke-as-waste argument fell by the wayside. Although the Civic Club of Allegheny County in Pittsburgh sponsored a poster contest that said that the waste of precious fuel was tantamount to aiding the Kaiser, the smoke continued to pour forth. The number of "smoky" days recorded by the weather bureau in Milwaukee jumped from 47 in 1916 to 212 in 1918. The war effort made no distinction between those cities where smokemakers had been prosecuted or where they had been "educated." As Secretary of the Interior Franklin B. Lane told Pittsburgh's bureau chief, J. W. Henderson, "war meant smoke and . . . people should stand it in contributing their 'patriotic bit.' "[43]

Entry into the Great War dashed whatever chance there was for an immediate cleansing of the urban atmosphere, but the crusade for clean air was set aside only temporarily. Despite the fact that the war convinced many that smoke symbolized prosperity, and even victory, the women's groups, civic associations, and engineers were once again calling for smoke abatement by the early 1920s. In 1924, St. Louisans were rallying against the "Black Smoke Tax." Various engineering journals published occasional pieces addressing the problem. But, in the early twenties, protests were raised against the smoke nuisance less frequently than before.[44]

In the business era of the twenties, the prosecution forces were almost completely routed by the advocates of education. Advance in smoke abatement technology made this possible. However, inspectors like H. B. Meller in Pittsburgh and Raymond R. Tucker in St. Louis played a key role in the post-war developments. Meller, who succeeded Henderson as Pittsburgh's bureau chief, wrote as early as 1920 that "many of the men who were active opponents of [smoke abatement] . . . became warm supporters when they found that compliance . . . saved them money." Meller later began work on a smoke abatement project financed by the Works Progress Administration. When he died in 1936, Tucker completed the project—and by 1940 unveiled a "showcase" program of smoke elimination in St. Louis. This example impressed the remnant of the anti-smoke crusaders in Pittsburgh greatly, so much so that the city that had in the late thirties scrapped smoke elimination programs as wasteful began to emulate St. Louis. The irony was that once again war, this time World War II, precluded Pittsburgh and other cities from engaging in a massive cleanup.[45]

Cities like Pittsburgh and St. Louis, which depended heavily on bituminous coal, conquered the smoke problem only with the technological advances of the thirties and forties. Other urban areas, such as Kansas City, saw their smoke problem disappear with the introduction of a new energy source—natural gas. The cleanup in all these cities indicated that the smoke nuisance was conquered not so much as a result of stricter controls but because of a technological breakthrough that placed a heavier emphasis on natural gas, diesel fuel, and electricity. All these new energy sources combined to replace the "black smoke nuisance" with less visible yet sometimes more irritating forms of pollution.[46]

The postwar developments led engineers like Tucker, who studied the anti-pollution crusades before World War I, to comment on their futility and naiveté. Tucker was amused by the fact that the earlier crusaders believed that they could legislate pollution out of existence. E. G. Halliday was mystified that the engineers of that time actually believed that "if smoke were to be heated to a sufficiently high temperature, it would be consumed." But these critics forgot that those interested in abating smoke were utilizing available engineering theories and that those who felt that smoke should be legislated out of existence believed that it could be done. From the sophisticated engineering perspective of the 1940s, the early smoke abatement campaigns were certainly futile and naive.[47]

The smoke abatement crusades were futile during the Progressive era, however, precisely because the proponents of clean air were limited in their options. They constantly encountered a pro-growth mentality that reinforced the idea that smoke was a sign of prosperity. Especially after the Panic of 1907, opponents of prosecution argued that smoke meant jobs, prosperity, and progress. Such notions would not soon be dispelled and were in fact reinforced by the preparations for World War I. Nevertheless, these seemingly futile efforts to cleanse the urban atmosphere in the Progressive era were a starting point and thus merit the attention of students of anti-pollution politics.

Notes

1. Michael Starr, "Anti-Pollution Efforts in the Progressive Era: The Case of New York's Smoke" (seminar paper, University of Wisconsin, 1970); *Proceedings of the Engineers' Society of Western Pennsylvania* 8 (February 1892): 43.

2. *St. Louis Globe-Democrat*, 17 November 1906 [emphasis added].

3. John C. Van Dyke, *The Money God* (New York, 1908), pp. 113–14; Charles Richard Williams, ed., *Diary and Letters of Rutherford Birchard Hayes, Nineteenth President of the United States* (Columbus, O., 1924), 3: 262, 6 December 1874; Oscar Handlin, "The City Grows," in *Pittsburgh: The Story of an American City*, ed. Stefan Lorant (Garden City, N.Y., 1964), pp. 81–82.

4. Booth Tarkington, *The Turmoil* (New York, 1915), pp. 1–2.

5. See, for example, the *St. Louis Globe-Democrat*, 28 May 1905; the *Pittsburgh Dispatch*, 29 October 1906; and the *Pittsburgh Times*, 16 June 1906.

6. J. B. Stoner, "The Ill Effects of Smoke on Health and Comfort," *Military Surgeon* 32 (1913): 373; *Cincinnati Times-Star*, 29 October 1906; *Cleveland Leader*, 7 April 1906; Herbert M. Wilson, "Smoke Worse than Fire," *American City* 4 (May 1911): 212.

7. Stoner, "Ill Effects of Smoke," p. 373; *Chicago Examiner*, 11 February 1909; Dr. Charles A. L. Reed, "An Address on the Smoke Problem," delivered before the Women's Club of Cincinnati, 24 April 1905, p. 3; *Milwaukee Sentinel*, 10 November 1903.

8. See *Medical News* 1 (8 January 1914): 1; *St. Louis Post-Dispatch*, 22 January 1893; *Cleveland Press*, 13 April 1904; *Milwaukee Sentinel*, 10 November 1903.

9. *Milwaukee Sentinel*, 9 November 1903.

10. Civic League of St. Louis, *Report of the Committee on the Smoke Nuisance*, 1906, p. 5; *Cleveland Leader*, 2 March 1904; *Allegheny Construction*, 14 April 1906.

11. *Pittsburgh Press*, 29 June 1906.

12. *Pittsburgh Times*, 16 May 1895.

13. *Medical News* 1 (8 January 1914); Civic League of St. Louis, *Yearbook, 1911*, p. 34.

14. See, for example, the *Chicago Journal*, 4 February 1909; Mrs. Ernest Kroeger, "Smoke Abatement in St. Louis," *American City* 6 (June 1912): 907–09.

15. *Proceedings of the Engineers' Society* 8 (February 1892); Reed, "Address on the Smoke Problem"; see also the *Cincinnati Enquirer*, 20 November 1904; *Pittsburgh Gazette-Times*, 18 February 1912; Tarkington, *The Turmoil*, pp. 16–17. See chap. 8 of this volume for a more thorough discussion of the role of women in environmental reform.

16. See, for example, Everett E. Carlson, "The Engineers' Club of St. Louis: A Century of Its History," *Missouri Historical Society Bulletin* 25 (July 1969): 211; and the Civic Club of Allegheny County File on Smoke and Smoke Control, typescript, n.d., p. 1; Lucius H. Cannon, comp., *Smoke Abatement: A Study of the Police Power as Embodied in Laws, Ordinances and Court Decisions* (St. Louis, August–September 1924), p. 211; *Proceedings of the Engineers' Society* 8 (February 1892 and November 1892); *Pittsburgh Sun*, 15 October 1906; *Pittsburgh Post*, 10 November 1906. See chap. 6 of this volume for more discussion of the role of engineers in environmental reform.

17. John M. Cox, "Smoke Abatement in Kansas City" (seminar paper, University of Kansas, 1977); *St. Louis Post-Dispatch*, 8 May 1899.

18. Chamber of Commerce of Pittsburgh, *Yearbook 1899*, address by Andrew Carnegie, 10 November 1898, pp. 95–97; Chamber of Commerce of Pittsburgh, *Yearbook 1900* (Pittsburgh), "Report of the Special Committee on Smoke Prevention," pp. 59–69; *Pittsburgh Post*, 30 October 1906; *Pittsburgh Gazette-Times*, 16 December 1912.

19. Chicago Association of Commerce and Industry *Smoke Abatement and Electrification of Railway Terminals in Chicago* (Chicago, 1915).

20. James Cox, *Old and New St. Louis* (St. Louis, 1894), p. 89; *St. Louis Republic*, 24 November 1906.

21. *Journal of the Senate of the 41st General Assembly* (Jefferson City, Mo., 1901), p. 294. See also the *St. Louis Republic*, 14 March 1901, and the *St. Louis Globe-Democrat*, 15 March 1901. The amendment is significant also because the same language emerged in the law that was passed in Pittsburgh in 1906.

22. *Chicago Record-Herald*, 13 July 1906.

23. James Willard Hurst, *Law and the Conditions of Freedom in the Nineteenth Century United States* (Madison, Wis., 1956); Lawrence Friedman, *A History of American Law* (New York, 1973), p. 411.

24. Joel Franklin Brenner, "Nuisance Law and the Industrial Revolution," *Journal of Legal Studies* 3 (June 1974): 408.

25. Morton J. Horwitz to R. Dale Grinder, 17 March 1975; Murray N. Rothbard, "Conservation in the Free Market," in *Egalitarianism as a Revolt against Nature and Other Essays*, ed. Roy A. Childs (Washington, D.C., 1974), p. 114; Horace Gay Wood, *A Practical Treatise on the Law of Nuisances in Their Various Forms*, 1st ed. (Albany, N.Y., 1895), p. 475.

26. Wood, *Practical Treatise*, p. 475; *St. Paul v. Gilfillan*, 26 Minn. 298, cited in Cannon, *Smoke Abatement*, p. 215.

27. Wood, *Practical Treatise*, pp. 510–12.

28. Hurst, *Law and the Conditions of Freedom*, p. 101; Friedman, *American Law*, pp. 409–27; Samuel B. Flagg, *City Smoke Ordinances and Smoke Abatement*, U.S. Bureau of Mines Bulletin no. 49 (Washington, D.C., 1912).

29. *Chicago Inter-Ocean*, 16 January 1907; *Pittsburgh Times*, 28 August 1909;

Tarkington, *The Turmoil*, pp. 16–17.

30. *Cleveland Plain Dealer*, 3 December 1902; *Cincinnati Enquirer*, 20 December 1904.

31. *Toledo Blade*, 23 January 1906; *Chicago Record-Herald*, 22 June 1906; E. P. Roberts, " '100 Per Cent Efficiency in Smoke Abatement': The Province of the Smoke Inspector," *Industrial World* 47 (2 February 1913): 89–97; J. W. Henderson, "Up-to-Date Smoke Regulation," *Proceedings of the 11th Annual Convention, Smoke Prevention Association* (1916), pp. 89–97.

32. *St. Louis Post-Dispatch*, 15 May 1911; *St. Louis Republic*, 17 May 1911.

33. See George Roeder, "Milwaukee Smoke: Problem and Response" (seminar paper, University of Wisconsin, 1970); *Industrial World* 48 (2 February 1914): 140; *Steel and Iron* 49 (15 February 1915).

34. [St. Louis] *Mayor's Message with Accompanying Documents*, Annual Report of the Inspector of Boilers, Elevators and Smoke Abatement, 1911–1912, p. 69.

35. See the petition to the General Assembly of Missouri concerning Senate Bill 204, manuscript collection, the State Historical Society of Missouri, Columbia, Missouri.

36. *Pittsburgh Press*, 23 October 1906; *Pittsburgh Sun*, 10 November 1906.

37. *Industrial World* 48 (2 February 1914): 135.

38. F. L. Rose, "The Smoke Inspector," *Chicago Record-Herald*, 11 August 1903; *St. Louis Globe-Democrat*, 22 March 1905; *Cleveland Tribune*, n.d., in the Cleveland Scrapbook Collection, pp. 243–47; Municipal Platform of the Socialist Party of St. Louis, 7 January 1911; *St. Louis Republic*, 5 February 1911.

39. *St. Louis Republic*, 9 February 1911; *St. Louis Post-Dispatch*, 12 July 1911.

40. [St. Louis] *Mayor's Message with Accompanying Documents*, Annual Report of the Inspector of Boilers, Elevators and Smoke Abatement, 1912–1913, p. 536; *Cleveland Plain Dealer*, 30 December 1902; John Krause, "Smoke Prevention," *Proceedings of the Engineers' Society of Western Pennsylvania* 24 (March 1908): 107–8.

41. Chicago Assciation of Commerce, *Smoke Abatement*, with an appraisal by Benjamin Linsky, p. iii.

42. *Chicago Record-Herald*, 29 June 1906.

43. The posters are in the *Monthly Bulletin* of the Civic Club of Allegheny County, 18 April 1918. Statistics from weather bureau observation forms from Milwaukee in 1916 and 1918. For a fuller elaboration of the effect the war had on the number of smoky days not only in Milwaukee, but also in St. Louis and Pittsburgh, see R. Dale Grinder, "The Anti-Smoke Crusades: Early Attempts to Reform the Urban Environment" (Ph.D. diss., University of Missouri–Columbia, 1973). *Pittsburgh Post*, 15 July 1917.

44. Chamber of Commerce of St. Louis, Committee on Smoke Regulation, *Smoke Problem Not a Modern or Social One* (St. Louis, 1924), p. 1.

45. H. B. Meller, "Some Features of Smoke Regulation in Pittsburgh," *Municipal and County Engineering* 50 (October 1920): 127.

46. John M. Cox, "Smoke Abatement in Kansas City" (seminar paper, University of Kansas, 1977).

47. Raymond R. Tucker, "A Smoke Elimination Program That Works," *Heating, Piping and Air Conditioning* 17 (September 1945): 463.

5. Refuse Pollution and Municipal Reform: The Waste Problem in America, 1880–1917

By Martin V. Melosi

> *If the entire year's refuse of New York city could be gathered together, the resulting mass would equal in volume a cube about one eighth of a mile on an edge. This surprising volume is over three times that of the great pyramid of Ghizeh, and would accommodate one hundred and forty Washington monuments with ease. Looked at from another standpoint, the weight of this refuse would equal that of ninety such ships as the "Titanic."*[1]

The graphic imagery of Franz Schneider's remarks dramatically illustrates the severity of the refuse problem in American industrial cities. The ever-increasing mounds of waste, combined with arbitrary methods of collection and disposal, made solid waste pollution a major urban blight during the late nineteenth and early twentieth centuries. Of course, garbage and other forms of refuse date back to the cavemen, but it was not until the late 1880s that public awareness of the problem brought forth outcries for a permanent solution in the United States. The story of the efforts to resolve the refuse problem in American industrial cities is one of ephemeral successes and long-term frustrations.

As thousands of rural Americans and foreign immigrants poured into the cities in the nineteenth century, the piles of wastes became heaps and mountains. Cramped living quarters and congested streets only aggravated the situation, especially near the central business districts. Not only was there more garbage and rubbish, but there was less space to store it until collection. These problems were at their worst in the large industrial cities of the Northeast, but soon refuse pollution became a nationwide phenomenon. Ironically, increased industrial productivity, which spawned a higher material standard of living for many Americans, also compounded the problem of waste. Consumption of more goods meant a perceptible increase in discarded materials.[2]

Contemporary statistics on refuse, although incomplete, indicate the mag-

Table 5.1 *Tons of Garbage Collected by City, 1916*

City (Population)	Tons of Garbage Collected
Baltimore (593,000)	37,915
Boston (781,628)	52,650
Bridgeport, Conn. (172,113)	19,897
Cincinnati (416,300)	40,692
Cleveland (674,073)	59,708
Columbus, O. (220,000)	20,393
Dayton, O. (155,000)	16,621
Detroit (750,000)	72,785
Grand Rapids, Mich. (140,000)	8,678
Indianapolis (271,758)	23,267
Los Angeles (600,000)	51,062
New Bedford, Mass. (118,158)	10,162
New York (5,377,456)	487,451
Philadelphia (1,709,518)	101,678
Pittsburgh (579,090)	73,758
Rochester, N.Y. (275,000)	30,782
Toledo, O. (220,000)	23,971
Washington, D.C. (400,000)	46,293

SOURCE: Rudolph Hering and Samuel A. Greeley, *Collection and Disposal of Municipal Refuse* (New York, 1921), p. 40.

nitude of the problem for most industrial cities. For instance, between 1910 and 1916, each citizen of New York City produced approximately 1,625 pounds of garbage, rubbish, and ashes per year. In other cities, the annual per capita production ranged from 185 to 1,840 pounds during the early twentieth century.[3] Table 5.1 shows the amount of garbage collected in eighteen major cities during 1916.

Urbanites were not responsible for all the refuse created. Horses, the major source of transportation during the period, contributed a substantial share. Sanitary experts calculated that the average city horse produced approximately fifteen to thirty pounds of manure daily. An official of the Automobile Chamber of Commerce, a lobbying group that hoped to substitute motor transportation for animal transportation, estimated that the 82,000 horses, mules, and cows that were maintained in the city of Chicago produced more than 600,000 tons of manure a year. Given the approximately 3.5 million horses in American cities at the turn of the century, the problem of manure was overwhelming—and every street cleaner knew it![4]

The crude state of collection and disposal practices added to the gravity of the refuse problem. During the late nineteenth century, cities were still grappling with the issue of who was ultimately responsible for providing scavenging service. Should individual householders and merchants dispose of their waste in any manner they saw fit? Should the municipality take charge of all matters related to sanitation? What about allowing private companies to bid for the right to collect and dispose of the refuse? Figure 5.1 shows that there was no national trend in favor of municipal responsibility in 1880, but it does reveal a correlation between city size and the propensity for some citywide method of collection. Cities with a population of less than 30,000 tended to favor private collection more than did larger cities. These findings reinforce the notion that urban growth, in and of itself, had an impact on the extension of city services—in this case, refuse collection.

Figures for street cleaning show a much more significant trend toward municipal responsibility than with refuse collection. Figure 5.2 shows that 70 percent of the cities surveyed in the 1880 census made public provisions for street cleaning. The arteries that allowed humans, animals, and goods to move from one place to another, by their very nature, had to be free of obstacles. The question of ultimate responsibility for street cleaning was determined more easily than that of refuse because, unlike households, streets had no clear territorial limits and transcended the question of individual responsibility.

Compounding the dilemma of ultimate responsibility were problems of waste disposal once it had been collected. The cities had to contend with a vast array of refuse, such as garbage (organic waste), rubbish (paper, cans, old shoes), human and animal excrement, dead animals, street sweepings, and ashes. The variety of solid wastes made collection and disposal complex. Collection and disposal methods for one substance, such as garbage, might not be suitable for another, such as dead animals. Not only was the type of waste a factor in determining proper collection and disposal methods, but also the city's geographic location, its climate, economic and technical factors, and local traditions figured in the decision. More often than not, expediency won out over health or aesthetic reasons. As figures 5.3 through 5.5 illustrate, methods in 1880 varied in form but were equally primitive. The one method that dominated, if any, was dumping refuse on land or into water, an immediate solution that merely shifted the problem from one location to another.

As parts of American cities became vast dumping grounds for waste, many urbanites could not help but recoil at the mounds of rubbish and garbage in the alleys and the streets. In the 1880s, some individuals and groups went beyond complaining about the stench from the dumps or the perpetual clutter in the streets and took direct action to ease the refuse problem. Historians

Figure 5.1. Responsibility for the collection of garbage/ashes, 1880

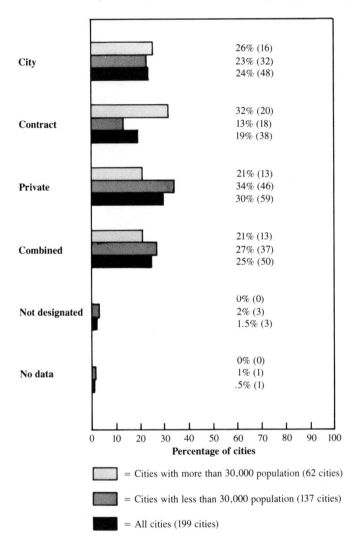

SOURCE: Drawn from data in Department of the Interior, Census Office, *Report on the Social Statistics of Cities, 1880*, comp. George E. Waring, Jr. (Washington, D.C., 1886).

Figure 5.2. Responsibility for street cleaning

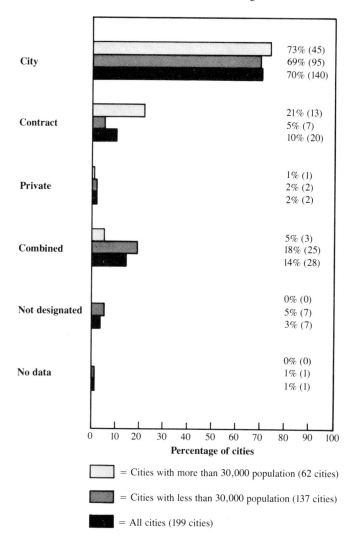

SOURCE: Same as fig. 5.1.

Figure 5.3. Garbage disposal methods (199 cities)

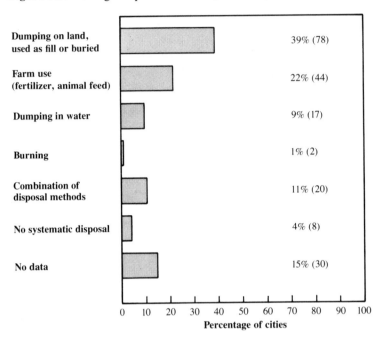

SOURCE: Same as fig. 5.1.

argue that any distinguishable movement for general urban reform did not gain national impetus until the mid-1890s, after the disruptions and dislocations of the Panic of 1893. Reform efforts before that time, they assert, were of local derivation, loosely organized, and short-lived.[5] Refuse reform generally fits this model, but local demands for change fused with national medical and technical opinion to determine the nature of waste abatement in the late nineteenth century.

As recently as the eighteenth century, health officials and sanitarians had assumed an immutable connection between filth and disease. By the mid-nineteenth century, experiments in England and the United States indicated some direct relationship between communicable disease and unattended waste. The work of British sanitarian Sir Edwin Chadwick led the way to new sanitary laws in England and inspired American health officials to regard refuse collection and disposal as a health issue. This attitude was an important step toward improved sanitation in the United States, even though it was not until the late nineteenth or even the early twentieth century that the germ theory

Figure 5.4. Street sweepings disposal methods (199 cities)

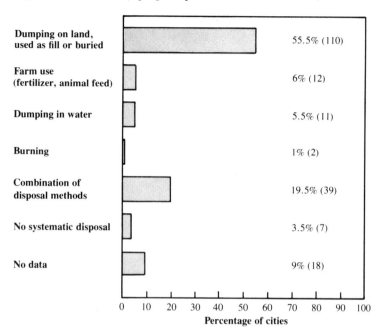

SOURCE: Same as fig. 5.1.

of disease supplanted the arcane filth (or miasmic) theory and revolutionized American public health.[6]

After mid-century, environmental sanitation, especially refuse disposal, increasingly became the responsibility of the cities' sanitary authorities.[7] The 1880 census reveals that at least 94 percent of the cities surveyed had a board of health, health commission, or health officer. Of these sanitary authorities, 46 percent had some direct control over the collection and disposal of refuse, and almost all had the power to deal with nuisances created by refuse. As might be expected, the larger American cities granted their health boards and commissions more direct control over refuse collection and disposal than did smaller cities, as table 5.2 indicates.

It would be naive, however, to assume that the health boards of the late nineteenth century were capable of thoroughgoing refuse reform. For instance, in 1880 few sanitary authorities operated without overt political interference. A large proportion of the boards of health were dominated by city officials, rather than by physicians or sanitarians. In fact, some boards

Figure 5.5. Ash disposal methods (199 cities)

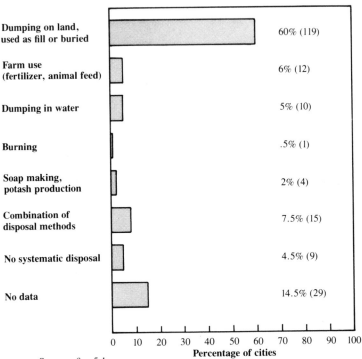

SOURCE: Same as fig. 5.1.

included no physicians as members. Without the communities' best-qualified public health experts in positions of immediate authority over health matters, political considerations were more likely to influence the boards' actions than sanitary considerations. Also, the politically dominated boards were less able to provide the leadership necessary to improve health conditions on a daily or periodic basis; they could merely react to cataclysmic events such as epidemics—and not very well in those cases.[8]

Despite the limitations, health officials tended to dominate thinking about refuse collection and disposal practices in the 1880s and 1890s. Now considered a health problem, refuse no longer could be regarded simply as a nuisance. In 1887, noting the unsatisfactory condition of refuse collection and disposal throughout the nation, the American Public Health Association (APHA) appointed the Committee on Garbage Disposal, chaired by the eminent sanitarian Dr. S. S. Kilvington. The committee was assigned the task of inquiring into the extent of the refuse problem in the United States. For ten

Table 5.2 *Responsibility for Refuse Collection and Disposal (Percentage of Cities)*

Cities with Sanitary Authorities by Population (Number of Cities)	Full/Some Authority	Little/No Authority	No Data
Under 30,000 (127)	38	61	1
30,000–99,999 (40)	55	45	–
Over 100,000 (20)	75	25	–

SOURCE: Same as Fig. 5.1.

years the group gathered statistics, examined European collection and disposal methods, and analyzed the various methods employed in the United States, in an effort to obtain some practical answers.[9]

Civic organizations that called for improvements in sanitary conditions in the city relied heavily upon the health argument to make their case. Dr. John S. Billings, founder of the Army Medical Library and *Index Medicus*, believed that public apathy was making way for increasing civic awareness of the problem of refuse. He noted:

> Quite recently . . . there seems to be a growing interest in sanitary matters in our cities, and people are asking whether the death-rates are higher than they ought to be; whether the city is in good condition to resist the introduction or spread of cholera; and to what extent it is worth while to expend money to secure pure water, clean streets, odorless sewers, etc.[10]

The Ladies' Health Protective Association (LHPA) of New York City became a leading civic force in the fight to bring about sanitation reform in American cities. Organized in 1884, the LHPA undertook a variety of projects, including slaughterhouse and school sanitation, street cleaning improvement, and refuse reform.[11] Although influenced by national trends in public health, the LHPA was a community organization without extensive medical or technical expertise. Thus its protests were often couched in broader, if not more simplistic, terms than that of danger to the city's health. Aesthetic considerations underscored much of the association's interests, as the following statement from one of its pamphlets suggests:

> Even if dirt were not the unsanitary and dangerous thing we know that it is, its unsightliness and repulsiveness are so great, that no other reason than the superior beauty of cleanliness should be required to make the citizens of New York, through their vested authorities, quite willing to appropriate whatever sum may be

necessary, in order to give to themselves and to their wives and daughters, that outside neatness, cleanliness and freshness, which are the natural complement and completion of inside order and daintiness, and which are to the feminine taste and perception, simply indispensable, not only to comfort but to self-respect.[12]

Possibly because of, rather than in spite of, its general outlook about the nuisance quality of waste and its defilement of the city's beauty, the LHPA put the problem of refuse in terms that citizens, as well as political leaders, could understand and accept. The association's successful efforts in lobbying for improved sanitary conditions in New York led to the formation of similar groups in other eastern cities.[13]

While the initial outrage over dirty streets and mounds of garbage came from those seeking to improve the health of the citizens, resolution of the refuse problem required several additional preconditions. Public awareness was important, but city governments had to commit funds to improving sanitary services. Furthermore, departments of public health and public works needed to implement efficient and effective methods of collection and disposal. In the 1890s, civic groups, journalists, and sanitarians publicized the need for improved collection and disposal methods, but with few practical results. Most cities were still grappling with efforts to increase "home rule" and thus found little time to promote broad-scale environmental reform.

The emergence of the sanitary (or municipal) engineering profession played a more important role in refuse reform than did municipal initiatives.[14] Sanitary engineers became intrigued with European, especially English, efforts to deal more efficiently and "scientifically" with refuse. The technological leadership of Europeans in this area was no surprise, since English and Continental cities had been struggling with the waste problem long before the United States was founded. American engineers were interested primarily in English experiments in incineration, which began on the municipal level in 1874. By 1876, Alfred Fryer built the first municipal refuse "destructor" in Manchester, marking the beginning of large-scale use of incinerators throughout England. The apparent success of British efforts led to the construction of similar "destructors" in the United States. (Americans called them "garbage furnaces," "cremators," and "incinerators".) In 1885, Lt. H. J. Reilly (United States Army) built the first American garbage furnace at Governor's Island, New York. In 1886-87, the first municipal cremators were built in Wheeling, West Virginia, Allegheny, Pennsylvania, and Des Moines, Iowa.[15]

To many engineers and sanitarians, the introduction of the incinerator harkened a new day for refuse disposal. Regulated disposal by fire seemed to be the technological panacea to a monumental problem. As

Doctor Kilvington told an audience at the APHA's annual meeting in Milwaukee in 1888:

> Everywhere interest in the question of cremation is awakening,
> and the present points to a future—a near future—in which every
> city, large or small, upon the American continent will consider
> the crematory a necessary part of its municipal outfit; forward to
> a time when our cities will be redeemed from the curse of accu-
> mulating waste, when the rivers will be unpolluted by the sewage
> which now converts them into common sewers, when the cess-
> vault and the garbage-pit and the manure heap and even the earth
> cemetery will be abandoned, when the age of filth-formation will
> be superseded by the era of filth-destruction, when fire will purify
> alike the refuse of the living and the remains of the dead—but
> also is it allotted to each one of us to help to bring in the coming
> of this sanitary consummation.[16]

Soon other technological breakthroughs were being tested and marketed. In 1886 a company in Buffalo, New York, introduced the so-called Vienna or Merz process for extracting oils from city garbage. The reduction process, as it became known, was intended to provide cities with salable by-products such as grease, fertilizer, and perfume base, which would offset part of the high cost of disposal. Like the incinerator, the reduction process was hailed as another ultimate solution to the waste problem.[17]

Enthusiasm over the new technologies imported from Europe led to substantial reevaluation of collection and disposal practices in the United States. However, the appointment of Colonel George E. Waring, Jr., as street cleaning commissioner of New York City (1895) was the major turning point in the development of modern refuse management. Waring was born in Pound Ridge, New York, in 1833. As a young man he studied engineering and agricultural chemistry, and by the mid-1850s he divided his time between farming in the spring and lecturing before farmers' clubs in the winter. A job on Frederick Law Olmsted's Staten Island farm proved to be the springboard into a career as a renowned engineer. Through his association with the pioneer landscape architect, Waring obtained an appointment as drainage engineer for the Central Park project. The Civil War temporarily interrupted his burgeoning career, but his experiences as a combat officer, rather than stunting his professional goals, sharpened them. "Colonel" Waring, as he would be called for the rest of his days, returned to civilian life strongly impressed by the sense of "duty and authority" that he acquired in the service. In fact, his passion for military discipline provided the foundation upon which his administrative style would be based in later years. In the late 1860s, he devoted almost total attention to drainage and sewerage engineering. By the 1880s, he became a well-known figure in sanitation, especially because of his extensive writings on the subject and his role in developing an effective sewer system for the city of Memphis.[18]

Waring's appointment as street cleaning commissioner of New York City in 1895 was the culmination of his career. In his effort to improve city services, reform mayor William L. Strong had appointed Waring and Theodore Roosevelt (police commissioner), hoping that these men of honesty and expertise would reform the city's corruption-ridden departments. Waring began his duties by clearing the Street Cleaning Department of its deadwood. "I made it a condition of my acceptance," he stated, "that I should be entirely exempt from interference and free of all political obligations. I would undertake to clean the streets if I could do it my own unhampered way, and not otherwise." After years of Tammany Hall domination, the Street Cleaning Department had become heavily laden with spoilsmen who misused the department's funds and provided only marginal service to the city. After expelling the political cronies, Waring selected young men with engineering backgrounds or military training, thus staffing the department with a technical elite. Even in hiring men for the most menial tasks, he sought to put "a man instead of a voter" behind every broom. The efficient operation of the Street Cleaning Department undergirded Waring's extensive refuse reform program.[19]

To implement the extensive cleansing program that he had in mind, Waring drew together a variety of necessary changes for dealing with street cleaning and refuse collection and disposal. His ideas were not revolutionary or unique; they represented instead an accumulation of the best methods that had been attempted piecemeal throughout the country. It was the commissioner's ability to perceive of the refuse problem broadly that allowed him to establish the most comprehensive environmental sanitation program of that time.

The collection of refuse posed many difficulties. Waring's first step was to initiate a system of "primary separation" at the household level. Garbage, rubbish, and ashes were to be kept in separate receptacles awaiting collection. This method allowed the Street Cleaning Department to dispose of the disparate material using the appropriate methods for each.[20] He also initiated the building of the first municipal rubbish sorting plant in the United States, where salvageable materials were picked out of the discarded rubbish and then resold. Profits from the plant were returned to the city to offset collection costs.[21]

Street cleaning was the commissioner's most serious collection problem. The streets of the city were crudely constructed; littering was acceptable public behavior; and horse manure was everywhere. Relying on his staff of superintendents and foremen to keep watch on the daily cleaning, he enlarged the corps of sweepers as well as improving their competence and attempting to raise their morale. Street cleaning was far from an honored job in the 1890s, but the Colonel gave his men an esprit de corps by increasing their pay, improving work conditions, and impressing upon them the importance of their work. His "White Wings" (as the sweepers were called) were issued white uniforms, which, although clearly impractical for the job, associated the men with cleanliness, on a par with doctors and nurses. Over 2,000 strong, the "White Wings" performed admirably under Waring's guidance and brought unprecedented attention to the department. Citizens of New York and local newspapers quickly took note of the unaccustomed cleanliness of their streets.[22]

Waring's separation program and his improvements in street cleaning were intended to raise public consciousness about the need for broad-scale sanitary improvements. The colonel relied heavily upon mustering human resources, not only to keep the citizenry apprised of the city's sanitary needs but also to inspire active community participation in that venture. Unlike some of his engineering colleagues, he relied more upon human initiative and involvement than upon technological advancements to solve sanitary problems. The most dramatic example of this emphasis was the formation of the Juvenile Street Cleaning League. Initially, more than five hundred youngsters participated in this program to disseminate information about proper sanitation and to inspire community involvement in keeping the streets clean. Waring hoped that the children, especially from "the ignorant populations in some East Side districts," would set an example for their "less enlightened" parents and thus promote civic pride. Despite the bigoted overtones of the plan, Waring's ultimate goal was the extension of public knowledge about proper sanitation and the development of a sense of personal commitment to cleanliness of the city. As an effective popularizer and propagandist, he spread the word of cleanliness more effectively than ever before.[23]

Waring faced his greatest test on the question of final disposition of refuse. Characteristically, he employed a combination of old and new techniques. Although he considered dumping wastes at sea to be the simplest and most traditional method of disposal, he realized many of its pitfalls and sought alternatives whenever possible. The only improvement the colonel initiated in this area was to commission new types of dumping scows, which ostensibly would empty the wastes more efficiently and farther from shore. Although the new dumpers helped retard the pollution of beaches along the New York - New Jersey coastlines, they were only stopgap measures at best.[24]

The commissioner's treatment of garbage was based upon more innovative methods. He sought not only to eliminate the wastes but also to retrieve resalable by-products. For this purpose, he installed a reduction plant on

Barren Island that extracted ammonia, glue, grease, and dry residuum for fertilizer from the garbage. These salvageable materials were to be sold in the city's behalf, just as the items from the rubbish plant. Waring also encouraged experimentation to find newer and more economical ways to reduce garbage and, simultaneously, began an extensive land reclamation program on Rikers Island by using waste as landfill.[25]

By the end of his short tenure as street cleaning commissioner in 1898, Waring had generated considerable local and national attention, which led to similar programs in many other cities.[26] At the peak of his influence as a sanitarian and municipal engineer, Waring was appointed by President William McKinley to study sanitary conditions in Cuba in 1898. Soon after returning to New York, he died of yellow fever contracted in Havana. His tragic death cut short an active public service and a prolific writing career, although it certainly enhanced his reputation by exaggerating his already considerable accomplishments. Helen Gray Cone, in a eulogistic poetic tribute, called him the "soldier who died to save," and his longtime admirer, Albert Shaw, editor of *Review of Reviews*, proclaimed, "Colonel Waring's work for the protection of human life and physical and moral health, through cleaning the cities, has been so successful and so vast, that he stands out as the great Hercules of modern times."[27]

Despite the inflated compliments of friends and admirers, Waring's accomplishments were many and significant in their own right. His program for New York City indicated an important shift from viewing the refuse problem simply as a question of health to confronting it as a multifaceted urban problem. Waring's comprehensive collection and disposal methods helped improve sanitary conditions in the nation's leading city, but they also took into account the broader requirements for making the city aesthetically palatable. Waring's efforts emphatically demonstrated a nascent urban environmentalism that sought to upgrade the quality of urban life. He also demonstrated a faith in municipal government to lead the way in environmental reform, aided by a technical elite freed from the influences of patronage. His actions mirrored the emerging Progressive reform spirit of his day, as he sought to place the public welfare above private gain. He was optimistic about the prospects for change and exhibited the familiar faith in the inherent good of "the people," which could transcend the limitations of a hostile environment (with the proper guidance from an elite of experts). He recoiled in moral outrage at the physical and social degradations of city life, envisioning himself as a noble crusader against the forces of evil. Thus, in a real sense, Waring was a product of his times as well as a pioneer in his own field. His example provided a bridge between the arcane refuse practices of the nineteenth century and the increased sophistication of the twentieth century.[28]

By the late 1890s, the refuse question had clearly entered a new phase. The upsurge in reform spirit throughout the country brought many and varied issues under its sway; sanitation reform was one such issue. Waring's efforts had set the tone for change in that field, and throughout the first two decades of the twentieth century the heightened reform interest in American cities gave the impression that a final solution to the refuse problem was at hand.

Debate within the public health community over environmental sanitation contributed greatly to the broadening in perspective about the refuse problem. The acceptance of the germ theory of disease had not only enlivened interest in preventive medicine but had brought into question the importance of environmental sanitation in curbing disease. Furthermore, the responsibility of health officials for dealing with garbage collection and disposal came under heavy fire. Some members of the medical community argued that bacteriology had not advanced sufficiently to rule out the impact of decaying organic waste as an indirect cause of disease. Dr. P. M. Hall, commissioner of health in Minneapolis, told an APHA gathering in 1912:

> In handling the outbreaks of infectious diseases we now look to
> the individual as the carrier. Why should we ignore the surround-
> ings? Will not the individual carrier of diseases appreciate the
> lessons of personal hygiene better in clean surroundings than in
> those that are dirty?

He further asserted that proper collection and disposal methods helped reduce the occasion for waste to create problems and thus contributed to the public health.[29] Some members of the audience questioned Hall's conclusions, arguing that garbage collection and disposal had no relation to health questions and therefore should not be a health department function. These differences of opinion were typical of the cleavages within the public health community over the value of environmental sanitation; they provided an important forum for the reevaluation of the refuse problem.[30] It was clear that the simplistic conclusions about the refuse issue that had dominated the thinking of the nineteenth century were being seriously challenged.

More than the sanitary implications of street cleaning and refuse disposal was under scrutiny in these early years of the twentieth century. Emphasis began to shift from simply an awareness of the refuse problem to a major effort to determine its extent and thus better gauge what methods could be applied to a solution. Once the extent of the problem was determined, refuse reform began to move along two important lines: (1) a careful analysis of the available technological solutions conducted by sanitary engineers and (2) a program of community involvement generated by civic organizations. These two approaches were by no means mutually exclusive but simply represented a sophistication of the efforts of nineteenth-century refuse reformers, including Waring.

The engineering community actually began to take more of a leadership role in finding a technical solution to the refuse problem in the late 1890s. Although engineers claimed that the sanitary considerations of the refuse problem were central, thus clinging to the value of environmental sanitation to improve health, they more often stressed that collection and disposal of waste was primarily a technical problem that should be left to those with specialized training in such areas. Neither the public health official nor the municipal bureaucrat, the argument went, had the breadth and depth of training of the sanitary engineer. Health officials could uncover the source of the refuse problem, but it was the new professional, the sanitary engineer, who would be called upon to find a solution.[31] As the famed sanitarian Ellen H. Richards suggested:

> The sanitary engineer has a treble duty for the next few years
> of civic awakening. Having the knowledge, he must be a "leader"
> in developing works and plants for state and municipal improve-
> ment, at the same time he is an "expert" in their employ. But he
> must be more; as a health officer he must be a "teacher" of the
> people to show them why all these things are to be. The slowness
> with which practicable betterments have been adopted among
> the rank and file is, partly at least, due to the separation of func-
> tions, of specialization, and partly to the exclusiveness of agents
> in the work.[32]

William P. Gerhard went even further than Richards in suggesting an almost spiritual calling for the sanitary engineer: "Much of the sanitary engineer's work is necessarily of a missionary character, as the public must be educated to appreciate the benefits of sanitation."[33]

By this time, sanitary engineering had come into its own as a formal branch of engineering. The growth and complexities of urban problems, such as ventilation, sewerage, water supply maintenance, street cleaning, and garbage collection and disposal, had led the way for the advent of a technical specialist who could deal with those problems. The sanitary engineer quickly became the logical successor to the health officer in dealing with refuse problems. The ambivalence within the health community toward environmental sanitation was in sharp contrast with the sanitary engineers' dogged adherence to it. The technical training and expertise of the sanitary engineer seemed to promise an efficient and tangible solution to the waste problem. It is not surprising that the sanitary engineer quickly assumed the leadership in refuse reform, for he was the practical embodiment of the reformist spirit of the day and a fitting heir to Colonel Waring, who, after all, was a pioneer in the field.[34]

Sanitary engineering became a powerful force in municipal affairs not only because of the apparent local demand but also through the efforts and actions of important national engineering associations and committees. With respect to the refuse issue, one of the earliest and best-known groups was the APHA's Committee on the Disposal of Garbage and Refuse. Its major functions included gathering statistics, inspecting local sanitation operations, and analyzing local and national sanitation trends.[35] The American Society for Municipal Improvements (ASMI, later the American Society of Municipal Engineers), founded in 1894, was another important group that devoted substantial attention to the problem of refuse. It was the first national organization that attempted to unite all municipal engineers.[36] Other engineering groups, with broader interests than ASMI, such as the American Society of Civil Engineers (ASCE), still devoted some attention to the refuse problem. Almost every convention of ASCE included a panel related to sanitation matters. From time to time, very specialized groups formed, such as the Society for Street Cleaning and Refuse Disposal of the United States and Canada, which aimed to "guide the thought and concentrate the effort to secure better conditions in street cleaning and refuse disposal methods."[37]

All these groups and organizations helped establish a vital communications network and a means to disseminate ideas about the problem of refuse and how to deal with it. They also played a major role in collecting statistics about the refuse problem from American and Canadian cities as well as from abroad. The data gathered, although often incomplete, provided a reservoir of information not available to refuse reformers in the nineteenth century. Despite expected differences of opinion and local variations, sanitary engineers began to establish a consensus about many important aspects of the refuse problem gleaned from these statistics. A national focus, which had been lacking in nineteenth-century refuse reform, was beginning to emerge in the early twentieth century. The APHA's "Report of the Committee on Garbage Disposal" (1897) was the first comprehensive analysis of national collection and disposal trends. It inspired other such studies and several special municipal investigations between 1900 and 1917, when cities such as Buffalo, Chicago, Louisville, and Washington, D.C., carried out extensive inquiries of their garbage collection and disposal practices.[38]

Realizing the problems inherent in interpreting disparate data from a large number of cities, the APHA's refuse committee devised the "Standard Form for Statistics of Municipal Refuse" in 1913 to bring some order out of the chaos.[39] Attempts to standardize statistics also led to a universal recommendation from engineering groups for cities to keep better records, especially in such areas as quantities of wastes produced, seasonal variations, and cost factors in collection and disposal. As an editorial in the *Engineering Record* stated,

> It is not enough to make a few estimates in the winter and in the summer, but a year's records obtained at least once every month and preferably more often should be secured. Unless this is done, any system of collection and disposal that is adopted is based on guess-work, and every intelligent citizen has had enough opportunity to observe the results of guesswork in municipal affairs to be loath to encourage anything of that sort.[40]

Sanitary engineers also did much to lobby for municipal control of street cleaning and garbage removal and disposal. The question of ultimate responsibility, which was often avoided in the 1880s and early 1890s, received considerable attention in the early twentieth century. In their important book, *Collection and Disposal of Municipal Refuse*, Rudolph Hering and Samuel Greeley state flatly, "The collection of public refuse is a public utility."[41] If there remained any support for the contract system of collection and disposal, it was modified substantially to include more rigorous municipal supervision.[42] Surveys taken from the 1890s through World War I demonstrate the impressive shift to increased municipal responsibility. In the 1880 census, 70 percent of the cities surveyed cleaned their own streets; in a 1914 study the proportion had increased to 90 percent.[43] Great strides were made in municipal responsibility even in garbage collection and disposal. By World War I at least 50 percent of American cities had some form of municipal collection system, compared with only 24 percent in 1880.[44]

Once sanitary engineers began to have a firmer grasp of the refuse problem, they turned their energies to analyzing collection and disposal methods. Almost immediately they began to condemn the practices of the nineteenth century. Dumping on land or in water, open burning, and the use of untreated waste as land or street fill came under the most serious scrutiny. More sophisticated criteria for selection than simple convenience began to emerge. As pragmatists, the sanitary engineers placed increasing emphasis upon the need to examine local conditions before determining the proper collection and disposal methods for a community. In planning for new systems, the engineers felt it necessary to take into consideration not only the types and quantities of wastes but also the quality of local transportation facilities, the character of the body in charge of the work, and physical characteristics of the city that might determine location and type of disposal system, plus the receptivity of the local government and the citizenry to changes in practice. The reliance of the engineer upon a technical solution to the problem of refuse, therefore, was increasingly being tempered by an awareness of the complexity of the problems faced.[45]

Because of the general low regard for "primitive" methods of collection and disposal, sanitary engineers focused their attention on newer methods, meant to fulfill sanitary and aesthetic requirements. Although no single type of refuse technology came to dominate, incineration and reduction were most often discussed during the period.[46] Each method had its advocates and detractors, but both methods came under more careful analysis than they had when first introduced. The success of the English destructors had led to the APHA refuse committee's provisional endorsement of incineration and quick implementation of the method in several American cities.[47] Further study of the application of British systems to American cities indicated that some municipalities had made a hasty decision in building untested and questionable incinerators. Colonel William F. Morse, an influential sanitary engineer and incinerator developer, suggested that several failures could be attributed to insufficient professional analysis of incineration principles, faulty incinerator designs, overconfidence in the capabilities of the apparatus, and unskillful management of the crematories themselves.[48] With further study, it became clear to many engineers that British destructors were not designed to handle the kinds of wastes encountered in the United States. For example, American garbage had more water in it, making it more difficult to burn. Consequently, they recommended design changes to take into account the differences in the composition of waste. They also recommended that incinerators should be considered only after a careful analysis of costs and municipal needs.[49]

The reduction process, which appeared in the United States about the same time as incineration, underwent a similar development: impulsive implementation, severe criticism, reevaluation. The 1897 refuse committee report indicated a great deal of interest in reduction because of its promise to return revenue to the city.[50] However, after a period of operation, several undesirable side effects led to an increased criticism of the method. The foul odors emanating from the plants raised the greatest protests. As one critic, Mayor J. J. Williams of Memphis, stated:

> The air for miles and miles around them is so contaminated that
> the courts and lawmakers have been appealed to, and have, as a

Table 5.3   *Methods of Garbage Disposal (Percentage and Number of Cities)*

	1880	1890
Dumping on land, used as fill or buried	39 (78)	46.5 (33)
Farm use (fertilizer, animal feed)	22 (44)	29.5 (21)
Dumping into water	9 (17)	13 (9)
Burning	1 (1)	7 (5)
Reduction	—	—
Incineration	—	—
Combination	10 (20)	—
No systematic disposal	4 (8)	—
No data	15 (30)	4 (3)
Total number of cities per survey	199	71

*a*Includes open burning.
SOURCE: Gleaned from George E. Waring, Jr., comp., *Report on the Social Statistics of Cities, Tenth Census of the United States, 1880,* 2 vols. (Washington, D.C.); "Street Cleaning and the Disposal of Refuse," *Engineering Record* 22 (29 November 1890): 410; "Some Statistics of Garbage Disposal for the Larger American Cities in 1902," in APHA, *Public Health: Papers and Reports* 29 (October 1903): 152–53; "Disposal of Municipal Refuse," *Municipal Journal and Engineer* 35 (6 November 1913): 627–28; "Refuse Collection and Disposal," pp. 728–30; Capes and Carpenter, *Municipal Housecleaning,* pp. 194–99.

rule, given relief to the sufferers by abating the foul, disease-breeding business. . . . if for no other cause, the laws should prohibit these establishments, because it is degrading and inhuman for human beings to spend their days in such an occupation as assorting the filth of our cities.[51]

In 1916, ASMI's Committee on Refuse Disposal and Street Cleaning recommended a compromise: reduction was fine for large cities where the revenue derived from it might warrant its use, but for small cities incineration appeared to be more sanitary and less costly.[52]

The debate over the merits and weaknesses of incineration and reduction had a positive effect upon their use. Improvements in technology and more careful applications of the methods led to more rational use. As table 5.3 indicates, both methods gained in popularity throughout the early twentieth century. However, neither method dominated the field of disposal. In fact, primitive methods still represented from 26 to 66 percent of those employed in American cities between 1900 and 1920.[53]

1902	1909	1915	1918
24 (39)	18.5 (25)	11 (21)	27 (29)
21 (33)	28 (25)	7.5 (37)	20 (21)
6 (10)	7.5 (10)	1 (2)	1 (1)
3 (4)	–	–	–
9 (15)	19.5 (26)	10 (19)	20 (21)
19 (31)	26.5 (35)	30.5[a] (58)	13 (14)
12.5 (20)	–	7 (13)	18 (19)
–	–	–	–
5.5 (9)	–	33 (63)	1 (1)
161	133	190	106

Clearly, cost factors played a major role in determining the methods used. And, like Waring before them, sanitary engineers sought to present their proposals for new methods with increasing emphasis upon efficiency of operation and possible return of revenue through the sale of by-products.[54] Waring had explored the means of selling grease, oils, and other residue from organic waste and had attempted to resell usable items found in New York's rubbish. But, by the early twentieth century, an additional approach—energy retrieval from waste—was commanding increasing interest. Once again England and other European countries led the way. The English had adapted many of their destructors to produce residual sources of heat, such as steam, and had even developed a process of generating electricity for running trolley cars.[55] Based on European experiments, American engineers began to develop their own methods of generating heat and light from wastes. In a related experiment, E. L. Culver built an experimental plant in Austin, Texas, where he manufactured fuel bricks—"oakcoal"—out of garbage.[56] Wide application of energy retrieval methods in the United States was retarded because of the high costs of operation of such facilities and the cheaper and more plentiful sources of energy available at the time. Nonetheless, these innovations demonstrated some intriguing and more creative possibilities for the use of waste than simple destruction. It was an idea, however, whose time had not yet come.

While sanitary engineers were evaluating the new methods of collection and disposal of wastes, the spirit of the time infused nontechnical reformers with an urge to relieve the refuse problem in their own way. Inspired by the efforts of the engineering community and imbued with a compulsion to improve the urban quality of life, a variety of reform groups sought solutions to the problem of refuse as part of their more comprehensive attempts to rid the cities of vice, corruption, and disease. Many of the most important national municipal organizations that formed during this period, such as the National Municipal League and the League of American Municipalities, incorporated refuse reform into their array of goals.[57]

In the tradition of the Ladies' Health Protective Association, several middle-class women's groups assumed the leadership in civic efforts to end the refuse problem. Mildred Chadsey, commissioner of housing and sanitation in Cleveland, used the term "municipal housekeeping" to define those sanitation functions of the city that were previously performed by individuals.[58] Samuel Greeley noted:

> It is unfortunately true that cleanliness and efficiency in the house treatment of refuse are sometimes defeated by careless and infrequent collection service or by improperly conducted disposal works. This condition must be very trying to the careful housekeeper, and is, perhaps, one reason why women have taken an active interest in promoting the efficiency of the larger phases of the work.

Greeley went on to suggest that two qualities were required for success in refuse disposal work—common sense and expert professional skills. As he said, "Women are doing much to bring these qualities to bear upon the refuse disposal problems of the communities in which they live."[59]

The interest of women in refuse reform was not simply a topic of conversation at a monthly civic club meeting or an expression of good intentions. Women became aggressive promoters of refuse reform. In Boston, Duluth, Chicago, and other cities, women's municipal organizations began investigations into disposal methods. The Women's Health Protective Association of Brooklyn sought and obtained new ordinances for collection and disposal. The Louisville Women's Civic Association published and distributed four thousand pamphlets about the garbage problem and even produced a movie entitled *The Invisible Peril*. Shown to thousands of citizens, the movie depicted how an old hat discarded in an open dump spread disease. The women of Reading, Pennsylvania—some in their sixties—banded together in a street cleaning brigade to protest poor methods. The local alderman, embarrassed by the action, soon discovered that his position was in jeopardy for not addressing the problem himself.[60]

The city cleanup campaigns were the most dramatic and highly publicized form of citizen involvement in refuse reform. They were extensions of Waring's civic awareness efforts on a grander scale. At least once a year, most cities sponsored a "cleanup week" to generate interest in sanitation and other related problems, such as fire prevention, fly and mosquito extermination, and city beautification. Interest in the campaigns often brought together several civic organizations for a coordinated effort. In Philadelphia, the municipal government assumed the leadership of the city's cleanup campaign and transformed it into a major event. The city distributed 3,400 personal letters, 750,000 gummed labels, 260,000 bulletins, 20,000 colored display posters, 750 streamers, 1,000,000 cardboard folders, 300,000 badges, 300,000 blotters, 350,000 circulars, and various other paraphernalia. Some communities, such as Sherman, Texas, used the opportunity to campaign for better collection and disposal ordinances. Too often, however, the cleanup campaigns were merely cosmetic exercises. Any truly substantive and far-reaching sanitary benefits of the efforts are difficult to determine.[61]

The efforts of the sanitary engineer and the zealousness of civic reformers, although great, did not resolve the refuse problem by 1920. The coming of World War I partially explains the delay, because it diverted attention from urban reform by readjusting societal priorities. The war, however, also played a role in the curious resurgence of one of the "primitive" disposal methods— feeding garbage to swine. The wartime food conservation campaign, led by Food Administrator Herbert Hoover, temporarily tightened enforcement of garbage collection ordinances and ultimately resulted in a de facto reduction in the quantity of garbage.[62] What garbage remained, it was argued, could more profitably be fed to hogs instead of being incinerated or reduced at a time when food production had a high priority. The United States Food Administration waged a vigorous campaign to disarm critics who believed that garbage-fed hogs were unsanitary, and prepared massive reports stating the contrary.[63] The efforts of the Food Administration, however, did not have a lasting impact upon the refuse question, nor did the temporary reduction in the amounts of garbage continue to be a trend after the war. The problems of the early twentieth century were still unresolved.

Sanitary engineers had gone a long way toward gaining a firmer grasp on the refuse problem in the first two decades of the twentieth century and, to their credit, helped publicize the extent of the waste inundating the cities. Yet the faith of Americans in the ability of technology and science to resolve the refuse problem was excessive. On the one hand, scientific knowledge had not advanced sufficiently to determine the precise impact of specific disposal methods in broad ecological terms. For instance, with the advent of the automobile as a primary source of transportation, many people believed that the streets would be free of pollution. Unfortunately, no one realized the cruel irony—horse manure would be supplanted by a greater danger in the form of noxious gasoline fumes.[64] On the other hand, few if any Americans gave much thought to the cause-and-effect relationship between the consumption of goods and the production of waste. Some contemporaries bemoaned the wasting of natural resources, but few made the connection with the production of refuse. In the largest sense, then, the uncritical faith in science and technology was not sufficiently tempered with a sense of its limitations.

The growth of civic awareness with respect to sanitation was a step, but only one step, forward in bringing the refuse problem to the attention of the citizenry. The cleanup campaigns were ephemeral, since they were most often an extension of the contemporary reformist mood and hardly a vehicle for long-range solutions. Even efforts to obtain new ordinances or more effective methods of collection and disposal were inherently difficult. It was one thing to write new laws requiring householders to separate garbage from rubbish or to make littering illegal; it was quite another to enforce such laws. Forcing citizens to change their habits, let alone understanding the more complex problems associated with sanitation, could not be accomplished overnight. Furthermore, city officials had to be convinced that improving waste collection and disposal methods was a high priority among voters, and not excessively costly. Cost of improvements quickly became a prime determinant of what kind of system the city should acquire, and no new system would come cheaply.

Therefore, a bottleneck could impede refuse reform at any level. Changes could not be easily made if citizens were apathetic, if city officials were skeptical of the political benefits of change, if engineers were uncertain about the best technical solution to the problem, or if other societal priorities competed for municipal funds. What had seemed to be such a simple problem to cope with down on the farm became an extremely complex dilemma in the modern industrial city.

Notes

The author would like to thank the Rockefeller Foundation and Texas A&M University for the financial support that made this study possible.

1. Franz Schneider, Jr., "The Disposal of a City's Waste," *Scientific American* 107 (13 July 1912): 24.

2. See census statistics for disposable personal income, gross national product, consumer expenditure patterns, and food consumption for some hint as to the kinds of increases in consumption of goods. United States Department of Commerce, Bureau of the Census, *Historical Statistics of the United States* (Washington, D.C., 1975), pp. 224–25,

320-21, 328-32. For contemporary views, see Austin Bierbower, "American Wasteful-
ness," *Overland Monthly* 49 (April 1907): 358-59; William F. Morse, "The Disposal of the
City's Waste," *American City* 2 (April 1910): 177; Rudolph Hering, "Sewage and Solid
Refuse Removal," in *A Half Century of Public Health: Jubilee Historical Volume of the
American Public Health Association*, ed. Mazyck Porcher Ravenel (New York, 1970;
orig. pub. 1921), pp. 188-89.

    3. Statistics gleaned from Rudolph Hering and Samuel A. Greeley, *Collection and
Disposal of Municipal Refuse* (New York, 1921), pp. 13, 28.

    4. Joel A. Tarr, "Urban Pollution: Many Long Years Ago," *American Heritage* 22
(October 1971): 65-66; "Clean Streets and Motor Traffic," *The Literary Digest* 49
(5 September 1914): 413.

    5. See Ernest S. Griffith, *A History of American City Government: The Conspicuous
Failure, 1870-1900* (New York, 1974), pp. 97-98; Melvin G. Holli, "Urban Reform in
the Progressive Era," in *The Progressive Era*, ed. Lewis L. Gould (Syracuse, 1974),
pp. 133 ff.; David P. Thelen, "Social Tensions and the Origins of Progressivism," *Journal
of American History* 56 (September 1969): 336-41.

    6. During much of the nineteenth century, the miasmic theory dominated American
sanitary thinking. According to this theory, gases emanating from putrefying matter or
sewers were the cause of contagious diseases. Consequently, civic cleanliness, drainage,
sewerage, proper ventilation, and other measures associated with environmental sanitation would suffice to arrest contagious diseases. The discovery of specific pathogenic
organisms—bacteria—enabled public health officials and sanitarians to understand the
actual cause of many contagious diseases for the first time. This "germ theory" of
diseases eventually replaced older notions about the relationship between filth and
disease and led to the use of the bacteriological laboratory as the chief means of controlling epidemics. See John Duffy, *A History of Public Health in New York City, 1866-1966*
(New York, 1974), pp. 91 ff.

    7. See James H. Cassedy, *Charles V. Chapin and the Public Health Movement* (Cam-
bridge, Mass., 1962), pp. 44-45; Wilson G. Smillie, *Public Health: Its Promise for the
Future* (New York, 1955), pp. 351-52; William F. Morse, "Methods of Collection and
Disposal of Waste and Garbage by Cremation" (paper read at the Sanitary Convention of
State and Local Boards of Health of Pennsylvania, Erie, Pa., 1892), p. 3.

    8. Data from *Social Statistics of Cities, 1880*. See also Smillie, *Public Health*, p. 352.

    9. Ravenel, *A Half Century of Public Health*, pp. 190-91; Hering and Greeley, *Col-
lection and Disposal of Municipal Refuse*, p. 2.

    10. John S. Billings, "Municipal Sanitation: Defects in American Cities," *Forum* 15
(May 1893): 305.

    11. Mary E. Trautmann, "Women's Health Protective Association," *Municipal Affairs* 2
(September 1898): 439-43; Duffy, *Public Health in New York City*, pp. 124, 130, 132.

    12. New York Ladies' Health Protective Association, *Memorial to Abram S. Hewitt on
the Subject of Street Cleaning* (New York, 1887), pp. 4-5.

    13. Philadelphia Department of Public Works, Bureau of Street Cleaning, *Annual
Report*, 1893, p. 58; Mrs. C. G. Wagner, "What the Women Are Doing for Civic Cleanliness," *Municipal Journal and Engineer* 11 (July 1901): 35.

    14. The title, "sanitary engineer," is most appropriate for identifying engineers who
dealt with the refuse problem. "Municipal engineer" is acceptable, but it suggests a range
of functions that includes more than sanitation.

    15. W. Francis Goodrich, *Refuse Disposal and Power Production* (Westminster, Eng.,

1904), pp. 3, 9-10; Hering and Greeley, *Collection and Disposal of Municipal Refuse*, pp. 311-13; Chamber of Commerce of the United States, Construction and Civic Development Department, *Refuse Disposal in American Cities* (Washington, D.C., 1931; rep. 1940), p. 15; William F. Morse, "The Disposal of the City's Waste," *American City* 2 (May 1910): 223.

16. S. S. Kilvington, "Garbage Furnaces and the Destruction of Organic Matter by Fire," in APHA, *Public Health: Papers and Reports* 14 (1889): 170.

17. Morse, "Disposal of the City's Waste," *American City* 2 (May 1910): 271.

18. Martin V. Melosi, "Pragmatic Environmentalist: Sanitary Engineer George E. Waring, Jr.," *Essays in Public Works History*, no. 4 (Washington, D.C., 1977), pp. 6-12.

19. George E. Waring, Jr., "The Cleaning of the Streets of New York," *Harper's Weekly* 39 (29 October 1895): 1022.

20. Waring, "The Disposal of a City's Waste," *North American Review* 161 (July 1895): 4, 51-54; Waring, *A Report on the Final Disposition of the Wastes of New York by the Dept. of Street Cleaning* (New York, 1896), pp. 3-6; Waring, "The Cleaning of a Great City," p. 919; John McGraw Woodbury, "The Wastes of a Great City," *Scribner's Magazine* 34 (October 1903): 388-90.

21. Hering and Greeley, *Collection and Disposal of Municipal Refuse*, p. 299; Waring, "The Cleaning of a Great City," pp. 917-19; Waring, "Disposal of a City's Waste," pp. 49-52.

22. Waring, "The Cleaning of a Great City," pp. 917-21. E. Burgoyne Baker, "The Refuse of a Great City," *Munsey's Magazine* 23 (April 1900): 83-84; "Street Cleaning," *Outlook* 66 (20 October 1900): 427; Waring, "The Garbage Question in the Department of Street Cleaning of New York," *Municipal Affairs* 1 (September 1897): 515-24.

23. Baker, "The Refuse of a Great City," p. 90; Waring, "The Cleaning of a Great City," pp. 921-23; David Willard, "The Juvenile Street-Cleaning Leagues," in Waring, *Street Cleaning and the Disposal of a City's Wastes: Methods and Results and the Effects upon Public Health, Public Morals, and Municipal Prosperity* (New York, 1898), pp. 177-86.

24. "The Delehanty Dumping-Scow," *Harper's Weekly* 40 (24 October 1896): 1051; Waring, "The Fouling of the Beaches," *Harper's Weekly* 42 (2 July 1898): 663; Waring, "The Cleaning of a Great City," pp. 917-19; Waring, *Street Cleaning and the Disposal of a City's Wastes*, p. 47; Baker, "The Refuse of a Great City," p. 89.

25. Waring, "The Utilization of a City's Garbage," *Cosmopolitan* 24 (February 1898): 406-10; Waring, "The Cleaning of a Great City," pp. 919-21; Waring, *Street Cleaning and the Disposal of a City's Wastes*, pp. 47-49; Baker, "The Refuse of a Great City," p. 87.

26. Charles Zueblin, *American Municipal Progress*, rev. ed. (New York, 1916), pp. 75-76, 82; Delos F. Wilcox, *The American City: A Problem in Democracy* (New York, 1906), pp. 118, 224; George A. Soper, *Modern Methods of Street Cleaning* (New York, 1907), p. 165; John A. Fairlie, *Municipal Administration* (New York, 1906), pp. 258-59; "Tammany and the Streets," *Outlook* 66 (20 October 1900): 427-28; "The Disposal of New York's Refuse," *Scientific American* 89 (24 October 1903): 292-94; Duffy, *Public Health in New York City*, pp. 125-26.

27. Helen Gray Cone, "Waring," *Century* 59 (February 1900): 547; Albert Shaw, *Life of Col. Geo. E. Waring, Jr.: The Greatest Apostle of Cleanliness* (New York, 1899), preface, pp. 10-11, 14, 30-34.

28. See Roy Lubove, "The Twentieth Century City: The Progressive as Municipal Reformer," *Mid-America* 41 (October 1959): 199, 202-3, 209; Holli, "Urban Reform in the Progressive Era," pp. 133 ff.; Ernest S. Griffith, *A History of American City*

Government: The Progressive Years and Their Aftermath, 1900-1920 (New York, 1974), pp. 150 ff.

29. P. M. Hall, "The Collection and Disposal of City Waste and the Public Health," *American Journal of Public Health* 3 (April 1913): 315.

30. Ibid., pp. 316-17. See also C. E. Terry, "The Public Dump and the Public Health," *American Journal of Public Health* 3 (April 1913): 338-41; R. H. Bishop, Jr., "Infantile Paralysis and Cleanable Streets," *American City* 15 (September 1916): 313.

31. "Report of the Committee on Refuse Collection and Disposal," *American Journal of Public Health* 5 (September 1915): 934; Harry R. Crohurst, *Municipal Wastes: Their Character, Collection, Disposal* (Washington, D.C., 1920), p. 84; M. N. Baker, "Condition of Garbage Disposal in the United States," *Municipal Journal and Engineer* (October 1901): 147-48; "The Unsatisfactory Condition of Garbage Disposal in America," *The Sanitarian* 40 (January 1898): 20-21; H. deB. Parsons, *The Disposal of Municipal Refuse* (New York, 1906), pp. 8-9; George A. Soper, "Modern Methods of Street Cleaning" (address before the New England Conference on Street Cleaning, Providence, R.I., 1910).

32. Ellen H. Richards, *Conservation by Sanitation* (New York, 1911), p. v.

33. William P. Gerhard, *Sanitation and Sanitary Engineering*, 2d ed. (New York, 1909), p. 58.

34. See Richards, *Conservation by Sanitation*, pp. 216 ff.; Gerhard, *Sanitation and Sanitary Engineering*, pp. 59 ff.; Parsons, *The Disposal of Municipal Refuse*, p. 8; M. N. Baker, *Municipal Engineering and Sanitation* (New York, 1902), p. 164; Carl S. Dow, "Sanitary Engineering," *The Chautauquan* 66 (March 1912): 80-98; R. Winthrop Pratt, "Sanitary Engineering," *Scientific American, Supplement* 77 (7 March 1914): 150; "The Sanitary Engineer—A New Social Profession," *Charities and the Commons (The Survey)* 16 (2 June 1906): 286-87. See also chap. 7 of this volume for a more incisive analysis of the role of municipal engineers in urban government.

35. See "Report of the Committee on the Disposal of Garbage and Refuse," in APHA, *Public Health: Papers and Reports* 23 (1897): 206 ff.

36. American Society for Municipal Improvements, *Proceedings*, 1918, pp. 296 ff.

37. *Municipal Journal and Engineer* 41 (23 November 1916): 646. The society formed in 1915. For a more thorough discussion of the role of sanitary (or municipal) engineers in environmental reform, see chap. 7 of this volume.

38. Hering and Greeley, *Collection and Disposal of Municipal Refuse*, pp. 12-20.

39. "Report of the Committee on Refuse Collection and Disposal," pp. 933-34.

40. "Refuse Disposal in America," *Engineering Record* 58 (25 July 1908): 85. See also Baker, "Condition of Garbage Disposal in United States," p. 147; S. Whinery, "How to Keep the Streets Clean," *American City* 10 (January 1914): 23-24.

41. Hering and Greeley, *Collection and Disposal of Municipal Refuse*, p. 4.

42. Baker, "Condition of Garbage Disposal in United States," p. 148. See also William P. Capes and Jeanne D. Carpenter, *Municipal Housecleaning* (New York, 1918), p. 5; Frederick C. Wilkes, "Should the City Remove Rubbish?" in League of American Municipalities, *Bulletin* 4 (October 1905): 134-36.

43. Gleaned from "Statistics of Cities," in United States Department of Labor, *Bulletin* 36 (September 1901): 880-85; *Municipal Journal and Engineer* 37 (10 December 1914): 836-44.

44. Gleaned from "Refuse Collection and Disposal," *Municipal Journal and Engineer* 39 (11 November 1915): 527-727; B. F. Miller, "Garbage Collection and Disposal," in ASMI, *Proceedings, 1915*, pp. 10-11.

45. "Report of the Committee on the Disposal of Garbage and Refuse" (1897), p. 207; Crohurst, *Municipal Wastes*, pp. 79 ff.; ASMI, *Proceedings, 1916*, pp. 244–45; Baker, "Condition of Garbage Disposal in United States," pp. 147–48; "Report of the Committee on Street Cleaning," *American Journal of Public Health* 5 (March 1915): 255–59.

46. "Sanitary landfill," which would come into wide use by the mid-twentieth century, was still in its early experimental stage at this time. See Crohurst, *Municipal Wastes*, pp. 44–45; Capes and Carpenter, *Municipal Housecleaning*, pp. 175–78.

47. "Report of the Committee on the Disposal of Garbage and Refuse," p. 108.

48. William F. Morse, "The Disposal of Municipal Wastes," *Municipal Journal and Engineer* 22 (6 March 1907): 232–35.

49. William F. Morse, "The Sanitary Disposal of Municipal Refuse," *Transactions of the American Society of Civil Engineers* 50 (1903): 114 ff.; "Refuse Disposal in America," *Engineering Record* 58 (25 July 1908): 85; "Why American Garbage Crematories Fail." *Municipal Journal and Engineer* 13 (November 1902): 234.

50. "Report of the Committee on the Disposal of Garbage and Refuse," pp. 215 ff.

51. "Garbage Collection and Disposal," *City Government* 7 (September 1899): 50. See also Joseph G. Branch, *Heat and Light from Municipal and Other Waste* (St. Louis, 1906), pp. 7–8.

52. "Report of Committee on Refuse Disposal and Street Cleaning," in ASMI, *Proceedings, 1916*, p. 245.

53. Capes and Carpenter, *Municipal Housecleaning*, pp. 194–99. See also "Garbage Collection and Disposal," *Engineering News* 42 (28 September 1899): 214; B. F. Miller, "Garbage Collection and Disposal," in ASMI, *Proceedings, 1915*, pp. 12–13; "Methods of Collection and Disposal," *Municipal Journal and Engineer* 41 (7 December 1916): 701–2; Pittsburgh Commission on Garbage and Rubbish Collection and Disposal, *Report on Methods of Garbage and Rubbish Collection and Disposal in American Cities* (1918), pp. 14–15; "Garbage Collection and Disposal," *City Manager Magazine*, July 1924, pp. 12–14.

54. George H. Norton, "Recoverable Values of Municipal Refuse," *Municipal Engineering* 45 (December 1913): 550–52; "Revenue from Municipal Waste," *Municipal Journal and Engineer* 32 (6 June 1912): 868; Morse, *The Disposal of Refuse and Garbage* (New York, 1899), pp. 3–7.

55. "Running Municipal Trolley Cars with Garbage and Refuse," *Scientific American* 96 (1 June 1907): 446; W. Francis Goodrich, *Refuse Disposal and Power Production*, pp. v–vii.

56. Robert H. Moulton, "Turning Garbage into Fuel," *Independent* 89 (5 February 1917): 222. See also Norton, "Recoverable Values of Municipal Refuse," pp. 550–52; Peter T. Austen, "The Utilization of Waste," *The Forum* 32 (September 1901): 74–84; Branch, *Heat and Light from Municipal and Other Waste*, pp. 1 ff.

57. For example, see League of American Municipalities, *Proceedings, 1899*, pp. 13–27; *City Government* 7 (September 1899): 49 ff.; Carol Aronovici, "Municipal Street Cleaning and Its Problems," *National Municipal Review* 1 (April 1912): 218–25.

58. Mildred Chadsey, "Municipal Housekeeping," *Journal of Home Economics* 7 (February 1915): 53–59. See chap. 8 of this volume for a more thorough examination of the role of women in sanitation reform.

59. Samuel Greeley, "The Work of Women in City Cleansing," *American City* 6 (June 1912): 873–75.

60. See "A Street-Cleaning Nurse," *The Literary Digest* 52 (18 March 1916): 709–10; "Street Cleaning Brigade of Women," *Municipal Journal and Engineer* 9 (December

1900): 152; Mrs. Lee Bernheim, "A Campaign for Sanitary Collection and Disposal of Garbage," *American City* 15 (August 1916): 134-36; Mrs. C. G. Wagner, "What the Women Are Doing for Civic Cleanliness," p. 35; Greeley, "The Work of Women in City Cleansing," pp. 873-75; Hester M. McClung, "Women's Work in Indianapolis," *Municipal Affairs* 2 (September 1898): 523; Ewing Galloway, "How Sherman Cleans Up," *American City* 9 (July 1913): 40.

61. Capes and Carpenter, *Municipal Housecleaning*, pp. 6-9, 213-32; Gustavus A. Weber, "A 'Clean-up' Campaign Which Resulted in a 'Keep Clean' Ordinance," *American City* 10 (March 1914): 231-34; "Philadelphia's Second Annual Clean-up Week," *Municipal Journal and Engineer* 37 (10 September 1914): 348-49; Galloway, "How Sherman Cleans Up," pp. 40-41.

62. "Effect of the War on Garbage Disposal," *Municipal Engineering* 53 (September 1917): 110-11; "Save the Garbage Waste," *American Municipalities* 33 (July 1917): 105; Irwin S. Osborn, "Effect of the War on the Production of Garbage and Methods of Disposal," *American Journal of Public Health* 7 (May 1918): 368-72; "Quantity and Quality of Garbage Lowered by War Conditions," *Engineering News-Record* 79 (13 December 1917): 1092.

63. F. G. Ashbrook and A. Wilson, "Feeding Garbage to Hogs," *Farmer's Bulletin*, no. 1133 (Washington, D.C., 1921), pp. 3-26; Charles V. Chapin, "Disposal of Garbage by Hog Feeding," *American Journal of Public Health* 7 (March 1918): 234-35; United States Food Administration, *Garbage Utilization, with Particular Reference to Utilization to Feeding* (Washington, D.C., 1918), pp. 3-11.

64. See "Clean Streets and Motor Traffic," pp. 413-14; Woodbury, "The Wastes of a Great City," pp. 396-98; "The Municipal Collection of Manure in Columbus, Ohio," *American City* 10 (April 1914): 379.

6. Toward an Environmental Perspective: The Anti-Noise Campaign, 1893–1932

By Raymond W. Smilor

The new technological era of post-Civil War America brought affluence and power; it did not necessarily bring satisfaction. While Americans accepted the benefits of industrial expansion without much question, they preferred to ignore its accompanying social problems and tensions. The depression of 1893-97 changed that by raising serious and disturbing doubts about the whole direction of industrialism. The crisis of the 1890s that resulted from the dynamic yet wholly uncoordinated changes of the post-Civil War period led people to cross social barriers in order to solve problems and thus participate in the developing social progressivism.

Concern for the urban environment was part of this emerging sense of reform arising from a larger desire to oversee industrial expansion and to cope with the machine age. Expanding industrialization aggravated environmental problems of smoke, garbage, dirty water, and noise. Believing that established ideas and institutions had failed to respond to these issues, people felt an urgent responsibility to find new remedies for pollution. In 1895, the *New York Daily Tribune* expressed this new awareness toward urban noise:

> Bedlam has at last broken loose and can't be corralled. The
> question naturally presents itself, whether mere unadulterated
> noise has not been allowed to get the better of us, while we have
> been attending to other matters, and whether it is not about
> time to direct our energies toward keeping down the uproar that
> arises on every hand.[1]

The anti-noise campaign reveals the development of an early consumer activism. Noise was a problem that affected everyone intimately, part of the common experience that all people shared. Men and women were consumers not only of high prices and defective products but also of a polluted environment. Their roles as consumers cut across social barriers and led them to join forces for environmental change.[2] The middle-class reformers who directed the anti-noise movement gained the support of all segments of the community because all individuals could agree on the harmful effects of noise. Noise came to represent a danger to health, a threat to civilization, a hindrance to efficiency, and an invasion of privacy.

Like other progressive reformers, anti-din advocates optimistically believed that rational analysis could solve the problems of the industrial age. They put their faith in the power of law and the application of scientific principles. From the early 1900s until World War I, citizen groups translated their anxiety over noise into a host of laws. During the 1920s, experts and scientists took over the campaign and began to examine every aspect of the noise issue.

Noise was not a new problem, but during the industrial age its variety and intensity increased markedly. Unprecedented clamor reverberated from cobblestone and rough pavement, steam whistles and sirens, garages, car barns, factories, junk shops, stoveworks, and freight yards. Congested cities echoed with the racket of elevated railroads above and subways below, automobiles and motorcycles (usually without mufflers), flat wheels on street cars, steam compressors, internal combustion engines, pneumatic chisels and riveting hammers. Peddlers, hucksters, newspaperboys, early-morning milkmen, icemen, street musicians, itinerant bands, garbagemen, and ashmen added to the cacophony. American cities seemed to reflect "no adequate regard . . . for the sanitary virtues of quietness."[3] One observer described the situation metaphorically: "if uproar is the smoke of noise," the twentieth-century metropolis is "a bonfire of sound that is rapidly spreading beyond the control of any ordinary extinguisher."[4]

As some Americans confronted ubiquitous urban din, they learned that technological advancement was not an unmitigated blessing. Because noise damaged hearing and strained the nervous system, a professor of neurology at Harvard Medical School declared that "needless noises must be classified as common plagues, like flies, mosquitoes, rats and dirt."[5] The American Public Health Association believed that "never before in the history of the world has there been such a constant clamor as is produced in modern cities or one made up of so many startling, alarm-like elements."[6] The New York City commissioner of health maintained:

> Only since the beginning of our present mechanical age has the
> jar and clang of metal on metal become the accompanying sym-
> phony of our lives—a diabolical symphony prolonged for the
> entire twenty-four hours of the day in many parts of our city.[7]

The fight against noise emerged somewhat later than other environmental reform movements. Recognition of the necessity for general cleanliness of the city, purity of the water supply, and benefits of fresh air developed more rapidly. Citizens could recognize that illness and even death resulted from rotting garbage, contaminated water, and impure air. Since noise was an evasive pollutant, it was more difficult to recognize its potentially harmful impact on a person's health or a community's well-being. In addition, the feeling that noise was an inescapable product of industrialism hindered concerted action.

Two more subtle forces hampered the anti-noise campaign. Despite evidence to the contrary, most people associated noise with progress. A member of the Committee on Noise of the American Civic Association observed that "noise has usually been regarded as a necessary accompaniment of general progress."[8] The chairman of Chicago's anti-noise committee pointed out, "Many of us are still under the impression that noise and lots of it means progress and 'hustle' notwithstanding the real fact that most noises are superfluous and serve no useful end."[9]

The ostensible connection between noise and progress led reformers to distinguish between necessary and unnecessary noises. "Perfect silence and the opposite of prosperity are, indeed, close companions," noted the *New York Times*, "but a great part of our urban clangors and clamors serve no end whatever except to irritate nerves and impair health."[10] Reformers differentiated between those noises that served progress and those that damaged health and reduced efficiency. Necessary noises served a purpose: "All necessary noises are the more bearable because we know that in their making something useful is being accomplished."[11] An unnecessary noise was defined as a sound without apparent social utility.

Ironically, this distinction between necessary and unnecessary noises proved to be both the strength and the weakness of the anti-noise campaign. On the one hand, the distinction broadened the base of supporters. Reformers and civic officials could agree that din from yelling peddlers, loud pets, shrieking steam whistles and sirens, blaring horns, and screeching automobiles served no useful social function. Consequently, they passed laws banning such noises. Racket from construction work or factory machines, however, resulted in socially useful activities and therefore remained free from restraint. Industrialists, factory executives, and merchants could support legislation against unnecessary noises, at the same time maintaining that noise from their business was necessary and unavoidable. Some of the worst noise producers sought to create a feeling of inevitability about the racket they caused.[12]

This loose definition of harmful noise, on the other hand, made fundamental changes in public policy impossible. Reformers aimed to broaden the environmental outlook of Americans, but their own limitations prevented them from accomplishing that goal. The division between necessary and unnecessary noise revealed a deeper ambiguity: most people wanted the best of both worlds. Although trying to secure a quiet environment, they were not willing to alter basic attitudes about business and production. They wanted the benefits of technology with quiet surroundings. If they could not have both, they were willing to sacrifice environmental quality.

Despite their own ideological limitations, anti-din advocates firmly believed that they could achieve a quiet environment by developing a new public awareness of the noise problem. They sought a broader environmental perspective in the context of a widening civic consciousness. Their approach combined education with legislative action, stemming from the conviction that the public would abate the noise nuisance "as soon as they fully understand that it injures the health and decreases the comfort of the people."[13] In creating popular sentiment against noise pollution and in favor of anti-din laws, reformers discovered a need for a communitywide citizens' noise abatement organization with a broad spectrum of members including health officials, police, doctors, clergymen, businessmen, teachers, and parents. Urban din would continue to be a problem "until community interests proponderate more than they do—and as much as they should—over those of individuals or small groups."[14]

Noise abatement reformers worked at the local level for several reasons, one of which was that local observations originally spurred their concern. In working for legislation, many factors entered into determining whether a particular noise constituted a legal nuisance. At common law, noise was not a nuisance per se, but it had the potential of becoming a legal nuisance. Courts evaluated the character, volume, time, place, duration, and locality of a sound properties that varied from one community to the next. A municipal ordinance, therefore, was the most effective way for a public authority to handle a local community problem.[15]

More important, reformers could mobilize public opinion against noise at the community level because people responded to noise disturbances in their own neighborhoods. Citizens supported the attack on noise not as members of a special class or a particular interest but as listeners concerned about the safety and quality of their surroundings. While middle-class and professional people assumed leadership roles in the crusade against noise, they were not the only group committed to the attack on din and not always the first to demand that municipalities take action to alleviate it.

Unlike the more well-to-do classes, the poor were unable to escape noise at any time. They often had to live near the strident factories in which they worked, and their surroundings seemed almost inevitably raucous. "Dirt and noise are inseparable adjuncts to life in a mill district, deplorable, but unavoidable."[16] Still, members of the working class protested. In the summer of 1907, working women from the tenement districts of Philadelphia asked for help in abating noise from the Civic Club and the board of health:

> What we can not stand is the noise. It never stops. It is killing us. We work hard all day and need sleep and rest at night. No one can sleep till midnight and all the noise begins again at five. Many of us have husbands who work all night and must get their sleep during the day, but they can get no sound sleep with all the noise that goes on about us. You can get away from the noise during the summer, but we can not. We are right in the middle of it all our lives. Now what can your civic club do for us?[17]

In response, the club organized a Committee on Unnecessary Noise with representatives from all civic associations in the city. After the committee notified newspapers of the clamorous conditions and began work on legislation, it received "a shower of grateful letters . . . from hard-working men and women in the tenement districts."[18]

The reform capabilities of working-class people, however, were severely limited. They did not have the time to follow all the various bureaucratic procedures of filing complaints, nor could they afford to be away from their jobs in order to initiate legal action or attend city hearings. Circumstances forced them to assume a more passive role, usually demonstrating their support for anti-noise measures through letters to organizations or through the approval their local representatives gave to anti-noise laws.

Petitions, complaints, or general concern over urban din resulted in the organization of anti-noise groups through local boards of health. As people became aware that noise pollution posed a serious hindrance to their well-being, they naturally turned to the board of health for relief. Since it often wielded substantial power, the board could force a person or a business to stop making a noise under the premise that the sound endangered life or health. The chairman of the Committee on Noise of the American Civic Association declared that, if boards of health could prevent a person "from polluting his neighbor's water-supply with typhoid germs, they can forbid him from congesting his neighbor's air with sounds that breed insanity."[19] As medical experts, health officials recognized that din could be detrimental to health, and their voices lent a special note of authority to the anti-noise campaign.

Police departments participated in a similar way. The New York commissioner of police admitted that it was "part of the duty of the police to suppress such noises as are not necessary."[20] Despite severe enforcement problems, police officials continued to respond to public pressure by issuing departmental orders to patrolmen to do all in their power to stop racket.

Some city councils approved investigative bodies to look into the noise pollution issue. In 1913, the Chicago City Council passed an order directing the health commissioner to examine the question of unnecessary noise and report his findings to the council. The Sub-Committee on the Reduction of Unnecessary Noise held a series of public hearings. After testimony from many citizens and hundreds of written complaints, the committee concluded that the number, character, and sincerity of complaints demonstrated "the widespread interest in the subject and the seriousness of the problem." It determined that the noise of downtown Chicago comprised "a bedlam which in its aggregate is unquestionably shattering our nerves and indirectly shortening our lives."[21]

Businessmen also combatted the problem, some by supporting the health and police departments through civic associations like the Chicago City Club, others by forming their own anti-noise groups through local chambers of commerce. The Atlanta Chamber of Commerce appointed an anti-noise committee in 1918. Civic boosterism played some part in the organization of the committee because the chamber had received "a great deal of complaint . . . to the effect that Atlanta is afflicted by unnecessary noise." The din seemed not only a mark against the city but also "an unnecessary strain upon the people whose lives are strenuous enough already." The committee received 140 letters from leading citizens and secured the ready cooperation of the police and the press.[22]

Businessmen who supported the anti-noise campaign were not wholly altruistic. Noise hampered efficiency and affected nerves—it also lowered property values and hurt business by keeping customers away. For these reasons, the New York Merchants' Association urged the Public Service Commission to reduce the racket of elevated railroads.[23] Moreover, by backing legislation that stopped peddlers from making a noise to sell their wares and limited them to certain areas of the city, merchants found an ideal way to restrict competition. They not only objected to the noise level but also disliked vendors obstructing the street and littering the premises. In a candid statement of self-interest, forty-six New York merchants and property owners petitioned the mayor to restrain peddlers because they "stand constantly without moving, in front of our stores, and they sell goods, wares and merchandise in opposition to us."[24]

Physicians not only played an important role in the anti-noise campaign but sometimes formed their own groups. The Baltimore City Medical Society appointed an anti-noise committee in 1912, which compiled a noise inventory by soliciting complaints from the public. The chairman declared that the campaign was "generously responded to by citizens in all walks of life."[25] After drawing up legislation, influencing the appointment of an anti-noise policeman, and heightening public awareness of the issue, members believed that they had established the anti-noise movement in Baltimore "on a permanent working basis where every day some specific noise is abated and many potential noises averted."[26]

The Society for the Suppression of Unnecessary Noise in New York City was the largest and best-known anti-din organization of the period. Its president and motivating spirit was Julia Barnett Rice, who had received a college education in classics and music and then had become a physician after attending Women's Medical College of the New York Infirmary in 1885 and completing a one-year internship. Instead of entering active practice, she married in 1885 and devoted herself to raising six children. From her hospital work, she retained an enduring concern for the sick that was the basis of her anti-noise crusade. Her husband pursued a varied career as an author, college professor, and lawyer before becoming wealthy as a businessman. While his money provided her with the freedom to focus on a specific issue, his ownership of *The Forum* supplied immediate access to the public. More important, Rice had a very strong desire to do something, to be active, to make use of her skills in order to benefit the public as a whole.[27] Endowed with time on her hands, with the means to become active, and with a strong sense of purpose, she turned her efforts to reform.

In 1905, at the age of 45, Rice threw herself into a tireless, one-woman crusade to stop the noises along New York City's East River. Shrieking tugboat whistles had become a bane to her home life in the exclusive Riverside section of the city and to patients in hospitals along the waterfront. The nuisance seemed inexcusable. Her attack on river whistling revealed the communitywide desire for quieter surroundings and the inherent shortcomings of environmental reform.

Rice immediately encountered a tangle of bureaucratic complications. Municipal and state authorities disclaimed jurisdiction on the grounds that the river was a federal waterway, and federal authorities refused to act because no law existed to deal with the problem. To prod officials, she collected three thousand signatures from rich and poor alike, protesting the racket. She acquired the support of hospitals in the vicinity and received the endorsement of the board of health. Despite the apathy on the part of officials, she encountered "gratitude from a long-suffering public, and much hearty encouragement from a sympathetic press."[28]

To settle the question of jurisdiction, Rice persuaded Representative William Stiles Bennet, a New York lawyer, to push a bill through Congress. The Bennet Act of 1907, which passed both houses without objection, regulated boat whistling in harbors across the country by "prohibiting useless and unnecessary whistling."[29] The bill placed the power for controlling indiscriminate whistling in the hands of the supervising inspectors of steamboats. It was the first anti-noise measure that Congress had ever authorized and the only piece of national legislation against noise during the period. Marine interests willingly supported the bill on the grounds of improved safety standards; their object was to eliminate the confusion that arose from discordant signaling.

While some ship captains did face disciplinary action and even suspension for a few days because of indiscriminate whistling, enforcement of the Bennet Act was haphazard. It was extremely difficult to prove that a particular whistle blast was unnecessary, given the demands for safety and the elusiveness of the sound. In the great majority of cases, value judgments of captains and pilots determined the use of whistles. Enforcement depended essentially on self-regulation. An economic argument also handicapped the bill. The *New York Times* admitted, "Nobody thinks of asking that all or any steamboats shall give up their whistles altogether. . . . The city is too fond of its commerce to attempt any interference with its rights or even its needs."[30] No one really expected a business to give up all its noise.

Despite its shortcomings, the Bennet Act did provide the first great impetus to the anti-noise cause. Rice's efforts publicized the issue of noise pollution and demonstrated that individuals could do something to improve their physical surroundings. Spurred on by success, she decided to combat the problem of urban din in its entirety. "If an individual could carry through what had appeared from the first foreordained to failure, much could certainly be accomplished by a regularly organized Association."[31]

Rice formed the Society for the Suppression of Unnecessary Noise in December 1906. The name was quite significant. Members maintained that much of the racket in a great city was unavoidable. Therefore, in their initial appeal to the public, they explained that they purposely had organized not an anti-noise society but "one which will confine its efforts to the suppression of unnecessary noise." They promised to "work along broad though conservative lines."[32] With this approach, the society secured a wide base of support but restricted its ability to effect a fundamental change in the public's attitude toward the environment. Because it never questioned the priorities of business, production, and "progress," the society attacked individual noise disturbances instead of the broader environmental implications.

To establish the society as a force in the community, Rice recruited impressive individuals of wide-ranging backgrounds. The association's three vice-presidents were novelist William Dean Howells; John Bassett Moore, professor of international law at Columbia University; and Rev. George M. Searle, superior general of the Paulist Fathers. The advisory board of the society boasted municipal officials including the commissioner of health and his predecessor, the commissioner of charities and correction, the city superintendent of schools, and the surveyor of the port of New York. College professors like Nicholas Murray Butler agreed to serve. Congressmen William Stiles Bennet, J. Van Vechten Olcott, and Herbert Parsons lent their support. The bishop and archbishop of the diocese of New York participated. Physicians on the board included the president of the State Commission in Lunacy, the editor of the *Medical Record*, and the president of the New York Academy of Medicine. The dean of Columbia University Law School, the head of the Association of Masters, Mates, and Pilots, and poet Richard Watson Gilder also joined. The board of directors consisted of representatives from fifty-nine hospitals. By the end of the first year, the membership had grown to about two hundred, and the society had attracted nationwide attention.[33]

With the backing of influential citizens, Rice could proclaim, "The beginning has thus been made, the beginning of a crusade against noise, one of the most insidious and harmful enemies to health to which city-dwellers are exposed."[34] In waging the crusade, the society's members looked beyond their own complaints. They hoped to come to the relief of the poor who constantly sent letters asking for help:

> . . . the unfortunate denizens of the city cannot leave it during
> the heated months, when the scourge of noise is hardest to bear.
> The rich can and do escape from the hot, noisy, sleepless city be-
> fore the open-window season really begins, but the tenement-
> house dweller and those who are cooped up in the limited space
> of cheap apartment houses know what suffering is imposed by
> unrestricted din.[35]

The society pursued an educational campaign, in conjunction with the passage of local ordinances, to convince the public to take action against the nuisance of unrestrained noise. For several reasons, the association shunned litigation to secure its goals. Environmental law was in its embryonic stages, and the legal pitfalls were numerous. The society did not want to assume the expense of litigation, and it refused to bring action against business and industry because it remained ambivalent on the idea of "progress." Firms also cooperated with noise abatement efforts by saying that they were doing all in their power to eliminate unnecessary racket from their enterprises.

Instead of legal action, the society turned to another effective technique of consumer activism to influence public opinion—the use of publicity. Newspapers and periodicals became ready allies. The willingness of the press to keep the issue before the public led Rice to assert that "perhaps never before has an absolutely untried work been so cordially and heartily welcomed."[36] The press responded because noise abatement efforts attracted community-wide interest.

The establishment of quiet zones around hospitals and schools was the most innovative anti-noise legislation, demonstrating the popular support for the movement. The zones were a new concept in urban planning, acting as protective shields within the urban environment to safeguard those to whom noise would be most distressing—the sick needing rest and children trying to learn. The defense of the sick and the welfare of children were issues that gained immediate, communitywide backing as individuals of all classes saw their own vital interests at stake.

The society brought an ordinance establishing quiet zones around hospitals before the board of aldermen in June 1907. The health and police commissioners endorsed the bill, civic organizations as well as prominent individuals in business and charitable work supported it, and the superintendents of fourteen hospitals signed a petition urging its passage. The board approved the ordinance unanimously.[37]

Rice further broadened the base of the movement when she recruited children into the campaign. She formed the Children's Hospital Branch of the society in 1908. Working with the board of education, she traveled to schools in all sections of the city and enlisted over twenty thousand members. Children took a pledge not to play in quiet zones and to help the sick by refraining from unnecessary noise. They signed a card and received a black-and-white badge with the word "Humanity" in the center. With "an abundance of sympathy for this movement," no less a personage than Mark Twain agreed to serve as honorary president of the branch.[38] Not only would the branch aid patients, but it also seemed a positive way to reinforce character development. "We believe that the ethical advantages to our boys and girls would be scarcely less than the added degree of peace and repose to be gained by the sick."[39]

The call for quiet zones around schools was even more popular, for it touched an emotional note in a generation deeply concerned about the development of its children. Rice found the "utter neglect" toward quiet conditions around schools "little short of incredible." Decrying the clamor that interfered with learning, she exclaimed, "And these are the conditions under which we force our children to study—to our shame be it said."[40] In 1911, the society launched a full-scale effort to secure quiet zones around schools. It gained the support of twenty-five state boards of education and health as well as the approval of heads of educational boards in seventy-five cities. The Bureau of Education of the United States Department of the Interior endorsed the idea. On the local level, teachers and parents banded together. Rice presented a petition with eleven thousand signatures to the board of aldermen. In the face of this kind of approval, the board passed the ordinance unanimously.[41]

As Americans supported these and other anti-noise ordinances, they reacted as listeners—as members of a community responding to a mutual problem. Because the campaign never really threatened vested interests, it could attract broad-based support. At the same time, the movement was unable to solve the problem of urban din completely. The issue was more complex than reformers had at first thought. Racket proved to be "an invisible, intangible, elusive enemy."[42] Neither did reformers anticipate the difficulties that arose in enforcing anti-din ordinances. On a personal level, individuals hesitated to complain about their neighbors unless the noise became a continual irritant. A more practical problem was that police forces were understaffed and overworked. Compared with other crimes, violations of anti-noise laws seemed of minor importance.

Reformers neglected to offer alternatives to ingrained values and never seriously questioned the direction that society should take. They did not ask citizens to make sacrifices for environmental quality because they themselves did not want to. Consequently, the problem of urban din seemed to become worse and its solution more puzzling. In 1914 Rice lamented, "But alas! needless noises abound, causing distress and wrecking health."[43] The anti-noise campaign, nevertheless, had moved toward a broader environmental perspective. Through the use of the press and information designed to educate the public, reformers increased public awareness of noise pollution. Local ordinances demonstrated that government had a responsibility to establish environmental safeguards. With the coming of World War I and in the midst of the growing complexity of urban din, however, reformers were no longer able to sustain their initial level of enthusiasm. As a result, a different group of anti-noise advocates began to direct the campaign.

While reformers believed that legislation was essential for lasting reform, they also hoped that mechanical and electrical engineers would make the city a tranquil place in which to live. Invention gave them some justification for that hope. Technological developments like the muffler, nonclattering ash cans, asphalt paving, and electric welding diminished some of the worst noise sources of urban life. The rubber tire revolutionized transportation. Acoustical engineers worked to reduce noise in buildings through use of soundproof foundations and materials that reduced vibration.[44]

To make the transition to the machine age less haphazard, the experts in science and technology took over the anti-noise campaign in the 1920s. Scientists responded to the need for more research to gauge the environmental effects of noise on people and for definite measurements of din to judge better the severity of the problem. Researchers at Ohio Wesleyan, Northwestern, Columbia, and Colgate universities conducted a battery of experiments. Noise caused violent emotional reactions in a hypnotized subject. The pitch of a sound was directly related to annoyance. Tests using white rats showed that din diminished food consumption and retarded growth. Scientists also confirmed that noise raised blood pressure, increased muscular tension, decreased efficiency, and caused fatigue. In 1925, Bell Telephone Laboratories invented the audiometer and opened a whole new area of investigation. Acoustical engineers began to gather scientific data on urban din under the premise that to stop racket one first had to measure it. As the evidence against noise accumulated, the National Safety Council warned:

> It is very unfortunate for us that we become gradually used to
> noise of any kind that at first was very disturbing, and that we
> do not actually recognize its damaging and insidious effects until
> it has undermined our health.[45]

Believing that their city had become "a veritable jungle of noises," New York City officials appointed a Noise Abatement Commission in 1929. The commission was the first of its kind in the United States and represented the first serious attempt to cope with noise pollution as a social problem. Over a period of two and a half years, it published two fascinating reports that reflected the changing moods of their authors. While optimism and certainty permeated the first, *City Noise* (1930), a sense of frustration pervaded the second, *City Noise, Volume II* (1932). In the course of the transition, the commission rejected the pat answers of earlier reform efforts and emphasized the need for a broader environmental perspective. The story of the commission reveals in microcosm the dynamics behind the rise and fall of an environmental issue. Combining scientific data with effective publicity, the commission made the issue of noise pollution a focal point of public concern. But it could not sustain that concern.

Urban din seemed eminently solvable, given the participation of the right individuals. New York City officials put their faith in scientists and businessmen. Experts, using a thorough scientific approach, would certainly find effective remedies. The commissioner of health appointed an impressive group of eleven authorities from the fields of neurology, otology, engineering, construction, and law to study the noise question and report their findings. He also secured the support of businessmen. The president of the Johns-Manville Corporation acted as chairman, while the vice-president of General Motors served as an adviser. The city could "well congratulate itself that the complex noise situation is in the hands of such distinguished specialists in whom the public has an abiding confidence."[46]

From the outset, the commission was an investigative body. To gather facts, it equipped a traveling laboratory for the scientific measurement of noise. Investigators measured the noise level in about 90 different areas of the city and made 10,000 observations. They utilized the audiometer and were one of the earliest research groups to employ the decibel as a unit of measurement for noise. They also used over eleven thousand public responses to a noise questionnaire to draw a noise map illustrating the citywide scope of the problem. The exhaustive study led the *New York Times* to remark that the "stupendous figures . . . indicate the ocean of sound in which we are all submerged."[47]

Confirming many fears that had disturbed people from the start of the anti-noise campaign, the commission concluded that "a state of emergency exists in New York as a result of the increase in noise." It determined that noise impaired hearing, lowered working efficiency, strained the nervous system, and gravely interfered with sleep. Din also seriously hindered the ability of children to think and retarded the normal development of infants.[48]

City Noise set forth the case against noise. The 308-page volume was impressive in scope, popular in appeal, and authoritative in presentation. Men of unquestioned eminence had produced it, and it immediately attracted international as well as national attention. Civic groups and newspapers hailed it as a landmark in the anti-noise crusade. The book demonstrated that noise pollution had become "a monster, bred and born of the city itself and preying upon the health and happiness of city dwellers."[49]

While this first volume defined the noise pollution problem, the second dealt with ways and means to eliminate it. Commission members discovered that it was considerably easier to define the problem than to solve it. The commissioner of health became aware of the "herculean task" of ridding the city of noise and admitted that "noise is even more our enemy than we had suspected."[50] As an investigative body, the commission always possessed limited authority, with no personnel to establish the validity of noise complaints and no power to enforce laws. Compounding these problems was the fact that no central agency existed to deal with noise pollution or any other environmental issue. The commission could only forward complaints to the proper municipal agency with the hope that some kind of action would follow. Determining the right agency for a particular noise disturbance was often a chore in itself. Once located, these agencies frequently had more pressing problems to deal with than noise complaints. The commission regretted that it had sometimes "not been our privilege" to see noise abatement methods enforced.[51]

The commission, however, perceived something more significant behind the failure of the anti-noise campaign than bureaucratic entanglements. It pointed to the lack of a socially and culturally developed environmental attitude and emphasized the need for education. To arouse public consciousness, the commission courted the cooperation of the press and used the radio to inform citizens. The commission reaffirmed the need for a new environmental attitude and a concern for community rights:

> We need not wait for further scientific proofs of ill effects from
> noise, our desire for peace and quiet is the justifiable foundation
> of the campaign against it. . . . only the development of a strong
> civic sense in each of us as to the care of the rights of the other
> fellow will make our city fit to live and grow in.[52]

The commission gradually converted thousands to noise abatement. However, nothing tangible resulted from this massing of public opinion except perhaps a few more complaints to city authorities and a few more letters to the newspapers. The process of conversion seemed to proceed at a snail's pace, leaving the commission open to criticism for the apparent futility of its efforts. Yet it continued to believe that permanent reform would come about only "when the haters of noise are numbered in millions, not thousands."[53] The anti-noise campaign, in other words, would have to bring about a change in the minds of men and women to insure a quiet environment. Indeed, a change in outlook was a prerequisite to improving the quality of urban life in general. The sense of frustration that marked the typewritten and little-publicized second volume reflected the difficulty of this task. Most of the thousands who complained to the commission were unwilling to take any further action to stop the clangor that bothered them. Rather, they expected the commission "to come to their rescue like a magic prince, solving their difficulties with a wave of a fairy wand and emphatically without any effort to themselves."[54]

The commission disbanded in May 1932, having neither established a new and broader environmental perspective nor appreciably diminished the noise pollution of New York City. In the wake of the Great Depression, issues other than noise abatement assumed priority for most Americans. Moreover, as people came to realize that no simple remedy existed for the noise problem, they lost their initial enthusiasm.[55]

Nevertheless, unlike earlier reformers, the commission did come to an important realization: law and technology alone were not enough to bring about environmental reform. The chairman admitted, "We do not believe that noise can be legislated out of existence."[56] While research and measurement contributed to an understanding of people's relationship to their surroundings, science was no panacea. Before substantive environmental improvement could occur, Americans would have to acquire a new environmental attitude, to rethink older values and reevaluate their relationship to their physical surroundings. They would then have to make hard choices through their governments. But this process collided with established values. As the commission's final report stated, "If man came first in the mind of man, noise abatement would be effective in a week. But the machine comes first and it is simpler for the machine to make noise."[57]

In the long run, environmental improvement would require sacrifices and a dramatic shift in priorities. Most people were not yet prepared for that. Before making sacrifices that involved changing lifestyle or economic loss, people first had to perceive that the costs to health and environmental quality from noise pollution were immediate, unavoidable, and exorbitant. The commission discovered that the costs were not yet high enough.

Notes

I wish to thank Resources for the Future, Inc., for their Doctoral Dissertation Fellowship in Natural Resources, which made the research and preparation of this essay possible.

1. *New York Daily Tribune*, 6 October 1895.

2. David P. Thelen discusses this consumer-oriented theme in *The New Citizenship: Origins of Progressivism in Wisconsin, 1885–1900* (Columbia, Mo., 1972), pp. 57–85.

3. "The Noise Nuisance," *Current Literature* 29 (November 1900): 508.

4. *New York Times*, 2 July 1905.

5. Professor James J. Putnam, "Discussion," *Transactions of the Fifteenth International Congress in Hygiene and Demography* (Washington, D.C., 23–28 September 1912), p. 540.

6. "What Is the Saturation Point for City Noise?" *American Journal of Public Health* 20 (July 1930): 758–60.

7. Shirley W. Wynne, M.D., Dr. P.H., Commissioner of Health, City of New York, untitled address before the Acoustical Society of America at the Westinghouse Lighting Auditorium, Grand Central Palace, 9 May 1930.

8. Elmer S. Batterson, "Progress of the Anti-Noise Movement," *National Municipal Review* 6 (May 1917): 372–78.

9. Dr. Willis O. Nance, "The Noise Problem in Chicago" (address to the City Club of Chicago, 17 June 1913); Nance's address appeared in *The City Club Bulletin* 6 (July 1913): 229–38.

10. *New York Times*, 6 August 1912.

11. John H. Girdner, M.D., "To Abate the Plague of City Noises," *North American Review* 165 (October 1897): 460–68.

12. For a listing of the municipal ordinances against noise, see *Anti-Noise Ordinances of Various Cities*, compiled for the Committee on Health of the Chicago City Council, Dr. Willis O. Nance, chairman, by the Municipal Reference Library, Chicago, 1913, pp. 1–36. This report draws together laws from thirty-one cities from every section of the country.

13. Lewellys F. Barker, M.D., Professor of Medicine, Johns Hopkins University, "Noise and Insomnia," *The Bulletin of the Medical and Chirurgical Faculty of Maryland* 5 (January 1913): 97–103.

14. *New York Times*, 13 September 1913.

15. William A. Lloyd, "Noise as a Nuisance," *University of Pennsylvania Law Review*

and American Law Register 82 (April 1934): 567–82. See also Horace G. Wood, *A Practical Treatise on the Law of Nuisances in Their Various Forms: Including Remedies Therefor at Law and in Equity* (Albany, N.Y., 1875), p. 583.

16. Elizabeth Crowell, "Painter's Row: The Company House," in *The Pittsburgh District: Civic Frontage*, ed. Paul Underwood Kellogg (New York, 1914), p. 131.

17. Imogen B. Oakley, "Public Health Versus the Noise Nuisance," *National Municipal Review* 4 (April 1915): 231–37.

18. Imogen B. Oakley, "The Protest against Noise," *Outlook* 90 (17 October 1908): 351–55.

19. Oakley, "Public Health Versus the Noise Nuisance," p. 236.

20. *New York Times*, 9 December 1915.

21. Nance, "The Noise Problem in Chicago," p. 234.

22. Atlanta Chamber of Commerce, "Anti-Noise Committee," *The City Builder* 2 (August 1918): 9–10 and 3 (September 1918): 7–8.

23. *New York Times*, 19 March 1912.

24. *New York Times*, 20 August 1908.

25. William T. Watson, M.D., "Eliminating Noise from Baltimore," *The Bulletin of the Medical and Chirurgical Faculty of Maryland* 5 (January 1913): 106–15.

26. William T. Watson, M.D., "Baltimore's Anti-Noise Crusade," *National Municipal Review* 3 (July 1914): 585–89.

27. Telephone interview with her daughter, Marjorie Rice Levis, September 2, 1976. See also John William Leonard, ed., *Woman's Who's Who of America: A Biographical Dictionary of Contemporary Women of the United States and Canada* (New York, 1914–15), p. 683.

28. Julia H. B. Rice, "An Effort to Suppress Noise," *Forum* 37 (April 1906): 552–70.

29. *Statutes of the United States of America*, passed at the Second Session of the Fifty-Ninth Congress, 1906–07, vol. 35, pt. 1, chap. 892, p. 881. See also *Congressional Record*, 59th Cong., 2d sess., 11–31 January 1907, p. 1093.

30. *New York Times*, 8 December 1906.

31. Mrs. Isaac L. Rice, "Our Most Abused Sense—The Sense of Hearing," *Forum* 38 (April 1907): 559–72.

32. Ibid., p. 569. See also *New York Times*, 15 January 1907.

33. Rice, "Our Most Abused Sense," pp. 568–69. See also *New York Daily Tribune*, 9 December 1906; *New York Times*, 27 February 1908.

34. Mrs. Isaac L. Rice, "First Annual Report of the Society for the Suppression of Unnecessary Noise" (New York, 1908).

35. Mrs. Isaac L. Rice, "Third Annual Report of the Society for the Suppression of Unnecessary Noise" (New York, 1910).

36. Rice, "First Annual Report," p. 2.

37. *New York Times*, 24 and 26 June 1907.

38. Julia H. B. Rice, "The Children's Hospital Branch of the Society for the Suppression of Unnecessary Noise," *Forum* 39 (April 1908): 560–67. See also *New York Sun*, 18 October 1908.

39. Mrs. Isaac L. Rice, "Report of the Society for the Suppression of Unnecessary Noise, 1907–1913" (New York, 1 April 1914).

40. Mrs. Isaac L. Rice, "Quiet Zones for Schools," *Forum* 46 (December 1911): 731–42.

41. Ibid., pp. 738–42. See also Rice, "Report, 1907-1913," pp. 5-6.

42. Rice, "Third Annual Report," p. 2.

43. Rice, "Report, 1907–1913," p. 20.

44. F. R. Watson, "Sound Interference in Buildings Cured," *Scientific American, Supplement* 68 (18 December 1909); E. P. Dorman, "Curing Noise in a Concrete Building," *Scientific American* 110 (14 February 1914): 140; "Reducing Noise in Factories," *Scientific American* 125 (6 August 1921).

45. "Report of Committee Investigating the Elimination of Excess Noise," *Proceedings of the National Safety Council*, Fourteenth Annual Safety Congress, pt. 1, Cleveland, Ohio, 28 September - 2 October 1925, pp. 192–99. For a description of the experiments, see *Transactions of the National Safety Council*, Eighteenth Annual Safety Congress, 30 November - 4 December 1929, pp. 382–96.

46. Edward F. Brown et al., eds., *City Noise: The Report of the Commission Appointed by Dr. Shirley W. Wynne, Commissioner of Health, to Study Noise in New York City and to Develop Means of Abating It, Noise Abatement Commission, Department of Health, City of New York* (New York, 1930), p. 17. For biographical information on the members, see pp. v–vii.

47. *New York Times*, 15 July 1930.

48. Brown et al., *City Noise*, p. 17.

49. Roxanne Amberson, "Crusading against Noise: An Account of What One City Is Doing to Control Noise," *The Forecast* 41 (June 1931): 347–48.

50. *New York Times*, 3 August 1930.

51. James Flexner, ed., *City Noise, Volume II: The Final Report of the Commission Appointed by Dr. Shirley W. Wynne, Commissioner of Health, to Study Noise in New York City and to Develop Means of Abating It, Noise Abatement Commission, Department of Health, City of New York* (New York, 1932), section 4, p. 1.

52. Dr. Foster Kennedy, Noise Abatement Commission, "What Noise Does to Human Beings" (radio talk given over station WEAF, New York City, 7 January 1930; from the Haven Emerson Public Health Library in New York City).

53. *City Noise, II*, section 2, p. 2.

54. Ibid., section 1, pp. 1–2.

55. The commission provides an interesting example of a five-stage cycle that applies especially to environmental issues. An individual or group takes an existing condition and arouses the public with a strong desire to do something to solve the problem. As the public comes to realize that the solution will be difficult and require some sacrifices, commitment wanes and the issue moves into limbo. See Anthony Downs, "Up and Down with Ecology–the 'Issue-Attention Cycle,'" *Public Interest*, no. 28 (Summer 1972): 38–50.

56. Lewis H. Brown, Chairman, Noise Abatement Commission, "What We Are Doing and How" (radio talk given over station WEAF, New York City, 28 January 1930; from the Haven Emerson Public Health Library in New York City).

57. *City Noise, II*, section 2, p. 4.

Group Participation
in Environmental Reform

7. Pollution and Political Reform in Urban America: The Role of Municipal Engineers, 1840–1920

By Stanley K. Schultz and Clay McShane

In 1905 Frederic C. Howe, a ten-year veteran of political wars to improve urban government, published his self-styled "manual of reform." In *The City: The Hope of Democracy*, Howe reflected the concerns of many urban reformers of his generation. For all his diatribes against misgovernment by political bosses and corruption from profit-hungry private corporations, he identified the "elemental problems" of cities as the building of sewers, the laying-out of streets, the provision of transit, and the development of park systems. Such public works, he claimed, had become "a necessity to the life, health, comfort, convenience, and industry of the city." With other reformers of the period, Howe argued that the efficient administration of such matters—indeed, the running of government itself—was too important to be left in the hands of private individuals or unskilled, elected public officials. "All of these," he noted, "are executive matters requiring special training or scientific knowledge of the work to be done."[1]

Calling for administration by experts, Howe and others sponsored a variety of changes in the structures of urban governments during the early years of the twentieth century. Characteristic of their proposals was the city manager form of government. That approach, heralded by the recently organized National Municipal League, promised administrative unity, clear lines of responsibility, expertise in the head of the administration, and discipline and harmony among the ranks of government servants. During the first few decades of the century, scores of small and middle-sized cities initiated this managerial revolution in urban government. The majority of the new city managers were men who had first proved their skill as municipal engineers.[2]

This route to the position was no historical coincidence. Engineers had long before demonstrated their abilities as the skilled few capable of solving the physical problems of cities. No wonder, then, that urban reformers and civic-minded citizens came to believe that engineers might also solve the administrative problems of governing the twentieth-century city. During the preceding half century, the job of municipal engineer had developed into a profession that had reshaped the physical landscape of urban America. It also had provided a corps of experienced experts and a model of administrative skill that early-twentieth-century Americans could use as a basis for the structural reform of urban government. The story of those experts who had engineered the nineteenth-century metropolis explained their exalted reputations as urban problem solvers during the early twentieth century.

Of the many crises confronting nineteenth-century urbanites, none loomed more obvious or important than environmental pollution. Despite ordinances in many cities requiring property owners to clean their frontage areas, urban streets were still mired in filth. Garbage collection remained a province of private companies and was spotty at best. A New Yorker recalled that the "householders swept as often as they pleased; and for the matter of being carried away, the dirt often remained in heaps for several days; or rather the heaps were trodden and scattered about again; and required to be swept and collected anew." Even into the 1860s herds of swine roamed the streets of such large cities as Cincinnati and New York, serving as inexpensive garbage collectors. In southern cities turkey vultures and cattle performed scavenger duties. The animals also contributed to the pollution problems, particularly the thousands of horses who remained the principal source of transit throughout the century. Inadequate sewage facilities kept many streets and yards cesspools of filth. Poor or nonexistent pavement only added to the mire, especially during the wet seasons when the movement of human and animal traffic churned dirt streets into mudholes. A visitor to Chicago in the 1850s observed that planks resting on cross ties of heavy timber provided the only pavement for streets and sidewalks. "Under these planks," he noted, "the water was standing on the surface over three-fourths of the city, and as the sewers from the houses were emptied under them, a frightful odour was emitted in summer, causing fevers and other diseases, foreign to the climate." Occasionally, a loose plank would give way, and "the foul water would spurt into the air high as the windows."[3]

Air pollution was no less a problem than street filth. Sanitationists—physicians and health officials—attributed most of the yellow fever, cholera, and typhus epidemics, among other diseases, to foul air and its inadequate circulation. Anticontagionism was still the predominant theory of disease causation throughout the 1880s. Allegedly harmful miasmas or vapors arose from swampy or damp places, from backyard privies, from decomposing organic matter in the streets, and from "vitiated" or "poisoned" air caused by inadequate circulation in the ever more densely crowded urban environment. In addition, the iron hooves of horses pulverized the garbage and manure of the streets into a fine dust that blew through the air, soiling clothing and choking lungs. As the number of small manufacturing establishments increased, so did the soot and smog that fouled the air. A major iron and steel city like Pittsburgh or a principal railroad center like Chicago experienced heavy air pollution, but even a smaller community like Atlanta, with its guano and fertilizer plants and its slaughterhouses, suffered as well.[4]

Mid-century urbanites found all these problems threatening their physical comfort and safety. Compounding the difficulties was the lack of efficient water supply and sewerage systems. In 1850, only New York City, Boston, Chicago, and Philadelphia had even partially adequate public water supplies. Integrated sewer systems were unknown; at best, cities contained a few private sewers or a few large storm sewers. There was no quibbling with the conclusion drawn by the Massachusetts sanitary surveyors in 1850:

> It has been ascertained that the inhabitants of densely populated
> places generally deteriorate in vitality. . . . This is a significant
> fact, which should be generally known. Cities are not necessarily
> unhealthy, but circumstances are permitted to exist, which make
> them so.[5]

Why did citizens permit such circumstances to exist? Part of the explanation lay in the structure of mid-century municipal governments. Most more closely resembled their colonial predecessors than today's municipal administrations. In most cities, mayors were mere figureheads. Citywide public expenditures for necessary services were a rarity, and so such important services as water supply, street sanitation, and even fire protection remained largely in the hands of private entrepreneurs, except in a few of the largest cities. Land-use decisions did not come from city government but from private individuals and real estate developers whose major goal was subdivision of land to maximize short-run profits. Because of their traditional mistrust of centralized government, urban Americans dispersed control over vital urban services among a hodgepodge of private property owners, private business concerns, and a host of city commissions whose authority overlapped in byzantine confusion. With the power to govern scattered in bits and pieces among a bewildering variety of offices, boards, and commissions, in effect no one governed. Decentralized and weak government reigned.[6]

The increasing incidence of epidemic diseases, along with changes in scientific knowledge and popular ideas about illness and death around the middle of the century, fostered new perceptions of the urban environmental crisis. Some citizens, of course, wanted to blame Providence or human frailty for the unhealthiness of cities and found convenient scapegoats in the growing numbers of native and foreign-born poor in their midst. But careful investigators of the cities' plight began to identify other sources of urban ills. As a sanitary survey of Lynn, Massachusetts, put the matter in the 1870s:

> In a contamination of water, soil, and air by accumulated filth,—
> in intemperance, careless habits of living, and general neglect of
> sanitary laws . . . combined in not a few instances with natural
> unhealthiness of site, must be found the explanation of the great
> variation in mortality between the different streets and districts
> of the city.

The writer concluded that, "if foreigners suffer more than natives, it is not because of any predisposition to disease, or any constitutional weakness of the races, or difficulty in becoming acclimatized, but because they are more exposed to the operation of the causes mentioned." An increasing number of urban Americans over the last half of the century came to believe that the solution to environmental problems lay in physical and technological innovations. A few also began to recognize that the implementation and administration of new technologies might require alterations in the reach and scope of municipal governments. Both in public propaganda for advanced technologies and in demands for greater public authority over urban services, a small number of new professionals led the way.[7]

Sanitarians, landscape architects, and civil engineers formed a troika that tried to pull citizens and elected officials alike out of the mire of government inaction to the higher ground of municipal planning and administration. From the mid-1840s throughout the rest of the century, urban public health officials and amateur statisticians surveyed the spatial distribution of diseases to demonstrate relationships between physical environment and disease causation. For example, in 1864 the Citizens' Association of New York City underwrote a building-by-building survey of the city by chemists, engineers, and physicians. Partly as a result of the survey, the first permanent public agency of its kind in the country, the Metropolitan Board of Health, appeared in 1866, and a model tenement reform act gained passage the following year. Urban sanitarians everywhere supported municipal regulation of foodstuffs, of air pollution, and of housing. They lent their support to the construction of new water and sewer systems, rapid transit systems, and parks. But rarely, except in times of epidemics, did public health officers and sanitarians exert influence over most matters of public policy and administration. Customarily, political clout in matters of public health lay with businessmen. Typical of such involvement was the formation in 1879 of the New Orleans Auxiliary Sanitary Association, whose membership included some physicians but was overwhelmingly composed of influential business leaders. That organization's motto was apposite: "Public Health is Public Wealth."[8]

From Andrew Jackson Downing in the 1840s to John Nolen in the early 1900s, landscape architects propagated physical solutions to urban ills. A number of them—for instance, Frederick Law Olmsted, Horace Shaler Cleveland, and George Kessler—had some training as engineers and therefore often championed public works such as water and sewer systems. Usually, however, the landscape architects urged the construction of large urban parks as "lungs" for the city and the creation of upper-class suburbs as escape hatches for the fortunate few. Occasionally their ideas roamed farther afield. Olmsted proposed parkways (thus coining the term) to serve as transportation arteries, recreational areas, pollution shields for urban watercourses, and the hubs of large-scale planned communities. In the early 1870s, Robert Morris Copeland offered a comprehensive plan for redoing Boston. Copeland predicted:

> The city whose area is carefully studied, which shows by plan
> where wharves may be built, where new avenues are to be laid
> out, and where factories may congregate; where parks, gardens,
> and palaces, if desired, may be made, will grow in a sure, orderly
> and progressive way.

He argued that competent engineering would satisfy all the city's needs, that "merchandise can be easily transported, business done, water and gas supplied, amusements furnished, fires limited, and sewage provided for." The city fathers chose not to adopt his plan. But Copeland had increased public awareness and discussion of the necessity of planning and had exemplified the enthusiasms of his fellow professionals. Still, with a few exceptions, the landscape architects contributed little to the reformulation of public policy or to changes in the administrative reach and authority of municipal governments.[9]

The sanitarians, landscape architects, and municipal engineers often worked together, supported similar goals, and exchanged ideas. Of the three groups, the engineers had the best-developed media, with numerous regional and national periodicals that provided a forum for communication and debate over urban issues. The engineering press assiduously reported the activities and ideas of the landscape architects and usually lent approval to their park planning schemes and suburban developments. Engineering periodicals were even stronger in support of the sanitarians' goals. In 1876, for example, *Van Nostrand's Eclectic Engineering Magazine* reprinted and lauded a utopian scheme advanced by the British sanitarian B. W. Richardson. "Hygeia—A City of Health" emphasized site selection, climate, sewerage, water supply, park systems, and housing design as the elements necessary to the ideal urban environment. J. M.

Gregory, a Chicago sanitarian, in a speech quickly reprinted by *Engineering News*, informed the Chicago Medical Society that

> a great city is a vast laboratory, in which the energies imported
> in the food supplies and stored in the atmosphere are transmitted
> into human life, or rather, into thousands of human lives, but
> which are momentarily and perpetually exposed to that further
> transmutation which crumbles organized being back to its chem-
> ical elements.

Engineers, accustomed to thinking about unified systems, joined sanitarians and landscape architects in viewing the city as an ecosystem, a large integrated unit with the efficient functioning of one part dependent upon the efficient functioning of the whole. On occasion, engineers even defined their role as over-seers of the ecosystem in medical metaphors. "The city engineer is to the city very much what the family physician is to the family," observed one writer in 1894. "He is constantly called upon to advise and direct in all matters pertain-ing to his profession. . . . He does know the character, constitution, particular needs and idiosyncracies of the city, as the family physician knows the con-stitutions of the family."[10]

The members of the troika, then, worked together on various schemes to improve the physical quality of the urban environment. Yet, for all the parks and suburbs designed by the landscape architects and all the health surveys undertaken by the sanitarians, the public works promoted and constructed by the municipal engineers proved the most decisive in improving the health and standard of living of urban Americans. Moreover, the techniques of administra-tion developed by the engineers had the longest-range impact upon the struc-ture and functions of urban government.

City officials long had understood the importance of adequate water sup-plies. Fears of epidemics and fires, together with the pollution of wells by seepage from graves and privies, forced city fathers to tap new sources and often to bring in water from outside municipal boundaries. Until the 1850s, most cities relied upon private firms to build and administer the water supply systems. Rarely was that reliance well placed. The outlay of capital and subse-quent maintenance expenditures were so large, and resultant profits so minimal, that most private firms failed to build systems that served the entire public. The companies left the poorer and more remote districts without water sup-plies. As these areas of the cities expanded rapidly in mid-nineteenth-century America and became ever more congested, health problems mounted according-ly. Unlike the municipal government, private firms could not exercise legal condemnation proceedings under nuisance law or the police power; therefore companies faced additional impediments to extending the water systems, even if they wished to do so.[11] Municipal ownership and administration of water supply systems gained slowly over the last half of the century, as city officials gradually discerned sanitary, technological, and politically expedient reasons to provide this service at public expense and under municipal control.[12]

The building of public waterworks, however, did not always solve the problem of water supply. Despite the creation in 1851 of the Chicago City Hydraulic Company and the passage in 1852 of a $400,000 bond issue, for example, Chicago's demand for water went unmet. By 1860 most Chicagoans still depended upon backyard wells and pumps whose water was constantly polluted by drainage from privy vaults. During the 1860s and early 1870s, the new Chicago Board of Public Works commissioned tunnels built several miles out into Lake Michigan to improve the city's water supply. Not until 1898 was the city able to integrate its facilities into a system that adequately supplied Chicago with water.[13]

Even when cities did construct waterworks, the addition of adequate water did not end environmental pollution. To some extent, it increased the problem, for cities then had to dispose of the vast quantities of water brought in by the new aqueducts. Existent surface drainage was inadequate. By mid-century, sanitarians and engineers began to demand replacement of the "elongated cesspools"—common sewers—with an innovation borrowed from English experience. The new system of pipe sewers, with interceptors to free shore lines of piles of filth, promised to rid cities of both household and street wastes and to replace privies with indoor plumbing. Initially, in cities like Boston and New York, the city councils empowered the construction of new sewer lines piecemeal, a few miles of line here, a few there. Without an integrated system, the sewers only made matters worse. The new water closets of the 1860s and 1870s overflowed the old privy waste disposal systems, soaked the urban water tables, and converted large portions of city land and streets into a stinking morass.[14]

There was little doubt in the minds of many sanitarians and engineers that a good sewer system meant investment in the present and future health of the citizenry. John Griscom, a pioneer health reformer in New York, observed in 1845 that sewers were "not only the most economical, but the *only* mode, in which the immense amounts of filth daily generated in this large city, can be effectively removed." During the mid-1850s in Chicago, Ellis S. Chesbrough, appointed chief engineer of the first sewerage commission, was so persuasive that the city expended more than $10 million to construct nearly fifty-four miles of sewers and to raise the grade of the streets, for drainage purposes, by as much as twelve feet in the emerging central business district. John Bell, a

Philadelphia physician reporting in 1859 for a Committee on the Internal Hygiene of Cities, argued that "paving ought to precede the erection of houses, and drainage follow habitation at a very early period. A neglect of these two preliminary conditions for public health has been productive, in all ages, of a fearful waste of life." By the late 1870s, George E. Waring, Jr., perhaps the most widely known sanitary engineer of the late nineteenth century, vividly stated the relationship between sewers and health. Speaking of the piecemeal construction of sewers in Boston and New York, Waring charged that they were "huge gasometers, manufacturing day and night a deadly aeriform poison, ever seeking to invade the houses along their course; reservoirs of liquid filth, ever oozing through the defective joints, and polluting the very earth upon which the city stands."[15]

Convinced of the necessity of expanding sewerage facilities, city officials authorized the construction of sewer lines, sometimes at public expense, sometimes at the expense of private developers. Chesbrough's work in Chicago provided the first systematic sewer plan under municipal ownership. During the immediate post-Civil War years engineers in other cities followed suit: Providence in 1869; New Haven in 1872; Fall River, Lawrence, and Boston in the mid-1870s. The discovery during the 1880s that many diseases, especially the killer typhoid, were waterborne accelerated drives for sewer construction, for pure water, and for the filtration of both water and sewage. By 1890, only twenty-six cities among those of ten thousand population or more had no sewers at all. By the early years of the twentieth century nearly every city in the nation had sewers. The filtration of water and sewage brought a dramatic decrease in typhoid mortality rates, a drop that averaged 65 percent in the major cities. The success of the sewerage campaigns lent additional weight to claims favoring technological solutions to public health problems.[16]

An important element in the demands for an integrated sewer system was the sewer gas theory of disease. Elaborate experiments and chemical analyses emerged to underscore the alleged dangers. Although widely debated, the theory gained substantial support from many involved in the public health movement, especially engineers. Engineering periodicals generally supported the theory, typically editorializing that "sewer gas, according to all the works on medical sanitary science, is one of the most destructive poisons and fruitful causes of disease in large cities, producing diphtheria, typhus, brain and bilious fevers, malaria and many other forms of disease." While George E. Waring, Jr., was the most prominent proponent of the theory, scores of engineers offered technical schemes for preventing the escape of the gas through sounder construction of sewer systems. The preventive medicine accomplishments of sewerage works, as one writer summed them, resulted in "actually creating an entire urinary and intestinal tract, and establishing . . . an artificial anus" for the city.[17]

The lessons were clear. Water and sewer systems were a city's lifelines. As such, they were too vital to be left to the piecemeal approach of either private enterprise or municipal construction. Comprehensive systems, built and administered by professional experts and funded by local government, had to replace the unsystematic methods of the past. Over the last three decades of the nineteenth century and the first decade of the new century municipal construction and control of unified systems gained public acceptance. By 1910, the standard text on urban public health, *Municipal Sanitation in the United States* by Charles V. Chapin, testified of sewers that "the public so well appreciates their advantages that they are usually demanded when needed, even if they must be entirely paid for by abutters." Chapin added that "in recent times, since sewers have been constructed by the municipality and with engineering advice, details have been wisely left to the engineers." Yet, it was not only details of design and construction that city officials "wisely" left to engineers. In allowing those new professionals to take charge of the construction of major public works, city fathers also turned over to municipal engineers the task of introducing system and method into their administration. Sometimes consciously, sometimes unconsciously, urban officials helped create new administrative strategies that eventually would foster the restructuring of municipal governments.[18]

The functions of modern municipal administration were inherent in water and sewerage technology. Sewer and water supplies required permanent construction and thus necessitated some kind of long-range planning. There were economies of scale in building only one reservoir and one main aqueduct. An integrated sewer system that accommodated present needs and anticipated future growth of the city might be expensive in the short run but relatively economical in the long run. By fits and starts city officials learned these lessons over the later years of the nineteenth century. They also came to recognize that the new technology called for a permanent bureaucracy to acquire land, oversee construction, administer on a day-to-day basis, and plan for long-term needs. Public works could be built most efficiently by technological and managerial experts who could bring their own expertise and the experiences of their counterparts in other cities to bear upon the task. Thus, city officials gradually turned to civil engineers.[19]

At a time when few clearinghouses for the exchange of ideas and experience benefited cities nationwide, the engineers had built up an impressive communications network among themselves. Their common training, either in the few engineering schools of the period or in shared apprenticeships on the major railroads, bound them together. Engineers belonged to local professional clubs that corresponded with one another, publishing and exchanging reports about conditions in their individual cities. Their numerous professional journals published reports on European developments and described water supply, sewerage, housing design, transportation, parks, and other elements of municipal planning. Engineers belonged to the same regional and national organizations. Over the late nineteenth century, the majority held membership in the American Society of Civil Engineers, which frequently printed papers on municipal engineering. By 1894, those professionals involved principally with urban problems formed their own specialized organization, the American Society for Municipal Improvements. The engineers offered city governments a corps of individuals skilled in the technology and management of large-scale enterprises, a professional group of experts who might solve the physical problems of the cities.[20]

In recognition of this fact, officials in a number of cities granted extraordinary powers to civil engineers. In the creation of administrative bureaucracies engineers apparently were the earliest municipal officials to achieve something resembling job security. Ellis S. Chesbrough, chief engineer of the Chicago Board of Sewerage (1855-61), served as that community's first city engineer from 1861 to 1879, an amazing longevity at a time when most municipal jobs changed hands every election. E. P. North, director of the Croton Water Works for New York City; Robert Moore, municipal engineer of St. Louis; George Benzenberg, city engineer of Milwaukee—all had at least twenty years of service in the same city before 1900. Engineers were among the earliest municipal employees to receive Civil Service protection, another indication of their vital role in managing the physical needs of the cities. Permanent administrative bodies, staffed by engineers, seem to have arisen during the 1880s and early 1890s. City officials gained state legislative approval to create metropolitan water and sewer districts such as Boston's Metropolitan Sewage Commission (1889) and similar districts in Chicago, the Passaic Valley, and elsewhere. These were the forerunners of twentieth-century metropolitan "authorities" such as the famed Port Authority of New York. In most cases, municipal governments vested control of such extramunicipal projects in their city engineer's office. By the early 1890s, also, engineers in a few cities obtained the power to approve plans in areas beyond city limits to insure that subdividers used street plans that would facilitate travel and accommodate the installation of subsurface utilities. In some cities engineers had the authority to abate nuisances beyond city limits, thus gaining the ability to protect watersheds and to engage in an early form of zoning regulation as well.[21]

In exercising their increasing responsibilities, municipal engineers helped rationalize the operating procedures of local governments. Through the establishment of their own offices, engineers contributed a model of hierarchical, bureaucratic organization that promised greater efficiency in the management of urban problems. They propagated division of responsibility, offered standardized systems of monitoring costs, and suggested new methods of formulating tax and budgetary policies. Since a substantial minority of engineers had legal training in addition to their technological training, they often advised other city officials on broadly defined administrative and legal questions. In the Boston of the 1870s, for example, engineers instigated, drafted, and oversaw enforcement of public welfare laws. Engineers and their projects served to centralize metropolitan administration of public works vital to the health and safety of urbanites. Due to successes in public works construction and management, engineers often found city councils receptive to their requests for additional responsibilities. In late-nineteenth-century Chicago, for instance, the public works department added the tasks of garbage collection and street cleaning to its specified duties. Gradually, the offices of city engineers and public works boards acquired the reputation of being wise managers who could streamline the operations of government.[22]

Interested in advertising their professional skills, engineers were not bashful about asserting their importance to municipal administration. They praised themselves, as one engineer observed, as having "a high reputation for fairness and a capacity to render wise and just decisions." They criticized the activities of citizens' associations, which offered proposals for needed public works by stating that such matters were best left to professionals. They even claimed a watchdog role over the acts of elected public officials, asserting that the city engineer was "to a large extent responsible for holding the successive political officials to a consistent, progressive policy. . . . To him, even more than to the successive mayors, falls the duty of serving as the intelligence and brains of the municipal government in all physical matters." They backed up that claim by institutionalizing the role of the consultant. Men like Chesbrough, Moses Lane of Milwaukee, Joseph P. Davis of Boston, and Julius W. Adams of Brooklyn were based in their home cities but traveled widely to consult on major projects in other cities. The consultant role was a measure of engineers' status and of their aloofness from the pendulum swings of partisan politics. Despite keen competition among urban centers, city engineers were so important as in-house experts that local politicians could not deny them the opportunity of advising hated rivals in other cities.[23]

Building from the initial base of public works construction and management, engineers developed centralized agencies capable of long-range planning and staffed by cosmopolitan experts. They advocated, with some success, that their organizational techniques be extended to municipal administration as a whole. Alfred F. Noyes, a leading city engineer of the period, echoed conventional wisdom among his colleagues in 1894 when he noted:

> The office of the municipal engineer is of the greatest importance
> to the community. . . . In fact, the city government of today is in
> a large measure a matter of municipal engineering, and the char-
> acter of the city engineer's department is a safe index to the
> intelligence shown in the development of a municipality.[24]

Many political reformers of the early twentieth century agreed with the opinions of Noyes and other engineers. However much reformers disagreed about specifics of structural change in urban government, they did concur that the proper direction led to government by skilled professional bureaucrats. Members of the National Municipal League left no room for doubt on this point. In 1899, a subcommittee composed "The Municipal Program," an attempt to advance the best theories about the "right organization" of municipal government. Reporting about the progress of that effort to the tenth annual meeting in 1904, Delos F. Wilcox, a transportation planner and political reformer, declared that one of the core principles of the "Program" was that city officials had to know their business. Wilcox observed:

> It is gradually dawning upon the American mind that special
> knowledge is required to run the machinery of city government,
> if we are to avoid a wreck. . . . The complex machinery of a city
> can be run only by those who know how to do that particular
> thing. . . . The whole body of municipal officials need special
> knowledge and long experience to give the city the benefit of
> good service.

The desirable characteristics of the ideal administrator were expertise, efficiency, and disinterested, incorruptible professionalism—all of which were traits embodied by municipal engineers who had demonstrated managerial skills of the highest order.[25]

In governing the early-twentieth-century city, the two most important new professions were city planners and city managers. Both promised to bring to the management of urban affairs the "special knowledge" and experience demanded by reformers. It was not surprising that municipal engineers and other individuals with some engineering training dominated both of the new professions.[26] Over the last half of the nineteenth century, urban Americans had become increasingly aware of the importance of technology to the comfort, health, and order of their daily lives. Virtually the only problems successfully attacked by urban leaders were those susceptible to engineering expertise. The physical problems of expanding cities had called forth a new profession of experts to provide solutions. In turn, those experts had developed administrative techniques and managerial skills that had enhanced their reputations as problem solvers. In both the technological and the political arenas, municipal engineers had played an important part. By the early years of the twentieth century, they provided a corps of efficient experts ripe for recruitment as skilled professionals to manage the new institutions of city government. The day of government by bureaucratic agencies and technical experts had dawned. In the vanguard stood municipal engineers.

Notes

1. Frederic C. Howe, *The City: The Hope of Democracy* (1905; rep., Seattle, 1967), pp. 50, 127, 131, 182. For historians' discussion of reformers' ambitions, see Samuel Haber, *Efficiency and Uplift* (Chicago, 1964); Ernest S. Griffith, *A History of American City Government: The Progressive Years and Their Aftermath, 1900-1920* (New York, 1974), chaps. 1–11; Samuel P. Hays, "The Changing Political Structure of the City in Industrial America," *Journal of Urban History* 1 (November 1974): 6–38; and Robert Wiebe, *The Search for Order, 1877-1920* (New York, 1967), pp. 164–95.

2. Griffith, *American City Government 1900-1920*, pp. 167–68; Nelson P. Lewis, *The Planning of the Modern City: A Review of the Principles Governing City Planning* (New York, 1916), p. 415; Harry A. Toulmin, Jr., *The City Manager: A New Profession* (New York, 1917), pp. 78–81; "City Manager Plan Widely Endorsed," *Engineering News-Record* 85 (7 October 1920): 703.

3. Quotations came from Warren S. Tryon, ed., *A Mirror for Americans: Life and Manners in the United States, 1790-1870 as Recorded by American Travelers*, 3 vols. (Chicago, 1952), 1: 169–70; Wilson Smith, ed., *Cities of Our Past and Present: A Descriptive Reader* (New York, 1964), p. 54. The most comprehensive survey of urban sanitation problems during the period is George E. Waring, Jr., comp., *Report on the Social Statistics of Cities, Tenth Census of the United States, 1880*, 2 vols. (Washington, D.C., 1887). Informative historical accounts include Lawrence H. Larsen, "Nineteenth-Century Street Sanitation: A Study of Filth and Frustration," *Wisconsin Magazine of History* 52 (Spring 1969): 239–47; David R. Goldfield, "The Business of Health Planning: Disease Prevention in the Old South," *Journal of Southern History* 42 (November 1976): 557–70; and Martin V. Melosi, "'Out of Sight, Out of Mind': The Environment and the Disposal of Municipal Refuse, 1860–1920," *The Historian* 35 (August 1973): 621–40.

4. On anti-contagionism, see Erwin Ackerknecht, "Anticontagionism between 1821 and 1867," *Bulletin of the History of Medicine* 22 (September-October 1948): 562–93; George Rosen, *A History of Public Health* (New York, 1958), pp. 103–8, 287–90; and Charles Rosenberg, "The Cause of Cholera: Aspects of Etiological Thought in Nineteenth Century America," *Bulletin of the History of Medicine* 34 (July-August 1960): 331–54. For discussion of problems in particular cities, see Thomas N. Bonner, *Medicine in Chicago, 1850-1950* (Madison, Wis., 1957); John H. Ellis, "Businessmen and Public Health in the Urban South during the Nineteenth Century," *Bulletin of the History of Medicine* 44 (May-June, July-August 1970): 197–212, 346–71; Stuart Galishoff, "Public

Health in Newark, 1832–1918" (Ph.D. diss., New York University, 1969); and John Duffy, *A History of Public Health in New York City, 1625-1866* (New York, 1968). The most useful contemporary account is John H. Griscom, *The Uses and Abuses of Air* (New York, 1850). See also Joel A. Tarr, "Urban Pollution—Many Long Years Ago," *American Heritage* 22 (October 1971): 65–69, 106. See chap. 4 of this volume for a more detailed discussion of smoke pollution problems.

5. *Report of a General Plan for the Promotion of Public and Personal Health, Devised, Prepared and Recommended by the Commissioners Appointed under a Resolve of the Legislature of Massachusetts, Relating to a Sanitary Survey of the State* (Boston, 1850), pp. 153–54; Nelson M. Blake, *Water for the Cities: A History of the Urban Water Supply Problem in the United States* (Syracuse, 1956). See chaps. 2 and 3 of this volume for a more detailed discussion of water supply and sewerage systems.

6. Jon C. Teaford, *The Municipal Revolution in America: Origins of Modern Urban Government, 1650-1825* (Chicago, 1975), pp. 47–110; Sam Bass Warner, Jr., *The Private City: Philadelphia in Three Periods of Its Growth* (Philadelphia, 1968), 49–157; Seymour J. Mandelbaum, *Boss Tweed's New York* (New York, 1965); Ernest S. Griffith, *A History of American City Government: The Conspicuous Failure, 1870-1900* (New York, 1974), pp. 52–62. For additional views on the role of government in environmental reform, see chap. 1 of this volume.

7. Quotation from J. G. Pinkham, M.D., *The Sanitary Condition of Lynn, Including a Special Report on Diphtheria* (Boston, 1877), p. 58. Among others, see Charles E. Rosenberg, *The Cholera Years: The United States in 1832, 1849 and 1866* (Chicago, 1962); Rosen, *History of Public Health*, pp. 237–46; and Barbara G. Rosenkrantz, *Public Health and the State: Changing Views in Massachusetts, 1842-1936* (Cambridge, Mass., 1972).

8. *Report of the Council of Hygiene and Public Health of the Citizens' Association of New York, upon the Sanitary Condition of the City* (New York, 1866); Rosen, *History of Public Health*, pp. 243–45; Dennis East II, "Health and Wealth: Goals of the New Orleans Public Health Movement, 1879–84," *Louisiana History* 9 (Fall 1968): 250 and 245–75 *passim*; cf. Richard J. Hopkins, "Public Health in Atlanta: The Formative Years, 1865-1879," *Georgia Historical Quarterly* 53 (September 1969): 287–304. For general discussion of the sanitarians' work, in addition to items cited above about public health campaigns, see Duncan R. Jamieson, "Towards a Cleaner New York: John H. Griscom and New York's Public Health, 1830–1870" (Ph.D. diss., Michigan State University, 1971); Jon A. Peterson, "The Impact of Sanitary Reform upon American Urban Planning, 1840–1890" (paper delivered at the Organization of American Historians meeting, St. Louis, 9 April 1976); Wilson G. Smillie, *Public Health: Its Promise for the Future* (New York, 1955); and James H. Cassedy, *Charles V. Chapin and the Public Health Movement* (Cambridge, Mass., 1962).

9. On the landscape architects, see Norman T. Newton, *Design on the Land: The Development of Landscape Architecture* (Cambridge, Mass., 1971); Laura Wood Roper, *FLO: A Biography of Frederick Law Olmsted* (Baltimore, 1973); Albert Fein, *Frederick Law Olmsted and the American Environmental Tradition* (New York, 1972); Marsha S. Peters, "The Natural City: Landscape Architecture and City Planning in Nineteenth Century America" (Master's thesis, University of Wisconsin, 1971); and John L. Hancock, "John Nolen and the American City Planning Movement" (Ph.D. diss., University of Pennsylvania, 1964). For the Copeland report, see Robert Morris Copeland, *The Most Beautiful City in America: Essay and Plan for the Improvement of the City of Boston* (Boston, 1872), pp. 10–12 and *passim*.

10. Dr. B. W. Richardson, "Modern Sanitary Science–A City of Health," *Van Nostrand's Eclectic Engineering Magazine* 14 (January 1876): 31–44; J. M. Gregory, "The Hygiene of Great Cities," *Engineering News* 7 (10 January 1880): 17; and John N. Olmstead, "Relation of the City Engineer to Public Parks," *Journal of the Association of Engineering Societies* 13 (October 1894): 594. See also James H. Cassedy, "Hygeia: A Mid-Victorian Dream of a City of Health," *Journal of the History of Medicine and Allied Sciences* 17 (April 1962): 217–29.

11. Blake, *Water for the Cities*; M. N. Baker, *The Manual of American Water-Works* (New York, 1897); and, for legal rights and privileges, see Horace G. Wood, *A Practical Treatise on the Law of Nuisances in Their Various Forms: Including Remedies Therefor at Law and in Equity* (Albany, N.Y., 1875).

12. Samuel W. Abbott, *Past and Present Condition of Public Hygiene and State Medicine in the United States* (Boston, 1900); C. E. A. Winslow, *The Evolution and Significance of the Modern Public Health Campaign* (New Haven, 1923), p. 38; J. J. Cosgrove, *History of Sanitation* (Pittsburgh, 1909), pp. 87–88; Louis P. Cain, "The Economic History of Urban Location and Sanitation" (unpublished manuscript, 1976), p. 5; and Ellis, "Businessmen and Public Health," p. 200.

13. "Early Sanitary History of Chicago, 1832–1874 and Sketch of the Early Drainage and Sewerage of Chicago 1847–1879," City of Chicago Municipal Reference Library, Frederick Rex, Librarian (n.d., n.p.); R. Isham Randolph, "A History of Sanitation in Chicago," *Journal of the Western Society of Engineers* 44 (October 1939): 227–40; Louis P. Cain, "Raising and Watering a City: Ellis Sylvester Chesbrough and Chicago's First Sanitation System," *Technology and Culture* 13 (July 1972): 353–72; and James C. O'Connell, "Chicago's Quest for Pure Water," *Essays in Public Works History*, no. 1 (Washington, D.C., 1976). See chap. 2 of this volume for more details on waterworks.

14. George E. Waring, Jr., *House Drainage and Sewerage* (Philadelphia, 1878), p. 11; Waring, *Social Statistics of Cities*, 1: 570–71; Eliot C. Clarke, *Main Drainage Works of the City of Boston* (Boston, 1885); Henry I. Bowditch, *Public Hygiene in America* (Boston, 1877), pp. 103–4; Leonard Metcalf and Harrison P. Eddy, *American Sewerage Practice*, 3 vols. (New York, 1914), vol. 1, *Design of Sewers*; Geo. W. Rafter and M. N. Baker, *Sewage Disposal in the United States* (New York, 1894), pp. 169–86; Richard Shelton Kirby and Philip Gustave Laurson, *The Early Years of Modern Civil Engineering* (New Haven, 1932), pp. 185–239. For a more thorough discussion of wastewater system technology, see chap. 3 of this volume.

15. John H. Griscom, *The Sanitary Condition of the Laboring Population of New York* (New York, 1845), p. 52. For Chicago, in addition to materials cited in n. 13, see E. S. Chesbrough, *Report and Plan of Sewerage for the City of Chicago, Illinois* (Chicago, 1855), and "Up from the Mud: An Account of How Chicago's Streets and Buildings Were Raised," Workers of the Writer's Program, WPA in Illinois for Board of Education (Chicago, 1941). The Bell and Waring quotations came from John Bell, *Report on the Importance and Economy of Sanitary Measures to Cities* (New York, 1859), p. 35, and Waring, *House Drainage and Sewerage*, p. 11.

16. Julius W. Adams, *Report of the Engineer to the Commissioners of Sewerage of the City of Brooklyn, upon the General Drainage of the City* (Brooklyn, 1859); Rudolph Hering, "Reports of an Examination Made in 1880 of Several Sewerage Works in Europe," *Annual Report of the National Board of Health, 1881* (Washington, D.C., 1882), pp. 200–12; Rafter and Baker, *Sewage Disposal*, pp. 177–85; George C. Whipple, *Typhoid Fever, Its Causation, Transmission and Prevention* (New York, 1908); Frederic L. Hoffman, "Amer-

ican Mortality Progress," in Mazyck Porcher Ravenal, ed., *A Half Century of Public Health: Jubilee Historical Volume of the American Public Health Association*, (New York, 1921), *passim*, esp. p. 102; United States Bureau of the Census, *Financial Statistics of Cities Having a Population of Over 30,000: 1910* (Washington, D.C., 1913), pp. 134–43; and two excellent pieces by Edward Meeker: "The Improving Health of the United States, 1850–1915," *Explorations in Economic History* 9 (Summer 1972): 353–73, esp. 366–73 and table 6, p. 370, and "The Social Rate of Return on Investment in Public Health, 1880–1910," *Journal of Economic History* 34 (June 1974): 392–421.

17. Quotations came from Editorial, *The Sanitary Engineer* 6 (19 October 1882): 412, and *New Orleans Times-Democrat*, 19 April 1894, as quoted in Ellis, "Businessmen and Public Health," p. 356. Among numerous contemporary accounts of sewer gas, see George E. Waring, Jr., *Earth Closets and Earth Sewage* (New York, 1870); A. de Varona, *Sewer Gases, Their Nature and Origin and How to Protect Our Dwellings* (Boston, 1879); "Sewer Gases and Their Evil Effects," *The Plumber and Sanitary Engineer* 2 (15 June 1879): 208; George Preston Brown, *Sewer-Gas and Its Dangers* (Chicago, 1881); D. H. Beckwith, "Sewage and Sewer-Gases," *The Sanitary News* 3 (15 March 1884): 124; "Sewer Gas Poisoning," *Scientific American* 63 (29 November 1890): 344; and "Sewer Gas Prevention in Houses," *Municipal Engineering* 13 (August 1897): 91. To date, the only adequate discussion of the sewer gas controversy is Deanna R. Springall, "The Sewer Gas Theory of Disease: A Period of Transition in Medical Etiology" (Master's thesis, University of Wisconsin, 1977).

18. "Report of the Massachusetts Drainage Commission, 1884–94," reproduced in Rafter and Baker, *Sewer Disposal*, p. 115; Charles V. Chapin, *Municipal Sanitation in the United States* (Providence, 1901), pp. 296–97.

19. For experiences in varies cities, see Samuel C. Busey, "History and Progress of Sanitation of the City of Washington and the Efforts of the Medical Profession in Relation Thereto," *The Sanitarian* 42 (March 1899): 205-16; M. L. Holman, "Historical Aspects of the St. Louis Water Works," *Journal of the American Engineering Society* 14 (January 1895): 1–9; A. L. Anderson, "The Sanitary Conditions of the Cincinnati Sewer," *Engineering News* 5 (14 and 21 November 1878): 324, 372; Arthur S. Hobby, "The Sewerage of Cincinnati," *Engineering News* 5 (28 November 1878): 377-78; Melvin G. Holli, *Reform in Detroit: Hazen S. Pingree and Urban Politics* (New York, 169), pp. 26–27; William Howard Travis, Jr., *Public Health Administration and the Natural History of Disease in Baltimore, Maryland, 1797-1920* (Washington, D.C., 1924); James B. Crooks, *Politics and Progress: The Rise of Urban Progressivism in Baltimore, 1895-1911* (Baton Rouge, 1968), pp. 132–36; and Alan D. Anderson, *The Origin and Resolution of an Urban Crisis: Baltimore, 1890-1930* (Baltimore, 1977), pp. 29–71, 86. Baltimore was the last major city to construct an integrated sewer system (1905–06) and, as a result, suffered one of the two highest typhoid mortality rates in the nation.

20. American Society of Civil Engineers, *A Biographical Dictionary of American Civil Engineers* (New York, 1972), *passim*; Daniel Calhoun, *The American Civil Engineer: Origins and Conflict* (Cambridge, Mass., 1960); Raymond H. Merritt, *Engineering in American Society, 1850-1875* (Lexington, Ky., 1969), *passim*, esp. pp. 136–76. For examples of publications by local clubs and by national periodicals, see "European Systems of Sewerage," *Engineering News* (28 January 1882): 33–35; "Municipal and Sanitary Engineering in the City of London," *Engineering News* 16 (21 and 28 August 1886): 122-23, 134–35; E. S. Chesbrough, *Report of the Results of Examinations Made in Relation to Sewerage in Several European Cities, in the Winter of 1856-7* (Chicago, 1858);

L. M. Haupt, "The Growth of Cities as Exemplified in Philadelphia," *Proceedings of the Engineering Club of Philadelphia* 4 (August 1884): 148–75; "St. Louis Boulevards in the Business District," *Journal of the Association of Engineering Societies* 12 (March 1894): 190; and Robert Gilliam, "Work for Our Engineers' Club," ibid. (June 1893): 305–13.

21. *Biographical Dictionary of American Civil Engineers*, pp. 23–24; Charles E. Eliot, "One Remedy for Municipal Misgovernment," *Forum* 12 (October 1891): 153–68; "Engineers of Commissioners of Public Works," *Engineering News* 31 (1 February 1894): 82; John Ficklen, "The Municipal Condition of New Orleans," *Proceedings of the Second National Conference on Good City Government* (8–10 December 1894); A. Marston and G. W. Miller, "The Methods of Choosing City Engineers," *Engineering Record* 47 (21 February 1903): 198–99. On the growth of "metropolitan authorities," see *Newark Aqueduct Board* v. *City of Passaic*, Court of Chancery of New Jersey, 22 July 1889, reprinted in Rafter and Baker, *Sewage Disposal*, pp. 579–85; Commonwealth of Massachusetts, *Acts of 1889* (Boston, 1890), chap. 439; and *First Annual Report of the Board of Metropolitan Sewerage Commissioners* (Boston, 1890); "Troy, N.Y.," *Engineering News* 4 (3 November 1877): 359–69; "The Better Water Supply of Northeastern New Jersey," ibid. 19 (24 March 1888): 230–31; "Municipal Co-Operation as a Possible Substitute for Consolidation," ibid. 41 (16 February 1899): 104–6; National Municipal League, *The Government of Municipal Areas in the United States* (New York, 1930), *passim*, esp. pp. 33–34. On extra-municipal powers, see, among others, Nelson Tibbs, "The Sanitary Protection of the Watershed Supplying Water to Rochester, N.Y.," *Engineering News* 19 (28 April 1888): 531; Olmsted, Vaux and Co., *Report on the Parkway Proposed for the City of Brooklyn* (1868); "How to Subdivide Land in Illinois," *The Engineer and Surveyor* 1 (April 1874): 4; and, for a general discussion of the broad context, Mel Scott, *American City Planning since 1890* (Berkeley, 1969), pp. 183–367.

22. On organization of their own offices and boards of administration, see a lengthy series of articles in *Engineering News* from 6 January 1886 through 25 December 1886; the March 1893 issue of the *Journal of the Association of Engineering Societies*; Albert F. Noyes, "Organization and Management of a City Engineer's Office," ibid. 13 (October 1894): 541 ff.; David Molitor, "Municipal Public Improvements and the Laws Governing Them," *Municipal Engineering* 13 (December 1897): 331–36; and August Herrman, "Rates of Taxation in the Larger Cities of the United States," *Proceedings of the American Society for Municipal Improvements* 5 (1898): 3–27. On the legal training of engineers, see entries in the *Biographical Dictionary of American Civil Engineers*. For the Boston and Chicago examples, see *Engineering News* 6 (10 January 1878); *The Sanitary News* 6 (10 October 1885); O'Connell, *Chicago's Quest for Pure Water*, p. 17.

23. Quotations came from *Journal of the Association of Engineering Societies* 12 (1893): 443, and Olmsted, "Relation of the City Engineer to Public Parks," p. 595. Cf. the series of articles titled "Municipal Government with Especial Reference to the Management of Public Works," *Journal of the Association of Engineering Societies* 11 (March 1892): 123–75. For general discussion of engineers' careers, see Merritt, *Engineering in American Society*, pp. 88–109, 136–76.

24. Noyes, "Organization and Management of a City Engineer's Office," p. 544.

25. Delos F. Wilcox, "The Municipal Program," *Proceedings of the Chicago Conference for Good City Government and the Tenth Annual Meeting of the National Municipal League* (Philadelphia, 1904), pp. 187–88.

26. In addition to citations in n. 2, see Scott, *American City Planning*, pp. 163–64, 228; Roy Lubove, *The Progressives and the Slums: Tenement House Reform in New*

York City (Pittsburgh, 1962), pp. 217–45; John L. Hancock, "Planners in the Changing American City, 1900–1940," *Journal of the American Institute of Planners* 33 (September 1967): 290–304; John W. Reps, *The Making of Urban America: A History of City Planning in the United States* (Princeton, 1965), pp. 497–525; John Porter East, *Council-Manager Government: The Political Thought of Its Founder, Richard S. Childs* (Chapel Hill, 1965); Clarence E. Ridley and Orin F. Nolting, *The City-Manager Profession* (Chicago, 1934); Richard J. Stillman II, *The Rise of the City Manager: A Public Professional in Local Government* (Albuquerque, 1974); and Harold Stone et al., *City Manager Government in the United States, A Review of the First Twenty-five Years* (Chicago, 1940).

8. "Municipal Housekeeping": The Role of Women in Improving Urban Sanitation Practices, 1880–1917

By Suellen M. Hoy

> *As society grows more complicated it is necessary that woman shall extend her sense of responsibility to many things outside of her home, if only in order to preserve the home in its entirety.*

Jane Addams
"Woman's Conscience and Social Amelioration"
(1908)

During the late nineteenth and early twentieth centuries, Americans witnessed the transformation of the United States from a predominantly rural-agricultural society to a primarily urban-industrial one. Many Americans, especially those living in cities, were disturbed by the rapidity and complexity of the change and were anxious about the future of traditional American values and institutions. Women, as individuals and in groups, found themselves particularly concerned about their homes and families. It is not surprising that many of them took on the important task of improving the urban environment.

Men and women alike believed that it was only natural for women to serve as "municipal housekeepers" in their communities. George E. Waring, the well-known sanitary engineer, was convinced that "city cleansing" was above all "woman's work." It required the "sort of systematized attention to detail, especially in the constantly recurring duty of 'cleaning-up,' that grows more naturally out of the habit of good housekeeping than out of any occupation to which man is accustomed."[1] Dr. Katherine Bement Davis, New York City's commissioner of correction, agreed. She observed that it had always been woman's responsibility "to do the spanking and the house-cleaning."[2]

Countless women in the United States joined a multiplicity of civic leagues, women's clubs, and village improvement societies.[3] Discussions at meetings and club publications reinforced the conviction that "city housekeeping was quite as much their vocation as taking care of the home" and that their own health and happiness as well as that of their families depended in large part on the sanitary conditions of their communities. Club officers also reminded members that women "are no less good mothers and devoted wives because they realize that many outside influences touch their domestic life."[4] Thus, women in large numbers came to believe that "the one calling in which they were, as a body, proficient, that of housekeeping and homemaking, had its outdoor as well as its indoor application."[5] This knowledge led them into the movement for sanitary reform.

In nearly every region of the country, groups of women became involved in activities that, among other things, included cleaning streets, inspecting markets, abating smoke, purifying water, and collecting and disposing of refuse. Several women were appointed to positions in local government and made responsible for improving the cleanliness of their cities. One woman, Caroline Bartlett Crane of Kalamazoo, Michigan, was hired as a consultant by over sixty municipalities to prepare sanitary surveys. And Mary E. McDowell, commonly referred to as the "Garbage Lady," was instrumental in effecting substantial changes in the solid waste disposal practices of Chicago, Illinois.

The early women's groups were rather exclusive, with membership ordinarily restricted to women of the upper and upper-middle classes who had extended periods of leisure, common interests, and congenial tastes. Women in these clubs typically met at each others' homes and at other social gatherings and discussed art, literature, and related subjects. Not until the late nineteenth century did they begin to concern themselves with philanthropic and civic affairs.[6]

Middle-class housewives made up the majority of club women interested in improving urban sanitary conditions. Many were middle-aged, had children in school, and often hired servants to clean their homes. There remained, however, a strong contingent of upper- and upper-middle-class women who kept active in civic affairs and who frequently retained leadership positions in women's organizations. For example, many of the women who followed Jane Addam's example and ran settlement houses in the nation's largest cities (Mary McDowell, Mary Simkhovitch, Lillian Wald, and others) belonged to the upper class.[7]

As early as 1894, the Civic Club of Philadelphia made its initial attack on littered and garbage-strewn gardens and streets. Established "to promote by education and active co-operation a higher public spirit and a better social order," the club obtained permission from city officials to place baskets for wastepaper and refuse in the zoological gardens, which visitors badly littered. The experiment proved so successful that the women devised a plan to place receptacles in other areas of the city. In 1896, after obtaining permission from the Philadelphia Department of Public Works, they purchased forty-five receptacles and positioned them on carefully selected street corners in the city's Seventh Ward. At the year's end, there had been a marked improvement in the appearance of the area. In June 1897, the club offered the receptacles to the city council, which accepted them with gratitude. The council also made a $400 appropriation for purchasing similar receptacles to be placed in other parts of the same district.[8]

The work of the Civic Club did not end with the council's action. Members were encouraged to become acquainted with municipal regulations on the collection of ashes and garbage and to report infringements to the Department of Public Works. Although their complaints "received prompt and courteous attention," the women of Philadelphia did not slacken their voluntary efforts on behalf of a clean community.[9] They were rewarded for their service in 1913 when Edith W. Pierce became the first female city inspector of street cleaning. In appointing Pierce to this position, Morris L. Cooke, the director of public works, noted that her responsibilities would be "somewhat different from that of the men inspectors." She was to inspect the entire city rather than a single district. Motivated by what she called the "three C's"—"Care, Common-sense, and Co-operation"—Pierce efficiently carried out her official assignments. She also organized sectional associations for keeping streets, sidewalks, homes, and schools clean and founded a Junior Sanitation League, modeled after George E. Waring's New York City organization.[10]

The Civic Club of Philadelphia was not the only women's club on the eastern seaboard to educate cities to "a sense of . . . their own needs" during the late nineteenth century. In 1884 a Ladies' Health Protective Association (LHPA) was formed in New York City to confront the problem of the ever-increasing amount of garbage, manure, and rubbish left in the streets. In the introduction of an appeal to Mayor Abram S. Hewitt, the women explained why they had become involved:

> It is the climax of aggravation to the painstaking housekeeper to
> look out of her windows and see ash barrels standing forgotten on
> the sidewalk from hour to hour and often from day to day; to
> have those barrels toppled over by sportive boys or raked over by
> grimy ragpickers, and the contents left in hillocks in the street
> from one month's end to another; and supposing even that she
> personally . . . carefully sweeps and washes her own area flags
> and space of sidewalk, to have these covered within two hours by
> the sticks, loose papers and powdered manure that blow upon
> them from all quarters alike.[11]

The women recommended to the mayor ways of improving the sanitary conditions of New York City's streets. They asked that the annual appropriation for street cleaning be adequate for the work; that street sweeping machines be used late in the night; that neither ashes nor garbage be allowed on pavements in front of residences; that householders be required to own galvanized iron receptacles; that crematories be built to dispose of house ashes, garbage, and street sweepings; and that the city be divided into convenient sections managed by foremen, responsible to a street commissioner-in-chief, and cleaned by laborers, paid by the piece and not by the day. The Ladies' Health Protective Association also suggested that women be appointed as inspectors, since "keeping things clean, like the training of children and the care of the sick, has ever been one of the instinctive and recognized functions of women."[12]

The Ladies' Health Protective Association continued its drive for clean streets through programs of its own and in cooperation with another group, the Sanitary Protective League, founded in 1890. Aside from creating a greater public awareness of the problem, the group achieved few significant results until Waring was appointed street cleaning commissioner in 1894 (see chapter 5). The LHPA was far more successful in its campaign to regulate public slaughterhouses. During the winter of 1884-85, it made a thorough investigation of the city's slaughterhouses and presented its findings to the board of health. On the basis of this report, the board persuaded the legislature to pass an amendment in June 1885 restricting slaughterhouses in New York City to an area bound by the Hudson River and Eleventh Avenue between Thirty-ninth and Fortieth streets. In 1895 the New York City Department of Health gave special thanks to the LHPA for its enduring support, noting that the women had been zealous in inspecting rendering companies and in reporting unsanitary conditions.[13]

The Woman's Municipal League of New York City followed in the tradition of the Ladies' Health Protective Association. Acting on a recommendation of the latter group and with the permission of the commissioner of street cleaning, the league's Committee on Streets raised funds to pay women to inspect the work of the Street Cleaning Department in various parts of the city and to award certificates and "Waring medals" to sweepers, drivers, and foremen who did the "best all-around work." William H. Edwards, commissioner of street cleaning, spoke warmly of the women's efforts at a conference of mayors and city officials in Binghamton, New York, in June 1913. He was grateful to the women for their "keen interest in his men" and for raising the standards of the department.[14]

From June to November 1912, the Chelsea Branch of the Woman's Municipal

League employed Belle Eddy Storrs to inspect five sections within Chelsea's boundaries. At various times during this seven-month period, Storrs addressed the employees of the Street Cleaning Department—explaining why the league was interested in them, praising them for their good work, and suggesting improvements. In one of her reports, Storrs observed that, although the sweepers' job was often "hard and uninteresting," only occasionally was there "a spirit of indifference" and it was usually found among the younger men. "The elderly men moved about briskly with purposeful motions." However, Storrs was disturbed that, from the sweepers' daily earnings of $2.19, they had to pay $1.23 for a white suit, $1.50 for a helmet, $3.00 for a rubber coat, and another $3.00 for rubber boots; that few men received more than half their normal pay when ill; and that there was no pension plan. The league chose to exert its influence on behalf of a pension fund, and a year later one was established. When a man served for twenty years and reached the age of sixty, he could be retired on half pay; the fund also took care of widows and children of the men who died while working for the department.[15]

One of the most active women in the league was Mrs. Julius Henry Cohen, chairman of the Committee on Streets. She faithfully attended the meetings of her committee as well as meetings of branch committees. She represented the league at municipal conferences and on civic committees, served as a member of the Department of Street Cleaning's Advisory Council, and was present at every ceremony to award medals and certificates to deserving department employees.[16] When informed by men of various grades in the department that children were "the cause of half the difficulties of street cleaning," she prepared a fifteen-page booklet on *What We Should All Know about Our Streets* for "Young Citizens in the City Schools." This well-illustrated pamphlet included a brief history of streets and the Street Cleaning Department, a description of the duties of householders, an explanation of ways to dispose of refuse, and suggestions on how "we can help" keep New York City clean.[17]

Cohen was also in the forefront of a league campaign to reduce the size of ash cans. Heavier loads, she reported, "frequently led to hernia in the drivers, even the more robust of them." Publications distributed by the Woman's Municipal League asked householders not to fill their ash cans to the top; they were advised to leave at least six inches empty. Because of this concern, the Medical Journal commended Cohen and the league for exercising "genuine charity."[18]

The Women's Municipal League of Boston, under the leadership of Katharine L. Bowlker, demonstrated the same concern for clean streets and alleys. Bowlker founded the league in 1908 because she believed that "the housekeeping of a great city was women's work."[19] In a speech before a public meeting of the

Women's Municipal League, she once remarked that the "one peculiar and inalienable function of woman" was "the provision of a suitable environment for her offspring. . . . By right of long inheritance, every woman knows how to make any place of sojourn a home."[20] Inspired by Bowlker, the league's membership grew from 72 in 1908 to 1,800 in 1912.

The Women's Municipal League of Boston was organized into four departments. Two of these departments—Streets and Alleys and Sanitation and Public Improvements—were directly responsible for bettering the city's sanitary conditions. Although both departments employed one woman inspector each to assist city officials in carrying out their duties, league members also worked together in active neighborhood groups to promote a cleaner environment through "study, education, inspection, and cooperation."[21] As part of a study and educational program, for example, the Department of Streets and Alleys conducted research on municipal ordinances and state statutes dealing with the collection and disposal of solid wastes and then printed their findings in a "Notice to Householders." After a series of these notices was distributed, the league sponsored numerous public meetings in various parts of the city to explain street and alley conditions in Boston and other cities.[22] The league was rewarded for its efforts in 1910 when the Massachusetts General Court, at the league's insistence, passed a bill forbidding the throwing of rubbish in the streets. The following year, Mayor John F. Fitzgerald stated in his annual report that there was "no doubt that the efforts of the Women's Municipal League had given a new impetus to the cleaning of streets."[23]

The most well remembered of the league's activities were those on behalf of Boston's markets. During the summer of 1909, the league shared with South End House the salary of an inspector, Louise R. Hemenway, who served as official market inspector for the Boston Board of Health. The league's "traveling exhibit" on markets, which was displayed in settlement houses and schools, inspired the founding of a Junior Municipal League. In recognition of its early market work, the league was invited to send a representative to speak at the International Congress of Hygiene and Demography in Washington, D.C., in 1912. The traveling exhibit went, too.[24]

In 1914 the league's reputation was further enhanced by a market survey conducted through its Department of Sanitation and Public Improvements. This investigation included every fish and meat market, provision shop, and grocery selling green vegetables, meat, or fish in the city of Boston. One of three paid inspectors and groups of volunteers from the league's sanitation department visited a total of 2,447 markets and shops.[25] Of the shops and markets investigated, 15 percent (376) were rated "bad"; 46 percent (1,126) were rated "fair"; and 39 percent (945) were rated "good." The league's final report noted that larger shops and markets, with few exceptions, maintained a high standard of cleanliness. But in small neighborhood shops and markets, owned for the most part by recent immigrants, the conditions were deplorable. Food was handled freely, flies were allowed to collect on meat and produce, wrapping paper was frequently obtained from local junk dealers, and cats were permitted to roam wherever they chose. In one grocery, an inspector found a fat gray tabby buried in the macaroni and remarked that it was an unusual place to find a cat. The owner agreed that it was strange; the pet usually liked "to lie on the spaghetti."[26]

The women's league realized that it lacked the authority to inspect and regulate the city's shops and markets on a regular basis. Therefore, at the conclusion of its report, the league simply offered suggestions for improvement. It recommended that city officials establish a well-planned market system. Such a system might include several large, general markets and some smaller shops and markets located in natural centers of the city. Such an arrangement would allow the city to inspect and regulate the markets more efficiently. The league also supported the passage of an ordinance that would eliminate the dangers of the combination shop and living apartment and called for the building of model markets that would include low-cost living compartments for some of Boston's poor. For its part, the league pledged to help educate consumers so that they would know what they had "a right to expect in the way of sanitary care and cleanliness in the distribution of food." In 1915 the Boston City Planning Board created a Market Advisory Committee and made the league a member. As a pioneer in market inspection, the Women's Municipal League often was sought out for advice by other cities, especially in Massachusetts.[27]

Years before the Women's Municipal League of Boston was formed, a young woman, committed to applying science to the improvement of human life, entered the newly established Massachusetts Institute of Technology as a special student in chemistry. In 1873 Ellen Swallow Richards became MIT's first female graduate. She then assisted Professor William R. Nichols in setting up a laboratory in the new discipline of "sanitary chemistry" and it 1884 was appointed to the MIT faculty as a full-fledged instructor of sanitary chemistry. In that capacity, Richards taught the analysis of food, water, sewage, and air to the first sanitary engineers, who later initiated experimental laboratories modeled after hers.[28]

One of Richards' most significant undertakings was her work with Thomas Messinger Drown in examining the Massachusetts water supply for the state board of health. For two years, they analyzed the water and sewage of nearly the entire state's population. Water and sewage samples were delivered to their laboratories where each sample was analyzed within two hours. If they arrived too late or were not handled properly en route, the samples were rejected and the next day's load doubled. Before the project was completed, Richards had analyzed in whole or in part some forty thousand water samples.

During these two years, Richards often spent fourteen hours a day in the laboratory. In the summer, if the days were too hot, she worked at night. However, she did not concentrate solely on water and sewage analysis. She spent hours perfecting the laboratory and, as the survey progressed, she modified procedures and equipment. At the end of the day, Richards placed the results of her analysis on a large map of Massachusetts and drew connecting lines between areas in the state where the water chemistry was similar. Soon she saw a pattern develop on the map. The lines connecting like kinds of water corresponded to the shape of the Massachusetts coastline.

Richards knew that chlorine was suspended in the water—the result of two factors: its proximity to the sea, the "great natural repository" of chlorine, or sewage disposal. Through testing, Richards hoped to determine if the chlorine content of a water supply was caused by its nearness to the sea or pollution. Systematic analysis indicated that the normal chlorine content of unpolluted water remained constant at certain distances from the sea. It also revealed that, if a water contained a higher content of chlorine than was consistent with its distance from the sea, the water was polluted. This, she observed, was "our one new fact."[29]

The water survey intensified Richards' and Drown's desire for a seaside laboratory. In 1888 the Annisquam laboratory was moved to Cape Cod and became known as the Marine Biology Laboratory. Dr. C. O. Whitman, a morphologist from Clark University in Worcester, was appointed director. By 1891 the facility had 189 students, teachers, and researchers from the United States and Canada. The most important results of the water survey, however, were that it produced the world's first water purity tables and established the first state water quality standards in the United States. Drown's and Richards' survey also resulted in the world's initial modern experiment station in Lawrence, Massachusetts.

Richards' environmental interests were not limited to water. In *Sanitation in Daily Life*, she advised her readers that their concerns about the environment should run along "two chief lines"—"first, what is often called municipal housekeeping . . . second, family housekeeping." She explained that the "first law of sanitation" required the "quick removal and destruction of all wastes" and that the second enjoined "such use of the air, water, and food necessary to life that the person may be in a state of health and efficiency."[30] It was not surprising that in 1878 Richards decided to investigate staple groceries in the state of Massachusetts. In 1885, as a result of her years of laboratory work on food materials, she prepared a book entitled *Food Materials and Their Adulterations.*[31] For Boston's Health-Education League, she wrote booklets on *Meat and Drink* and on *The Plague of Mosquitoes and Flies.* She also served as a member of the American Public Health Association's Committee on Standard Methods for the Examination of Air.

From the early 1890s, Richards' activities increasingly concentrated on what came to be known as the home economics movement. In 1899 she took the lead in bringing together individuals working "for the betterment of the home" in the first of a series of summer conferences at Lake Placid, New York. In December 1908, veterans of the Lake Placid conferences organized the American Home Economics Association and elected Richards as president, a position she held until 1910. During that period, she wrote many books and articles applying science to the problems of daily living. In 1910 Richards was appointed to the council of the National Education Association and was assigned the duty of supervising the teaching of home economics in schools. That October, Smith College awarded her the honorary degree of doctor of science. She died the following year at her home in Boston.

During these same years, Caroline Bartlett Crane, a resident of Kalamazoo, Michigan, became nationally known as a sanitary expert. In September 1912, she began a five-week inspection tour of nearly a dozen of Minnesota's largest cities. Earlier in the year, she had made sanitary surveys in Nashville, Tennessee, and several other cities in Kentucky and Pennsylvania. She went to these municipalities at the invitation of public officials, chambers of commerce, women's clubs, and various organizations of social workers. In making her surveys, she investigated the cities' water supply, street and alley conditions, solid waste collection and disposal practices, markets and food shops, parks and playgrounds, and public schools and hospitals. She then submitted a full written report to the groups that had paid for her services.

Carrie Bartlett, as she was known as a child, was born in Hudson, Wisconsin, on 17 August 1858. When she was fourteen, her family moved to Hamilton, Illinois, where two years later she decided to become a Unitarian minister. Since her family disapproved of her career choice, she attended nearby Carthage College and graduated in 1879. She taught school for three years in Iowa and then became a reporter and feature writer for the *Minneapolis Tribune*—at the time, she was the only newspaperwoman in the Twin Cities. She subsequently joined the *Oshkosh* (Wis.) *Morning Times* as city editor for six months during 1884.

Unhappy because her success as a newspaperwoman seemed to be taking her away from her "never-forsaken ideal of the ministry," Bartlett suddenly resigned as city editor, secured her father's blessing, and began a period of intensive preparation for the ministry. By late autumn of 1886, she had been accredited by the Iowa State Unitarian Conference and was at work on her first mission in Sioux Falls, South Dakota. Three years later, she was called to the First Unitarian Church of Kalamazoo. There, on 19 October, she was duly ordained and installed as pastor.[32]

The new minister believed that "a church—exempt from taxation—should minister to the needs of—not merely its own members—but, if possible, to the unsatisfied needs of the people at large."[33] Bartlett was responding not only to the Social Gospel and settlement house movements of the time but also to the "scientific" sociology she was learning in her summer courses with Professor C. R. Henderson at the University of Chicago. She was eager to transform Kalamazoo's First Unitarian Church into "an experiment station in social progress." In this goal, she was successful, eventually persuading the congregation to change its name to "The People's Church" and to attempt "new and untried kinds of social service."[34]

The church founded a kindergarten, a manual training and mechanical drawing department for boys and young men, a gymnasium for young women, and a Frederick Douglass Club for the community's black population. The People's Church opened a lunchroom for Kalamazoo's working women where they could obtain meals at low prices and use clean and quiet rest facilities before returning to work. The Reverend Bartlett organized research and study groups, known collectively as the Unity Club, to examine and discuss problems related to the city's charities, water supply, police and fire protection, sewage and waste disposal practices, and educational and recreational opportunities. However, the church and its pastor always maintained that they would relinquish any of their activities "as soon as the municipality or the school board could be persuaded to adopt it and finance it." By 1899 the kindergarten was completely closed, since it had become part of the curriculum of the Kalamazoo public school system.[35]

In December 1896, Caroline Bartlett married Dr. Augustus Warren Crane. Marriage changed her personal interests as well as her relationship with the People's Church, but it did not affect what she saw as her life's work. As she wrote some years later, she was "first and foremost a *preacher*—and always shall be."[36] Following her marriage, she realized that she was deficient as a housekeeper and enrolled in the household science courses offered by her church. She became increasingly interested in food processing and preparation, water purity, waste disposal, and public health. It was, in fact, her concern with these matters that prompted her to investigate Kalamazoo's slaughterhouses.

In 1902, as chair of a women's study group on household economics, Crane attempted to secure a speaker on meat inspection. When every invited official refused, she decided to speak on the subject herself. To prepare for the presentation, she and several prominent club women visited seven slaughterhouses, all located outside the city limits, which supplied meat to Kalamazoo's shops and markets. They were shocked by what they found. The buildings and grounds were amazingly unsanitary; they were "soaked with the rotten blood and filth of many years . . . unpainted, weather-beaten, warped," and decaying. Every surface was coated with "blood, grime, grease, hair, mold, and other quite unmentionable filth." The most dangerous discovery was that no distinction was made between healthy and diseased animals—both kinds were slaughtered and delivered to Kalamazoo's butchers.[37]

When these conditions were disclosed at a city council meeting and in the local newspapers, the community was incensed. City officials promised to remedy the situation, only to learn that they had no authority to regulate the practices of slaughterhouses located outside the city limits. Crane appealed to the state board of health, which took no action other than to appoint her to a state committee. Undaunted, she made a study of meat inspection laws in other states, drafted a model bill granting Michigan municipalities the right to pass inspection ordinances for meat sold within their corporation limits, and then consulted a lawyer and the assistant state attorney general on its constitutionality. When the bill was introduced in the state legislature, Crane traveled to Lansing to lobby for its passage. She was rewarded for her efforts when the bill became law in May 1903.[38]

Early in her career, Crane became convinced that public housekeeping was "the most vitally important function of city government," and she was eager "to make women feel their share of responsibility for the cleanliness of the city."[39] She advised:

> We certainly should keep our city—that is to say, our common
> house—clean. The floor should be clean. The air should be clean.
> The individual houses and premises, the schools, the places of
> public assembly, the places of trade, the factories, the places
> where foods are prepared, sold, served, should be clean. There
> should be sanitary collection and disposal of all the wastes that
> inevitably accumulate wherever human beings have a home and
> find habitation.[40]

It was only natural that in 1904 Crane should found the Women's Civic Improvement League of Kalamazoo, whose purpose was "the cultivation of higher ideals of civic life and beauty, and the promotion of out-door art, public sanitation, and the general welfare of the city."[41] One of the league's first projects was street cleaning. On 25 April 1904, the women petitioned the mayor and city council for permission to take charge of the cleaning of six and a half blocks of Kalamazoo's Main Street for a period of three months, beginning 2 May. They asked for an appropriation equal to the sum usually spent for this work and for the equipment customarily furnished. Their petition was granted and they received an amount of five dollars a day. According to the petition, the league's purpose in undertaking the work was, first, to ascertain "by investigation and experimentation the best, most sanitary, and most economical method of street cleaning" for a city of Kalamazoo's size (nearly 35,000) and, second, to put this method into operation in a limited area "for a time sufficient to demonstrate its worth and recommend its continuance" by municipal authorities.[42]

Before undertaking the three-month experiment, Crane carefully studied the street cleaning methods employed in other cities. She found that most street and sanitation departments were using a system initiated by Waring in New York City. The Women's Civic Improvement League decided to try the same methods in Kalamazoo. White uniforms were secured for the sweepers, who at first wore them grudgingly. Each man was then assigned to a particular section of the street, which was systematically swept and periodically flushed. Immediately following the sweeping, the dirt and refuse were bagged and deposited in convenient places along the streets or in alleys to be removed by horse-drawn carts.

In the beginning, the men found the new apparatus and methods strange and were sometimes reluctant to change their old habits. They did not like to use bags, and they frequently forgot or ignored an important injunction—"to sweep with the bricks, not across them." Crane, however, refused to give in. Those workers who could not or would not learn, who loafed, or who repeatedly complained were dismissed. Those individuals who adapted to the new ways and were industrious had their wages increased from $1.50 to $1.75 a day, which was what other city employees received. The sweepers eventually began to take pride in their work and finally became strong converts to Waring's methods. Throughout the three months, Crane personally inspected the work of the men each day and advised them on their problems.

The cleaning of streets was by no means the only concern of these women during the experiment. They also sought and obtained an ordinance against spitting on sidewalks. They visited merchants and asked them to clean their walks and not to sweep or throw anything from their stores into the streets. They took photographs of filthy alleys and showed them first to the adjacent property owners and then, if the alleys were not cleaned, to the public at large. They placed galvanized iron, aluminum painted cans on street corners and furnished members of their recently organized Junior Civic Improvement League with handouts to distribute, requesting residents and visitors not to litter the streets with refuse but rather to "put it in the waste-paper can at the corner."

At the end of the three-month period, the league had demonstrated that the Waring system was sanitary, efficient, and economical. The community agreed that Main Street was cleaner than it had ever been. The practice of quickly bagging the dirt assured that it would not be blown into nearby homes and businesses and that the sweepers did not waste their time gathering and handling the same dirt again and again. No longer were two-horse wagons used, with two men stopping to pick up bagged dirt and rubbish; one-horse carts, driven by one man, not only proved adequate but also saved time and labor. Even though the sweepers were paid higher wages under Crane, the city saved $3.39 each day. Despite the league's success, its methods were only partially adopted in 1904. Three years later, after a street cleaning study by an all-male civic committee, the city council fully implemented the practices advocated by the women's league.[43]

Crane received national attention as a result of her role in Kalamazoo's street cleaning experiment. Women's clubs across the country invited her to speak at their meetings, and municipalities wanted her to inspect their slaughter-houses and counsel them on their street cleaning problems. In 1907, at the request of the Neighborhood Center Committee of the Chicago Women's Club, Crane inspected Chicago's streets and gave a public lecture in the Art Institute's Fullerton Hall. Besides reporting on the Kalamazoo experiment, she outlined what she considered "principles for efficient and economical street cleaning": "(1) the kind of pavement that can be cleaned; (2) the intelligent use of brooms and other apparatus; (3) the intelligent application of water as a cleansing agent; and (4) the education of the public to refrain from littering the streets."[44] In nearly every speech and article, Crane emphasized the public's responsibility. She always argued that it was not the function of the departments of public works or streets and sanitation *alone* to keep the streets clean. "As a matter of fact," she observed,

> when we shall have really clean streets it will be an achievement
> of collaboration between the street cleaning department, the
> people who use the streets and the various municipal depart-
> ments or corporations that build the streets and install the water
> and sewer systems and other public utilities.[45]

As the demand for Crane's services increased, she gradually devised procedures for inspecting individual cities of different sizes, and by 1909 she was able to conduct sanitary surveys on a statewide basis. But she knew that every survey's success depended, in large part, on careful preparation. She insisted that her visit be widely advertised. It was not, she noted, "one person coming from a distant state to inspect conditions and criticize them in an official document which few people . . . would read and digest." Rather it was "a thoroughly advertised campaign participated in from start to finish by deeply interested citizens."[46] Thus, when Crane visited a city or a state, it was usually at the request of numerous official and nonofficial organizations.

Although support from women's groups was almost always present, Crane demanded a wider endorsement. On one occasion, she rebuked Mrs. C. G. Higbee, president of the Minnesota Federation of Women's Clubs, for failing in this respect:

> I have read the notices which you enclose. All the notices which I
> have received from every quarter (probably ten in all) have been
> strictly Women's Club notices. . . . I can assure you now that if
> this sort of thing continues, it will foredoom the whole campaign
> . . . to a feeble half-success. . . . I am doing the work for munici-
> pal sanitation which everywhere else but in Minnesota has com-
> manded the attention of the citizens of the State, men quite as
> much as women. . . . It is not a woman's campaign alone . . . but
> a campaign by men and women, and more prominence should be
> given . . . by the State Board of Health and the commercial or-
> ganizations. I am *alarmed* at the exclusively feminine aspect of
> this thing thus far.[47]

In Nashville, Tennessee, for example, the initiative for Crane's visit was taken by the Tennessee Federation of Women's Clubs; but, before Crane accepted, the state, city, and county boards of health, the mayor and city council, the board of trade, the Centennial Club, and the Anti-Tuberculosis League had joined in the invitation.

Another important part of Crane's preparation was the questionnaire. Before visiting a city, she required that a list of eight-two "Questions about Your City" be answered and returned to her. She wanted to know population, form of government, property valuation, tax rate, system of municipal accounting, bond issues for public improvements during the previous three years, charter amendments passed and defeated during the last five years, methods of supplying and treating water, miles of streets and sewers, and municipal provisions for cleaning and repairing pavements as well as for the collection and disposal of refuse. She asked for a map showing the location of the city's parks, playgrounds, schools, and recreation centers. She inquired about a smoke nuisance and efforts to abate it, if one existed. And she requested copies of municipal ordinances concerning meat, milk, and market inspections. Once these requirements were met, Crane asked that the city's daily newspapers be delivered to her for a two- to four-month period before her visit in order that she might better acquaint herself with "the city and its institutions and people."[48]

When Crane arrived in a particular city—such as Rochester, New York, or Montgomery, Alabama, which she visited in 1911 and 1912—she was escorted to whatever facilities and institutions she wished to see, usually during a period of three days to a week, by an official party capable of answering her questions. On the last evening of her stay, she scheduled a public address in which she reported on the community's sanitary conditions and offered specific suggestions for improvement. She always asked that the "largest and best place" be used for her "talk to the people." She did not want a church or a courthouse that would seat only a select few, for "the people will come . . . when they learn what it is about, and when the selection of a large and popular auditorium makes it plain that they are really *expected* to come."[49] For these services, she charged $100 a day plus expenses. She frequently asked for a higher fee if she prepared a lengthy, written report.

Crane was particularly suited to her work as municipal housekeeper and sanitarian. Her brief career as a journalist had made her aware of the importance of having press coverage of her campaigns. It was not unusual for her to prepare a series of news releases on a forthcoming visit and then distribute them to the sponsoring organizations for their publications and to the local newspapers.[50] As a minister, she had learned to speak effectively before large groups of people. Later, when she assembled an entire community to hear the closing address of one of her campaigns, it was often difficult to distinguish the sanitary expert from the civic revivalist. Most of the residents of the communities she visited agreed that she was a skillful communicator.[51]

The most significant results of Crane's efforts were the permanent civic improvements initiated by her investigations. A year after her visit to Calumet, Illinois, a public official stated that the sustained effort of the citizens had changed Calumet from a mining camp to a beautifully clean city. In Uniontown, Pennsylvania, her condemnation of the public water supply caused the state board of health to make an independent investigation, which confirmed her findings; shortly thereafter the dangerous conditions were eliminated. The year after her survey of twelve cities in Kentucky, the state legislature passed more health legislation than it had in its entire history, including an annual appropriation for a state bacteriological laboratory and provision for a school for county and city health officers. And, in at least twenty cities, municipal improvement leagues were created, under various names, to correct deficiencies noted by Crane either during her visit or in her final report.[52]

In nearly every public address, Crane emphasized her conviction that real civic improvements could best be made when partisan politics were removed from municipal administration. Mayors and aldermen, she contended, should be elected on the basis of their ability to direct the management of city affairs and not for reasons of party loyalty; medical officers were to be selected because of their medical competence and street commissioners because of their ability to keep streets clean and repaired.[53]

Few individuals could have agreed more with Crane than Chicago's Mary McDowell. In the fall of 1916, the Women's City Club of Chicago announced that it would not support a proposed $2 million bond issue increasing the garbage disposal facilities of the city unless its members were assured that a capable engineer would be placed in charge of the facilities. McDowell, the club's spokeswoman, said that the members wanted "a competent engineering expert at the head of the waste bureau" and that they would not "stand for putting the disposal of the city's wastes into politics." Residents of Chicago knew, as did *Engineering Record*, that "when Miss McDowell is against a measure in Chicago, even case-hardened politicians pay attention."[54]

McDowell, known to Chicagoans as the "Garbage Lady," was born in Cincinnati, Ohio, in 1854. The eldest of five children and nurse to an invalid mother, Mary matured quickly and grew especially close to her father, who in 1861 moved his family to Chicago, where he opened a steel rolling mill. While in Cincinnati, Mary followed her father's example and left the Episcopal church to join a more modest Methodist church composed mostly of laborers. But it was in Chicago that she was introduced to social service. During the fire of 1871, her father permitted her to use the family wagon to help move refugees to safety and to distribute supplies that were sent to the McDowell household from Ohio's Governor Rutherford B. Hayes, an old family friend.

In the 1880s, the McDowells moved to the near northern suburb of Evanston, where they attended the same church as Frances Willard, founder of the Women's Christian Temperance Union (WCTU). Mary assisted her father in teaching a young people's class on ways to apply Christian principles to daily living. She also became involved in the WCTU and by 1887 was serving as a national organizer for the young women's division. Through the WCTU, she learned of the kindergarten movement, attended a training school in New York City, taught the children of a private family for a year, and then returned to Chicago in 1890 to join Jane Addams and Ellen Gates Starr at Hull House. There she organized a kindergarten and a women's club before she was called home because of her mother's illness.[55]

McDowell did not lose interest in municipal affairs while in Evanston. In fact, during the Pullman strike, she persuaded a friend to accompany her on a visit to the pastor of Pullman's Methodist church, who described to her the difficult conditions under which the laborers in his congregation lived and worked. When the Christian Union's Philanthropic Committee of the University of Chicago decided to establish a settlement house in an industrial, immigrant neighborhood, it followed Jane Addams' advice and invited McDowell to direct the new settlement.[56] In September 1894, she moved from Evanston to the site of the University of Chicago's settlement—"Packingtown" as it was called—"two places," she observed, "as aesthetically and culturally far distant from each other as any in the world."[57]

"Back of the yards" resembled a frontier town. Only a few of the streets were paved, the sidewalks were wooden and several inches above the ground, the small frame houses were without sewer connections, and there was a saloon on nearly every corner. The neighborhood was bound on the east by slaughterhouses; on the west by city garbage dumps where each day open, horse-drawn wagons deposited refuse collected from other parts of Chicago; and on the north by "Bubbly Creek," a dead arm of the Chicago River covered with a thick scum through which carbonic gas occasionally oozed. The residents of Packingtown were stockyard workers of mainly Irish and German descent, although Poles, Slavs, Lithuanians, and Bohemians had begun to move into the community. Excited but apprehensive, McDowell made a home for herself in a second-floor tenement apartment on Gross Avenue and hoped that in time her neighbors would accept "the immigrant from Evanston."[58]

McDowell's first years in Packingtown were filled "with possibilities that were new and stimulating."[59] She responded initially to these opportunities by establishing a day nursery for preschool children and clubs for teenagers, both of which made it possible for her to become acquainted with working parents. She later offered courses in music, arts and crafts, and English for neighborhood workers. As a result of her initiative and leadership, a playground and gymnasium were completed in 1899; and seven years later, a permanent settlement building was constructed on Gross Avenue. McDowell also succeeded in securing a municipal bathhouse, a community park, and a branch public library.[60]

The activities for which McDowell is most remembered are those related to Chicago's sanitation practices. She first became actively interested in Chicago's refuse collection and disposal practices shortly after she moved to Gross Avenue. From her apartment she was continually annoyed by the unpleasant odors emanating from "Bubbly Creek," nearby garbage dumps and slaughterhouses, and the "hairfields," where hair disposed of by the slaughterhouses putrefied in the process of drying. She also watched the procession of uncovered garbage wagons that passed her windows daily. What disturbed her most, however, was the community's staggering amount of sickness and its unusually high mortality rate, especially among young children. Convinced that health and comfort of the citizens demanded better municipal house-keeping practices, she pleaded for more sanitary and scientific refuse prac-tices.[61]

An even earlier figure who demonstrated concern about Chicago's sanitation service was Jane Addams, the founder of Hull House. In 1895, five years after McDowell's stay at Hull House, the women's club that she had organized undertook a two-month investigation of the alleys of the Nineteenth Ward. During this period, the club reported to the health department a total of 1,037 violations of the law. As a result, city officials transferred three inspec-tors in succession out of the ward because of unsatisfactory work.[62] The work in the Nineteenth Ward was only the beginning of the concerted action taken by Hull House, however. The streets, like the alleys, were filthy. Fruit peddlers, slaughterhouses, bakeries, livery stables, and others habitually dumped their refuse into thoroughfares already filled with dirt and an occasional dead ani-mal. Under Addams' direction, settlement workers from Hull House conducted campaigns to teach neighborhood residents the importance of keeping streets and alleys clean. They regularly protested to city hall about the inadequate collection service, and they even built an incinerator at Hull House and tried to burn the refuse. Finally, out of desperation, Addams submitted a bid for the garbage removal contract in the ward. Her bid was thrown out on a tech-nicality, but, because of the publicity, the mayor appointed her the ward's garbage inspector at a salary of $1,000 a year.[63]

Addams kept the job for less than a year, but during that time she received national attention. The *Omaha Bee*, for example, reported that Addams and her associate, Amanda Johnson, had "made life . . . a burden to the garbage collectors" of Chicago but that their activity meant "a great deal in the way of cleanliness and health to a people who are greatly in need of both."[64] But the conditions of the streets were not substantially improved, and the ward's death rate remained one of the highest in the city. Addams argued that one of the reasons for this was the influence of Johnny Powers, a corrupt and powerful ward boss. The efforts of Hull House to unseat Powers, however, were unsuccessful.[65] Jane Addams' refuse reform activity left its mark on McDowell, who would later initiate similar kinds of work.[66]

From Addams, McDowell learned that the garbage collection and disposal practices of a community determined the standard of its life and that this life "should not be carried on for the benefit of a political party, but for the welfare of human beings." She also quickly perceived, from both Addams' counseling and her example, that "women must come to regard their city as their home"–that "home must not end with the front doorstep."[67] Thus, in 1905, McDowell and a few women from Packingtown made their first visit to city hall. They called on the commissioner of health, who directed them to the commissioner of public works. McDowell later recalled that the public works commissioner, Joseph M. Patterson, was "an intelligent, college-bred young man who had travelled and had a sentimental regard for the workers"; but he explained to them that, because the Department of Public Works had received such a meager appropriation for solid waste services, very little could be done. He advised McDowell and her companions "to make public opinion that will urge an appropriation from the Committee on Finance of the City Council."[68] Her task defined, McDowell set out to awaken the public and to alter the city's priorities regarding sanitation.

She offered to speak to any group in the city that would receive her. On one occasion, following a speech at the Hyde Park Presbyterian Church, a judge agreed to give her an injunction forbidding further dumping of garbage on Lincoln Street in Packingtown. McDowell went to court and received the injunction. The health commissioner, who had initially refused to discuss Packingtown's refuse problems with her, came to her in haste, pleading that there was no other place in which to dump the garbage and promising that he would disinfect the dump and see to it that "next year . . . no organic matter was put on Lincoln Street." Because it was near the time of the first frost, McDowell acceded to his request. However, little changed the following year.[69]

McDowell also persuaded Chicago's women's clubs to establish waste committees. She accepted the chair of the City Waste Committee of the Women's City Club, which financed a trip to Europe, where she studied, in particular, the sanitary practices of a number of German cities. In Frankfurt she was surprised to find one of the city's incineration plants "in the midst of a well-planned landscaped garden." During a tour of the plant, the public works officials told her that their incinerators could "take ugly stuff and make it over into that which is useful and beautiful." They also showed her how the heat from the incinerator generated electricity for one part of Frankfurt. These same officials inspired McDowell by their talk of the richness of American garbage–"such waste" and "so much grease." When she returned to Chicago, "primed with facts and pictures," McDowell took her story to "every social group from the aesthetic ball room on the North Side to the Chicago Federation of Labor in the center of the city."[70]

McDowell's waste committee chose to focus its attention on the city's refuse disposal practices. The city was hauling pure garbage to a private reduction company and paying it $47,000 a year "to extract good clean grease and a

useful dry material for fertilizer on which . . . [there was] a large profit."
McDowell argued that, although this was better than dumping garbage in her
neighborhood, it was certainly not the most economical practice. She suggested the possibility of a municipally owned reduction plant and requested
that a commission be formed "to study the whole question and report on a
city-wide plan for the scientific disposal of garbage and rubbish." These suggestions were met with "a futile politeness" until, in July 1913, the women
of Illinois received the municipal franchise.[71]

A week after acquiring the right to vote, McDowell and a few members of
her committee went to city hall with the same plea for a citywide plan based
on a scientific study. Much to their surprise, less than two weeks later, on
28 July 1913, the city council created the Chicago City Waste Commission to
"make a thorough, comprehensive, systematic and scientific investigation . . .
of the collection, transportation, and disposal of garbage and other waste in
the City of Chicago."[72] McDowell and ten other individuals constituted the
commission, which received an appropriation of $10,000 and held its first
meeting on 1 August. The commission hired two experienced engineers to
conduct the investigation—John T. Fetherston and Irwin S. Osborn. The former
was a recognized authority on incineration; the latter was well known for
designing, constructing, and operating a municipal reduction plant in Columbus, Ohio.[73]

In its sixty-nine-page final report, the Chicago City Waste Commission
stated that "the collection and disposal of a city's waste is essentially a community problem in the broadest sense" and must be dealt with without "defer-
ence to either personal interests or local prejudice." The report recommended
that Chicago should "both own and operate all the equipment and works necessary for a complete system of collection, transportation, and disposal of all
classes of city wastes." The commission also encouraged the disposal of sepa-
rated garbage by some form of reduction process at a central plant and the
construction of two modern high-temperature incineration plants. Finally,
the commission emphasized the importance of employing a competent technical staff "to develop, install and operate" the city's sanitation facilities and
"to make such further studies and tests as may be necessary to determine in
detail the most suitable type of receptacles and equipment for a motor collection service."[74]

The city council adopted the report of the Chicago City Waste Commission
on 15 June 1914. The first visible consequence was the construction of a small
reduction plant in Packingtown. With the elimination of the neighborhood
dumps, the health of Packingtown improved and the death rate dropped. One
of the tasks McDowell had set out to accomplish was completed. The central

reduction plant, recommended in the commission's final report, was also built; and it provided the beginning of a satisfactory solution to Chicago's waste problems. A change in the city's administration prevented the immediate construction of the proposed incineration plants, and a modified scheme eventually altered this feature of the original plan. The most significant factor, according to McDowell, was that the city of Chicago in 1914 made an effort to collect and dispose of its wastes in a scientific manner and went on record against the dumping of refuse in such a way or in a location that it might injure the health of the city's citizens. McDowell's long protests against "Bubbly Creek," however, fell on deaf ears until Upton Sinclair's *The Jungle* prompted Chicagoans to take action. Then the city council agreed to build a sewer, fill in the creek, and develop a manufacturing district.[75] Until her death in 1936, McDowell remained actively involved in the affairs of Packingtown and Chicago. In 1923 Mayor William Dever appointed her commissioner of public welfare, and in that capacity she made her department a clearinghouse for the city's social agencies.

The concern for the urban environment shown by individual women and groups of women in Chicago, Kalamazoo, Boston, New York, and Philadelphia was in evidence in almost every city of the United States during the late nineteenth and early twentieth centuries. In St. Louis, Cincinnati, and Pittsburgh, for example, middle-class women who considered themselves guardians of their families' health joined together and became the vanguard of the anti-smoke crusade. In St. Louis, for example, members of the Women's Organization for Smoke Abatement, known as the Wednesday Club until 1910, were tireless in their efforts to enforce existing smoke ordinances and to test new devices designed to abate the smoke nuisance.[76]

In other parts of the country, several individual women earned the respect of their communities for their work on behalf of improved sanitary standards. In 1899 New Orleans' Kate Gordon, founder of the city's ERA Club and a leading suffragist in Louisiana, directed a successful campaign in favor of a bond issue that insured completion of the municipal water purification and drainage system.[77] In Denver, Colorado, Sarah Platt Decker, president of the city's Woman's Club in 1894 and of the General Federation of Women's Clubs in 1904, became well known for her activities to secure cleaner streets and alleys. And in Portland, Oregon, Sarah A. Evans, who became president of the General Federation of Women's Clubs in 1914, led an early crusade that resulted in the nation's first municipal market sanitation ordinance and in her appointment as food and market inspector. Evans' work became a model for clubs throughout the United States.[78]

Although their efforts have been largely overlooked, women were a significant force in the movement to improve living conditions in the industrial cities of the United States. Motivated by a desire to protect their homes and families, large numbers of women believed that they, the nation's homemakers, could make a special contribution to the housekeeping practices of their communities. In so doing, they demonstrated the importance of citizen participation in civic affairs; for they not only awakened the general public to the ways in which cities were being managed and kept, but they were also directly responsible for the passage of needed legislation and the initiation of improved sanitation practices.

In general, the movement for sanitary reform attracted women who were satisfied with their traditional societal roles as wives, mothers, and homemakers. They were women who were seeking ways to enlarge their sphere of action "without touching the sources of their inequality."[79] They adopted goals that were conservative in nature: "to educate members, mentally and morally; to create public opinion; to secure better conditions of life."[80] Products of their age, they characteristically employed the three-pronged Progressive method of investigation, education, and persuasion to achieve their ends. Although not every program they espoused was completely implemented, women—as individuals and in groups—were particularly instrumental in making the urban environment a healthier and more comfortable place in which to live.

Notes

I wish to acknowledge financial assistance from the Penrose Fund of the American Philosophical Society.

1. George E. Waring, Jr., "Village Improvement Associations," *Scribner's Monthly* 14 (June 1877): 97–98. See also Samuel A. Greeley, "The Work of Women in City Cleansing: A Municipal Problem in Which Women Can Work with Peculiar Success," *American City* 6 (June 1912), 871–73.

2. *Woman's Journal*, 25 April 1914.

3. An example is the General Federation of Women's Clubs. In 1892, at its first biennial meeting, the membership roster listed some 20,000 women in nearly two hundred clubs. By 1900, 64,000 women were members, and, before the end of the Progressive era, close to a million women were part of the federation. "Statistics of the General Federation, May 1900," *Club Woman*, June 1900, p. 107; Mary I. Wood, *The History of the General Federation of Women's Clubs* (New York, 1912); and Mildred White Wells, *Unity in Diversity* (Washington, D.C., 1953).

4. "Men Are Too Busy," *American Club Woman* 2 (October 1911): 376; Mrs. John Hays Hammond, "Woman's Place in Civic Life," ibid. (November 1911): 405–6; and Mrs. Ellen Henrotin, "The Biennial Address of the President," *Fourth Biennial of the General Federation of Women's Clubs: Official Proceedings, Denver, Colorado, June . . . 27, 1898* (Louisville, 1898), p. 24.

5. Mary I. Wood, "Civic Activities of Women's Clubs," in *Women in Public Life: The Annals of the American Academy of Political and Social Science* (Philadelphia, 1914), p. 79.

6. Wood, *History of the General Federation of Women's Clubs*, pp. 22–34, 46–47.

7. Ibid., pp. 105, 297–310; William L. O'Neill, *Everyone Was Brave: A History of Feminism in America* (New York, 1971), pp. 84–90; and G. William Domhoff, *The Higher Circles: The Governing Class in America* (New York, 1970), pp. 44–54.

8. Edith Wetherill, "The Civic Club of Philadephia," *Municipal Affairs* 2 (September 1898): 477–78.

9. Mrs. F. Von A. Cabeen, *The Proper Disposal of Household Refuse and the Care and Cleanliness of Cellars: Paper Read at a Meeting of the Department of Social Science, Civic Club of [Philadelphia], February 21, 1895* (Philadelphia, 1896), pp. 5–7; Wetherill, "The Civic Club of Philadelphia," pp. 478–79.

10. "The First Woman Street Cleaning Inspector in Philadelphia," *American City* 9 (September 1913): 262; *Woman's Journal*, 2 August 1913.

11. Ladies' Health Protective Association, *Memorial of the New York Ladies' Health Protective Association, to the Hon. Abram S. Hewitt, Mayor of New York, on the Subject of Street-Cleaning* (New York, 1887), p. 4.

12. Ibid., pp. 5–12.

13. Mary E. Trautmann, "Women's Health Protective Association," *Municipal Affairs* 2 (September 1898): 440–43; John Duffy, *A History of Public Health in New York City, 1866-1966* (New York, 1974), pp. 118–32; Charles A. Meade, "City Cleansing in New York: Some Advances and Retreats," *Municipal Affairs* 4 (December 1900), pp. 721–41.

14. William H. Edwards, "Four Kinds of Cooperation Needed by Street Cleaning Departments," *American City* 9 (July 1913): 65; Louise Morgenstern, "Annual Report of the Committee on Streets of the Riverside Branch [for 1911]," Louise and Birdie Morgenstern Papers (New York Historical Society). Mrs. George E. Waring, Jr., served as honorary chair of the Committee on Streets.

15. Belle Eddy Storrs, "Street Investigator's Report," *Quarterly of the Woman's Municipal League of the City of New York* 1 (March 1912): 11–15; Edwards, "Four Kinds of Cooperation," p. 65.

16. Notes and clippings kept by Louise Morgenstern, 1910–15, Morgenstern Papers.

17. Mrs. Julius Henry Cohen, *What We Should All Know about Our Streets* (New York, 1915).

18. Mrs. Julius Henry Cohen, "Report of the Committee on Streets," *Quarterly of the Woman's Municipal League of the City of New York* 1 (June 1912): 12–17; New York *Evening World*, 4 May 1912.

19. Dorothy Worrell, *The Women's Municipal League of Boston: A History of Thirty-five Years of Civic Endeavor* (Boston, 1944), p. xiii.

20. "Suggestion from the Boston Women's Municipal League," *Quarterly of the Woman's Municipal League of the City of New York* 1 (June 1912): 6.

21. Mrs. T. J. (Katharine L.) Bowlker, "Woman's Home-Making Function Applied to the Municipality: Some Practical Lessons from the Work of a Thoroughly Democratic Women's Organization," *American City* 6 (June 1912): 863–64.

22. Worrell, *Women's Municipal League of Boston*, pp. 35–44. See also "Boston Club Activities," *The American Club Woman* 1 (March 1911): 94.

23. Worrell, *Women's Municipal League of Boston*, pp. 36–37; John Koren, *Boston, 1822 to 1922: The Story of Its Government and Principal Activities during One Hundred Years* (Boston, 1923), pp. 67–74.

24. Koren, *Boston, 1822 to 1922*, pp. 10–12.

25. "Untangling the Gray Cat from the Food Supply," *Survey* 31 (24 January 1914): 484.

26. Ibid. See also Catherine E. Russell, comp., *The Women's Municipal League of*

Boston's Report on the Conditions of the Provision Stores of Boston (Boston, 1914).

27. Russell, *Report on the Conditions of the Provision Stores of Boston*. See also Worrell, *Women's Municipal League of Boston*, pp. 10–12.

28. For biographical data, see Jane Wilson James, "Ellen Henrietta Swallow Richards," in *Notable American Women 1607-1950: A Biographical Dictionary*, ed. Edward T. James, Janet Wilson James, and Paul S. Boyer, 3 vols. (Cambridge, Mass., 1971), 3:143–46.

29. Robert Clarke, *Ellen Swallow: The Woman Who Founded Ecology* (Chicago, 1973), pp. 144–49; Madeleine B. Stern, *We the Women: Career Firsts of Nineteenth-Century America* (New York, 1963), pp. 130–31.

30. Ellen H. Richards, *Sanitation in Daily Life* (Boston, 1907), pp. v, vii–viii.

31. Ellen H. Richards was the author of numerous volumes on sanitation: *The Chemistry of Cooking and Cleaning: A Manual for Housekeepers* (1882); with Marion Talbot, *Home Sanitation—A Manual for Housekeepers* (1887); *The Art of Right Living* (1904); with Alpheus G. Woodman, *Air, Water and Food from a Sanitary Standpoint* (1904); *The Cost of Cleanliness* (1908); *Euthenics: The Science of Controllable Environment* (1910); and *Conservation by Sanitation* (1911). She also wrote extensively for scholarly journals and popular magazines.

32. Caroline Bartlett Crane, "The Story and the Results," typescript autobiography, ca. 1925, Caroline Bartlett Crane Papers (Western Michigan University Archives and Regional History Collections, Kalamazoo, Michigan), pp. 1-15. For a discussion of Crane as a Progressive, see Alan S. Brown, "Caroline Bartlett Crane and Urban Reform," *Michigan History Magazine* 56 (Winter 1972): 287–301.

33. Caroline Bartlett Crane, "Biographical Sketch," unfinished typescript, ca. 1933, Crane Papers, p. 2.

34. Ibid., p. 4.

35. Ibid., pp. 2–4; Thomas D. Brock, *History of the People's Church, 1856-1956* (Kalamazoo, 1956), p. 4.

36. Caroline Bartlett Crane to Mrs. Robert M. La Follette, 14 January 1911, Crane Papers. On 7 June 1898, the board of trustees of the People's Church accepted Crane's resignation.

37. Caroline Bartlett Crane, "Interest in Meat Inspection," typescript, 1909, Crane Papers, pp. 1-13.

38. Ibid. See also *Kalamazoo Gazette*, 28 March 1902, and *Kalamazoo Telegraph*, 31 March 1902. The bill was Senate Bill No. 306; it became effective on 17 September 1903.

39. Caroline Bartlett Crane, "The Work for Clean Streets," *The Women's Forum*, September 1905, p. 2.

40. Caroline Bartlett Crane, "The Making of an Ideal City," Crane Papers, no publication date or place.

41. "Constitution and By-laws of the Women's Civic Improvement League, Kalamazoo, Michigan," 1904, Crane Papers.

42. Crane, "Work for Clean Streets," p. 3.

43. Ibid. See also clippings from the Kalamazoo newspapers in the Crane Papers.

44. Caroline Bartlett Crane, *Clean Streets for Chicago*, pamphlet (Chicago, 1907), p. 1.

45. Caroline Bartlett Crane, "Roads and Pavements: Some Factors of the Street Cleaning Problem," *American City* 6 (June 1912): 895.

46. Caroline Bartlett Crane, "City Sanitarian," typescript, 1933, Crane Papers.

47. Crane to Mrs. C. G. Higbee, 21 September 1910, Crane Papers.

48. Caroline Bartlett Crane, "Questions about Your City," Crane Papers.

49. Crane to Mrs. Atwood, 13 August 1910, Crane Papers.

50. See, for example, Crane to Atwood, 13 and 27 August and 10 September 1910, Crane Papers.

51. "Cleaning Up American Cities," *Survey* 25 (8 October 1910): 83-84.

52. See Helen Christine Bennett, *American Women Civic Work* (New York, 1915), pp. 41-42; Caroline Bartlett Crane, typescript on Kentucky surveys and clippings from Kentucky newspapers, 1909, Crane Papers; *Journal of the American Medical Association* 53 (11 September 1909): 887-88. Katherine C. Halley of Nashville, Tennessee, wrote to Crane following her visit: "Plans are already on foot to clean up and paint the market house and the mayor wishes the city council to appropriate money for a three-storied market house, the two lower stories for produce and the top floor for a public hall. . . . There are also recommendations for flushing the streets two or three times a week" (Halley to Crane, 6 May 1910, Crane Papers). The Crane Papers are filled with such letters.

53. Crane, *Clean Streets for Chicago*, p. 3; Caroline Bartlett Crane, *General Sanitary Survey of Erie, Pennsylvania* (Erie, Pa., 1910), pp. 21-22.

54. "Women's Vote and the Engineer," *Engineering Record* 74 (28 October 1916): 518-19. See also Women's City Club of Chicago, "Report of Proceedings: Mass Meeting of Women to Protest against the Spoils System and Adopt a Woman's Municipal Platform," 18 March 1916, Women's City Club of Chicago Papers, Chicago Historical Society.

55. Miriam G. Rappe, "Mary E. McDowell," typescript, 1938, Mary E. McDowell Papers, Chicago Historical Society; Louise C. Wade, "Mary Eliza McDowell," in James, James, and Boyer, *Notable American Women 1607-1950*, 2:462-64; and "Mary McDowell," *American Magazine* 71 (January 1911): 327-29.

56. "Mary McDowell," pp. 327-29.

57. Mary E. McDowell, "Beginnings," autobiographical typescript, McDowell Papers.

58. Ibid.

59. Ibid.

60. Howard E. Wilson, *Mary McDowell: Neighbor* (Chicago, 1928), and Zona Gale, "Great Ladies of Chicago," *Survey* 67 (1 February 1932), 479-82.

61. Mary McDowell, "City Waste," in *Mary McDowell and Municipal Housekeeping: A Symposium*, Caroline M. Hill, comp. (Chicago, 1938), pp. 1-2.

62. Jane Addams, *Twenty Years at Hull House*, paperback ed. (New York, 1961), pp. 202-3.

63. Ibid., pp. 203-5.

64. *Omaha Bee*, 2 June 1895.

65. Anne Firor Scott, "Saint Jane and the Ward Boss," *American Heritage* 12 (December 1960): 12-17, 94-99; Allen F. Davis, *American Heroine: The Life and Legend of Jane Addams* (New York, 1973), pp. 121-25.

66. Mary E. McDowell, "The Spirit of Social Science in Chicago," typescript ca. 1923, McDowell Papers.

67. Caroline M. Hill, "Compiler's Preface," in Hill, comp., *Mary McDowell and Municipal Housekeeping*, p. vi; *Woman's Journal*, 27 June 1914.

68. McDowell, "City Waste," p. 3.

69. Ibid.

70. Ibid., pp. 4-5. See also Mary E. McDowell, "Chicago's Garbage Problem," *The*

City Club Bulletin 6 (20 December 1913): 336–38.

71. McDowell, "City Waste," pp. 5–6; *Woman's Journal*, 12 July 1913. Mary McDowell believed strongly that suffrage made the difference.

72. Chicago City Waste Commission, *Report of the Chicago City Waste Commission* (Chicago, 1914), p. 7. In a letter to the *Woman's Journal*, McDowell wrote:

> We very quickly sensed a new attitude of mind toward us. The Health Committee responded AT ONCE and voted to ask the Finance Committee for a Commission and an appropriation of the thousand dollars to make a study as a basis for a city-wide plan of the disposal of refuse. The Finance Committee AT ONCE voted the Commission and put two women on it. . . . The City Council at its very NEXT MEETING accepted the report of the Finance Committee. . . . ALL OF THIS ACTION HAPPENED IN ONE WEEK IN THE MONTH OF JULY, WHEN THE WOMEN WERE MADE VOTING CITIZENS. (*Woman's Journal*, 11 September 1915).

73. City Waste Commission, *Report*, p. 7.

74. Ibid., esp. pp. 8–9.

75. Wilson, *Mary McDowell*, pp. 156–64; McDowell, "City Waste," pp. 7–10.

76. R. Dale Grinder, "The Anti-Smoke Crusades: Early Attempts to Reform the Urban Environment, 1893–1918" (Ph.D. diss., University of Missouri-Columbia, 1973), pp. 95–102; R. Dale Grinder, "The War against St. Louis's Smoke, 1891–1924," *Missouri Historical Review* 69 (January 1975): 195–205; and Mrs. Ernest R. Kroeger, "Smoke Abatement in St. Louis," *American City* 6 (June 1912): 907.

77. Mrs. John B. Parker, "The Water Purification and Drainage System of New Orleans: A Great Public Works Undertaking for Which the Women Helped Vote the Bonds," *American City* 6 (June 1912): 884–86; *Woman's Journal*, 4 June 1910 and 15 April 1911; and Isabelle Dubroca, *Good Neighbor Eleanor McMain of Kingsley House* (New Orleans, 1955), pp. 54–56.

78. Marshall N. Dana, "From the Man's Point of View: The Civic and Educational Work of Women as Seen by the Secretary of a City Planning Association and a Well Known Municipal Official," *American City* 6 (June 1912); Mrs. Overton G. Ellis, "The Transfer of the Food Sanitation Committee from the Public Health Department to the Home Economics Department," Twelfth Biennial Convention of the General Federation of Women's Clubs: Official Report, June 9 to 19, 1914, Chicago, Illinois (Portland, 1914), pp. 480–81.

79. O'Neill, *Everyone Was Brave*, p. 143.

80. Martha E. D. White, "The Work of the Women's Club," *Atlantic Monthly* 93 (May 1904): 615.

A Bibliography
of Urban Pollution Problems

For several years, scholars in the social sciences—notably geography, political science, sociology, and psychology—have been actively engaged in the study of the urban environment. Yet most of the resulting books and articles have been present-minded, devoid of historical perspective. American environmental historians, while devoting considerable attention to the relationship between humans and nature, have virtually ignored "man as urbanite." Consequently, the body of historical research dealing with the urban environment has been sparse. What is available often represents pioneering ventures, the work of scholars with tangential interest in environmental questions, or antiquarian pieces. The following citations, nonetheless, provide a starting point for those interested in the study of urban pollution in the United States. For background, one should consult the work of such scholars as Carl Bridenbaugh, A. Theodore Brown, Carl W. Condit, Charles N. Glaab, Constance McLaughlin Green, Samuel P. Hays, Eric E. Lampard, Blake McKelvey, Lewis Mumford, Bessie L. Pierce, Arthur Schlesinger, Sr., Sayrd Still, Richard Wade, and Sam Bass Warner, Jr.

One approach to the study of urban pollution from a historical perspective is to analyze the causes and consequences of a single form of pollution over an extended period of time. To date, the most research has been conducted in the area of water pollution. Nelson M. Blake's *Water for the Cities: A History of the Urban Water Supply Problem in the United States* (Syracuse, 1956) is the classic study of the quest for pure water, but it is dated and often cursory. See also Moses N. Baker, *The Quest for Pure Water: The History of Water Purification from the Earliest Records to the Twentieth Century* (New York, 1948); Robert M. Ballard, "Pollution in Lake Erie, 1872-1965," *Special Libraries* 66 (1975): 378-82. For an examination of waterworks development, see Joseph W. Barnes, "Water Works History: A Comparison of Albany, Utica, Syracuse, and Rochester," *Rochester History* 39 (July 1972): 1-22; Elmer W. Becker, *A Century of Milwaukee Water: An Historical Account of the Origin*

and Development of the Milwaukee Water Works (Milwaukee, 1977); Roy
Morse, *Seattle Water Department History, 1854-1954* (1955). For city studies
dealing with the pure water question, see John Ellis and Stuart Galishoff, "Atlanta's Water Supply, 1865-1918," *The Maryland Historian* 8 (Spring 1977):
5-22; Jacob Judd, "Water for Brooklyn," *New York History* 67 (October
1966): 362-71; Adrian C. Leiby, *The Hackensack Water Company, 1869-
1969* (Bergen County, N.J., 1969); Roscoe E. Martin, *Water for New York*
(Syracuse, 1960); James C. O'Connell, "Chicago's Quest for Pure Water," *Essays in Public Works History*, no. 1 (Washington, D.C., 1976); Hermann K.
Platt, "The Jersey City Water-Rights Controversy, 1845-1850," *New Jersey
History* 94 (Winter 1976); Roland M. Smith, "The Politics of Pittsburgh Flood
Control: 1908-1936," *Pennsylvania History* 42 (January 1975): 5-24; William
Wright Sorrels, *Memphis' Greatest Debate: A Question of Water* (Memphis,
1976); Mark J. Tierno, "The Search for Pure Water in Pittsburgh: The Urban
Response to Water Pollution, 1893-1914," *Western Pennsylvania Historical
Magazine* 60 (January 1977): 23-36; Charles H. Weidner, *Water for a City:
A History of New York City's Problem from the Beginning to the Delaware
River System* (New Brunswick, N.J., 1974).

Probably the most lively area of research with respect to water pollution is
the study of wastewater systems and sewerage reform. Joel A. Tarr is the leading scholar on this topic. He has written a variety of articles, including "The
City and Its Wastes: Historical Turning Points in the Development of Urban
Sewerage Systems, 1800-1932," Eleutherian Mills Historical Library (forthcoming); (with F. C. McMichael), "The Evolution of Wastewater Technology
and the Development of State Regulations," in *Retrospective Technology Assessment*, ed. Joel A. Tarr (San Francisco, 1977); "From City to Farm: Urban
Wastes and the American Farmer," *Agricultural History* 49 (October 1975):
598-612; (with F. C. McMichael), "Historical Decisions about Wastewater
Technology, 1800-1932," *Journal of Water Resources Planning and Management* 103 (May 1977): 47-61; (with F. C. McMichael), "Historical Turning
Points in Municipal Water Supply and Wastewater Disposal, 1850-1932," *Civil
Engineering* 47 (October 1977): 82-91; "Out of Sight, Out of Mind: A Brief
History of Sewage Disposal in the United States," *American History Illustrated*
10 (January 1976): 40-47; "Sewage Disposal in America: Its Historical Evo-
lution," in *Alternative to Water-Carriage Waste Removal*, Carol E. Stoner, ed.
(Emmaus, Pa., 1977). For a good discussion of Chicago's sanitation efforts,
see the following pieces written by economist Louis P. Cain: *Sanitation Strat-
egy for a Lakefront Metropolis: The Case of Chicago* (DeKalb, Ill., 1978);
"Raising and Watering a City: Ellis Sylvester Chesbrough and Chicago's First
Sanitation System," *Technology and Culture* 13 (July 1972): 353-72; "The

Sanitary District of Chicago: A Case Study of Water Use and Conservation" (Ph.D. diss., Northwestern University, 1969); "Unfouling the Public's Nest: Chicago's Sanitary Diversion of Lake Michigan Water," *Technology and Culture* 15 (October 1974): 594-613. Two articles that deal with the important Refuse Act of 1899 merit attention: Albert E. Cowdry, "Pioneering Environmental Law: The Army Corps of Engineers and the Refuse Act," *Pacific Historical Review* 44 (August 1975): 331-49, and Ross Sandler, "The Refuse Act of 1899: Key to Clean Water," *American Bar Association Journal* 58 (May 1972): 468-71. See also Stuart Galishoff, "Drainage, Disease, Comfort, and Class: A History of Newark's Sewers," *Societas* 6 (Spring 1976): 121-38; Galishoff, "The Passaic Valley Trunk Sewer," *New Jersey History* 88 (Winter 1970): 197-214; Geoffry Giglierno, "The City and the System: Developing a Municipal Sewer Service, 1800-1915," *Cincinnati Historical Society Bulletin* 35 (Winter 1977): 223-47; James E. Herget, "Taming the Environment: The Drainage District in Illinois," *Journal of the Illinois State Historical Society* 71 (May 1978); Michelle Lincicome, "Sewage, Garbage and Rats," *Illinois History* 27 (April 1974): 162-63; Barbara G. Rosenkrantz, ed., *Sewering the Cities* (New York, 1977). Jon A. Peterson of Queens College (CUNY) has added an additional dimension to the study of sewerage in a paper delivered at the Organization of American Historians meeting in St. Louis in 1976. The paper, entitled "The Impact of Sanitary Reform upon American Urban Planning, 1840-1890," deals with the structural impact of sewerage systems on American planning.

The significant problem of air pollution has yet to attract much historical attention. However, four recent dissertations deal with some important aspects of the problem, especially abatement: Marvin Brienes, "The Fight against Smog in Los Angeles, 1943-1957" (University of California, Davis, 1975); R. Dale Grinder, "The Anti-Smoke Crusades: Early Attempts to Reform the Urban Environment, 1893-1918" (University of Missouri-Columbia, 1973); Donald MacMillan, "A History of the Struggle to Abate Air Pollution from Copper Smelters of the Far West, 1885-1933" (University of Montana, 1973); Richard H. K. Vietor, "Environmental Politics and the Coal Industry" (University of Pittsburgh, 1975). For a brief treatment of the automobile and air pollution, see James J. Flink, *The Car Culture* (Cambridge, Mass., 1975). See also Marvin Brienes, "Smog Comes to Los Angeles," *Southern California Quarterly* 58 (Winter 1976); Edward Greer, "Air Pollution and Corporate Power: Municipal Reform Limits in a Black City," *Politics and Society* 4 (1974): 483-510; Grinder, "The War against St. Louis's Smoke: 1891-1924," *Missouri Historical Review* 69 (January 1975): 191-205; Grinder, "From Insurgency to Efficiency: The Smoke Abatement Campaign in Pittsburgh before World War

I," *Western Pennsylvania Historical Magazine* 61 (July 1978): 187-202; Harold W. Kennedy and Andrew O. Porter, "Air Pollution: Its Control and Abatement [1890-1954]," *Vanderbilt Law Review* 8 (June 1955): 862-77.

Raymond W. Smilor has made the first comprehensive attempt to analyze the problem of noise in the industrial city in his dissertation, "Confronting the Industrial Environment: The Noise Problem in America, 1893-1932" (University of Texas at Austin, 1978). He has also treated the development of the anti-noise campaign in a number of articles, including "Cacophony at 34th and 6th: The Noise Problem in America, 1900-1930," *American Studies* 28 (Spring 1977): 23-38; "Creating a National Festival: The Campaign for a Safe and Sane Fourth, 1903-1916," *Journal of American Culture* (forthcoming); "Personal Boundaries in the Urban Environment: The Legal Attack on Noise, 1865-1930," *Environmental Review* 3 (Spring 1979).

On the refuse problem, the only study with a national perspective is Martin V. Melosi's "'Out of Sight, Out of Mind': The Environment and the Disposal of Municipal Refuse, 1860-1920," *The Historian* 35 (August 1973): 621-40. This study attempts to examine the reformist efforts to alleviate the problem of waste in the cities. Melosi is currently writing a book-length treatment of the refuse problem, entitled *Environmental Challenge in the City: The Refuse Problem and Municipal Reform, 1850-1920*. For a good overview of current refuse problems, see Wesley Marx, *Man and His Environment: Waste* (New York, 1971). See also Timothy Dial, "Refuse Disposal and Public Health in Atlanta during the Progressive Era: A Continuing Crisis," *Atlanta Historical Bulletin* 17 (Fall/Winter 1972): 31-40; Lawrence H. Larsen, "Nineteenth-Century Street Sanitation: A Study of Filth and Frustration," *Wisconsin Magazine of History* 52 (Spring 1969): 239-47; Joel A. Tarr, "Urban Pollution: Many Long Years Ago," *American Heritage* 22 (October 1971): 65-69, 106.

Studies of public health and sanitation are of general importance for understanding the urban quality of life. In many cases, however, the public health studies tend to deemphasize the significance of environmental sanitation and concentrate more heavily upon the impact of the biological revolution and preventive medicine. There has yet to be written a major study that deals exclusively with the important contributions of public health officials and sanitarians to urban environmental reform. Nonetheless, the following are some of the most significant general treatments of public health that provide substantial information about problems related to environmental sanitation: John B. Blake, *Public Health in the Town of Boston, 1630-1822* (Cambridge, Mass., 1959); James H. Cassedy, *Charles V. Chapin and the Public Health Movement* (Cambridge, Mass., 1962); John Duffy, *A History of Public Health in New York City, 1625-1866* (New York, 1968); Duffy, *A History of Public Health in New York, 1866-1966* (New York, 1974); Stuart Galishoff, *Safeguarding the Public Health: Newark, 1895-1918* (Westport, Conn., 1975); Howard D. Kramer, "History of the Public Health Movement in the United States, 1850-1900" (Ph.D. diss., State University of Iowa, 1942); George Rosen, *A History of Public Health* (New York, 1958); Charles S. Rosenberg, *The Cholera Years: The United States in 1832, 1849, and 1866* (Chicago, 1962); Barbara G. Rosenkrantz, *Public Health and the State: Changing Views in Massachusetts, 1842-1936* (Cambridge, Mass., 1972). See also Erwin Ackerknecht, "Anticontagionism between 1821 and 1867," *Bulletin of the History of Medicine* 22 (September-October, 1948): 562-93; Thomas N. Bonner, *Medicine in Chicago, 1850-1950* (Madison, 1957); Gert H. Brieger, "Sanitary Reform in New York City: Stephen Smith and the Passage of the Metropolitan Health Bill," *Bulletin of the History of Medicine* 40 (September-October 1966): 407-29; Cassedy, "The Flamboyant Colonel Waring," *Bulletin of the History of Medicine* 36 (March-April 1962): 163-76; Cassedy, "Hygeia: A Mid-Victorian Dream of a City of Health," *Journal of the History of Medicine* 17 (April 1962): 217-29; Cassedy, "The Roots of American Sanitary Reform, 1843-1847: Seven Letters from John H. Griscom to Lemuel Shattuck," *Journal of the History of Medicine* 30 (April 1975): 136-47; Robert Clarke, *Ellen Swallow: The Woman Who Founded Ecology* (Chicago, 1973); Abby Cohen, "Public Health and Preventive Medicine in Providence, 1913," *Rhode Island History* 36 (May 1977): 55-63; Jacqueline Karnell Corn, "Community Responsibility for Public Health: The Impact of Epidemic Disease and Urban Growth on Pittsburgh," *Western Pennsylvania Historical Magazine* 59 (July 1976): 319-39; Corn, "Municipal Organization for Public Health in Pittsburgh, 1851-1895" (Ph.D. diss., Carnegie-Mellon University, 1972); F. Garvin Davenport, "The Sanitation Revolution in Illinois, 1870-1900," *Journal of the Illinois State Historical Society* 66 (Autumn 1973): 306-26; Duffy, "Nineteenth Century Public Health in New York and New Orleans: A Comparison," *Louisiana History* 15 (Fall 1974): 325-37; Dennis East II, "Health and Wealth: Goals of the New Orleans Public Health Movement, 1879-1884," *Louisiana History* 9 (Fall 1968); John H. Ellis, "Businessmen and Public Health in the Urban South during the Nineteenth Century: New Orleans, Memphis, and Atlanta," *Bulletin of the History of Medicine* 44 (May-June 1970): 197-212; Ellis, "Memphis' Sanitary Revolution, 1880-1890," *Tennessee Historical Quarterly* 23 (March 1964): 59-72; David R. Goldfield, "The Business of Health Planning: Disease Prevention in the Old South," *Journal of Southern History* 42 (November 1976): 557-70; Michael J. Harkins, "Public Health Nuisances in Omaha, 1870-1900," *Nebraska History* 56 (1975): 471-92; Richard J. Hopkins, "Public Health in Atlanta: The Formative Years, 1865-1879," *Georgia Historical Quar-*

terly 53 (September 1969): 287-304; Duncan R. Jamieson, "Cities and the AMA: The American Medical Association's First Report on Public Hygiene," *The Maryland Historian* 8 (Spring 1977); Jamieson, "Toward a Cleaner New York: John H. Griscom and New York's Public Health, 1830-1870" (Ph.D. diss., Michigan State University, 1972); Philip D. Jordan, *The People's Health: A History of Public Health in Minnesota to 1948* (St. Paul, Minn., 1953); Jacob Judd, "Brooklyn's Health and Sanitation, 1834-1855," *The Journal of Long Island History* 7 (Winter-Spring 1967): 40-52; Earl E. Kleinschmidt, "The Sanitary Reform Movement in Michigan," *Michigan Historical Magazine* 26 (1942): 373-401; Kramer, "The Beginnings of the Public Health Movement in the United States," *Bulletin of the History of Medicine* 20 (May-June 1947): 352-76; Kramer, "The Germ Theory and the Public Health Program in the United States," *Bulletin of the History of Medicine* 22 (May-June 1948): 233-47; Judith W. Leavitt, "Public Health in Milwaukee, 1867-1910" (Ph.D. diss., University of Chicago, 1975); R. Isham Randolph, "A History of Sanitation in Chicago," *Journal of the Western Society of Engineers* 44 (October 1939): 227-40; Dorothy T. Scanlon, "The Public Health Movement in Boston, 1870-1910" (Ph.D. diss., Boston University, 1956); Henry W. Splitter, "Health in Southern California, 1850-1900," *Journal of the West* 8 (1969): 526-58; Manfred Waserman, "The Quest for a National Health Department in the Progressive Era," *Bulletin of the History of Medicine* 49 (Fall 1975): 353-80.

Some of the best sources of information about the relationship between pollution and the physical development of the industrial city are studies dealing with public works and engineering. The American Public Works Association's *History of Public Works in the United States, 1776-1976* (Chicago, 1976), edited by Ellis C. Armstrong, Michael Robinson, and Suellen Hoy, is a major contribution to this field. This large volume includes twenty essays dealing with key public works and facilities from a historical perspective. Although several of the essays are uncritical narratives, the volume as a whole provides valuable information about public works and urban technology and is a necessary departure point from which to begin more in-depth examination of such topics as the relationship between public works and urban growth and the impact of city services upon the urban quality of life. See also New York-New Jersey Metropolitan Chapter, American Public Works Association, *Public Works in Metropolitan New York-New Jersey* (New York, 1978). For background about the engineering professions, see Monte Calvert, *The Mechanical Engineer in America, 1830-1910* (Baltimore, 1967); Daniel H. Calhoun, *The American Civil Engineer: Origins and Conflict* (Cambridge, Mass., 1960); Morris M. Cohn and Dwight F. Metzler, *The Pollution Fighters: A History of Environ-*

mental Engineering in New York State (New York, 1973); Richard S. Kirby and Philip G. Laurson, *The Early Years of Modern Civil Engineering* (New Haven, 1932); Edwin T. Layton, *The Revolt of the Engineers: Social Responsibility and the American Engineering Profession* (Cleveland, 1971); Raymond H. Merritt, *Engineering in American Society, 1850-1975* (Lexington, Ky., 1969). For a fine historical treatment of municipal engineering, see Stanley K. Schultz and Clay McShane, "To Engineer the Metropolis: Sewers, Sanitation, and City Planning in Late Nineteenth-Century America," *Journal of American History* 65 (September 1978). For some useful biographical studies of important individuals in the engineering field, see Edward C. Carter II, "Benjamin Henry Latrobe and Public Works: Professionalism, Private Interest, and Public Policy in the Age of Jefferson," *Essays in Public Works History*, no. 3 (Washington, D.C., 1976); Neil FitzSimons, ed., *The Reminiscences of John B. Jervis* (Syracuse, 1971); Larry D. Lankton, "The 'Practicable' Engineer: John B. Jervis and the Old Croton Aqueduct," *Essays in Public Works History*, no. 5 (Washington, D.C., 1977); Martin V. Melosi, "Pragmatic Environmentalist: Sanitary Engineer George E. Waring, Jr., " *Essays in Public Works History*, no. 5 (Washington, D.C., 1977); Abel Wolman, "George Warren Fuller: A Reminiscence," *Essays in Public Works History*, no. 2 (Washington, D.C., 1976). See also Eugene P. Moehring, "Public Works and the Patterns of Urban Real Estate Growth in Manhattan, 1835-1894" (Ph.D. diss., City University of New York, 1976); Public Works Historical Society, *The Relevancy of Public Works History: The 1930s—A Case Study* (Washington, D.C., 1975).

Speculative overviews of the general significance of urban pollution are sorely needed. Until a reasonably large body of secondary accounts is made available, however, this task will be difficult. H. Wayne Morgan has written one of the very few general accounts, entitled "America's First Environmental Challenge, 1865-1920," in Margaret Francine Morris' *Essays on the Gilded Age* (Austin, 1973). This brief essay, which has inspired other research in urban environmental history, traces the roots of modern American ecological problems in the wake of accelerating industrialization. See also Morgan's edited volume, *Industrial America: The Environment and Social Problems, 1876-1920* (Chicago, 1974). Robert Detweiler et al. have put together an anthology of essays entitled *Environmental Decay in Its Historical Context* (Glenview, Ill., 1973), which includes a section on urban life that touches upon some of the themes of urban pollution from an international perspective. Donald Worster's edited volume of contemporary pieces, *American Environmentalism: The Formative Period, 1860-1915* (New York, 1973), contains a useful discussion of environmentalism and the American city in the introduction. Lynn White, Jr., "The Historical Roots of Our Ecological Crisis," *Science* 155 (March

1967): 1203-7, and Donald W. Whisenhunt, *The Environment and the American Experience: A Historian Looks at the Ecological Crisis* (Port Washington, N.Y., 1974), include important general discussion germane to urban ecology. Other studies that touch upon general themes relevant to urban environmental history include Nathaniel H. Bryant, "Urbanization and the Ecological Crisis: An Analysis of Environmental Pollution" (Ph.D. diss., University of Washington, 1975); Spenser W. Havlick, *The Urban Organism: The City's Natural Resources from an Environmental Perspective* (New York, 1974); Roy Lubove, *Twentieth-Century Pittsburgh: Government, Business and Environmental Change* (New York, 1969); Martin V. Melosi, "The Urban Physical Environment and the Historian: Prospects for Research, Teaching, and Public Policy," *Journal of American Culture* (forthcoming); Charles S. Olton, "Philadelphia's First Environmental Crisis," *Pennsylvania Magazine of History and Biography* 98 (January 1974): 94-100; Joseph M. Petulla, *American Environmental History* (San Francisco, 1977); James Ridgeway, *The Politics of Ecology* (New York, 1970); Nathan Rosenberg, "Technology and the Environment: An Economic Exploration," *Technology and Culture* 12 (October 1971): 543-61.

Bibliographic treatments of urban environmental history are very scarce. A starting point is Martin V. Melosi, "Urban Pollution: Historical Perspective Needed," *Environmental Review* 3 (Spring 1979), which deals narrowly with the problem of urban pollution. Other useful sources are *Environmental Review's* periodic *Bibliographic Supplement*, the Environmental Studies Institute's *Environmental Periodicals Bibliography*, and the American Historical Association's *Writings on American History*. All the standard bibliographic sources and thematic journals should be consulted for the widest possible selection of materials.

What is ironic about the paucity of historical treatments of American urban pollution is that there is no scarcity of data available for the would-be researcher. In fact, if one were to examine published materials only, the research possibilities would be endless. An outstanding source for information about the magnitude of many of the urban pollution problems is the United States census, especially the reports dealing with the statistics of cities. Although the reports are uneven in quality and do not always quantify the same data with each successive census, they do provide a reservoir of information with which to begin a study. The census should be supplemented with a variety of other government documents produced by such departments as Agriculture and Labor. Other important sources for statistics are contemporary engineering tracts, engineering journals (such as *Engineering News*), and proceedings of such groups as the American Society of Civil Engineers. Contemporary periodicals, such as *McClure's Magazine, Forum, Scribner's Magazine*, and others, provide numerous insights about pollution problems in the city. More specialized journals that deal with municipal affairs, such as *The American City*, *National Municipal Review*, and *Municipal Journal*, are valuable sources of information. Also, public health journals and scientific journals, such as the *American Journal of Public Health*, *Scientific American*, and *Science*, will provide important technical articles. On the local level, reports and proceedings of departments of health and public works, special municipal committees, and business organizations provide untold data. And newspapers are very useful for a variety of information and public reactions to pollution problems.

With such readily available information in virtually every city and numerous sources accessible in university and college libraries throughout the country, the study of urban pollution from a historical perspective provides great opportunity for professional historians, social science students of all levels, and anyone interested in the development of the American city and the state of its environment.

Hopefully, this volume will inspire additional work in urban environmental studies. There are varied opportunities for research on pollution problems, especially in the following areas: (1) quantitative measurement of the magnitude of pollution problems; (2) significant geographic, economic, political, and social variables that may have caused the concentration of a particular form of pollution in one area versus another; (3) public awareness of and attitudes about the problem of pollution; (4) environmental reform efforts; (5) the relationship between environmental pollution and conservation of resources; (6) the impact of nuclear wastes on the environment; (7) the contribution of forms of transportation to pollution (i.e., automobiles, buses, trains, etc.); (8) the role of various individuals as pollution fighters; (9) the development of public works; and (10) the impact of pollution on specific cities.

Notes on Contributors

Stuart Galishoff received a Ph.D. from New York University (1969) and was a Josiah Macy Fellow in 1967-68. Currently, he is associate professor of history at Georgia State University and a member of the College of Urban Life faculty. His major areas of interest are urban history, history of public health, and American medical history. His publications include *Safeguarding the Public Health: Newark, 1895-1918* (1975) and several articles in such journals as *Bulletin of the History of Medicine, Journal of the History of Medicine, The Maryland Historian, New Jersey History*, and *Societas*. He has recently completed a new book manuscript entitled "The Nation's Unhealthiest City: Sanitation and Public Health in Newark, 1832-1895."

R. Dale Grinder received a Ph.D. in history from the University of Missouri-Columbia, where he completed a dissertation entitled "The Anti-Smoke Crusades: Early Attempts to Reform the Urban Environment." His major interests include American environmental, urban, social, and intellectual history. In 1972-73, he served as a senior research analyst for the Environmental Protection Agency. In 1974-75 he was a fellow at the Institute for Humane Studies, Menlo Park, California. He has also taught history courses as adjunct professor for Old Dominion University and as visiting assistant professor for the University of Kansas. Currently he is employed by the American Coalition of Citizens with Disabilities in Washington, D.C. He has published several articles in *Libertarian Analysis, Missouri Historical Review, North Dakota History*, and *Western Pennsylvania Historical Magazine*.

Suellen M. Hoy is executive secretary for the Public Works Historical Society and assistant to the executive director of the American Public Works Association. In 1975, she received a Ph.D. in history from Indiana University, where she also served as editorial assistant for the *Journal of American History*. She has taught history courses at the State University of New York-Plattsburgh and Georgetown University. She has published several articles in such journals as *Albion* and *Indiana Magazine of History* and was associate editor for *History of Public Works in the United States, 1776-1976* (1976). Among her various professional activities, she serves as a chairperson of a resource group on state and local government for the National Coordinating Committee for the Promotion of History.

James McCurley is a doctoral candidate in the Carnegie-Mellon University Program in Applied History and Social Science. His dissertation involves the study of the evolution of federal wastewater policy, 1920-72.

Clay McShane is assistant professor of history at Northeastern University in Boston. He has also taught at Carnegie-Mellon University, University of Wisconsin-Madison, and University of Wisconsin-Waukesha. He received a Ph.D. in 1975 from the University of Wisconsin-Madison, where he completed a dissertation entitled "American Cities and the Coming of the Automobile, 1870-1910" (currently being revised for publication). Among his publications are *Technology and Reform: Street Railways and the Growth of Milwaukee, 1887-1900* (1974) (winner of the 1975 Gambrinus Prize for the outstanding book on the history of Milwaukee); with Stanley K. Schultz, "To Engineer the Metropolis: Sewers, Sanitation, and City Planning in Late-Nineteenth Century America," *Journal of American History* 65 (September 1978); "Water Quality Law in the United States, 1865-1920," in *Retrospective Assessment of Waste-water Quality Technology*, ed. Joel A. Tarr and Francis Clay McMichael (1977). His work in progress includes a study of street railway use and a book-length project (in collaboration with Stanley K. Schultz) entitled "Planning before the Planners: The Origins of Modern City Planning."

Martin V. Melosi received a Ph.D. in history from the University of Texas at Austin in 1975. Currently, he is assistant professor of history at Texas A&M University. In 1973 he received Phi Alpha Theta's George P. Hammond Prize for an essay on solid waste management and has been the recipient of several fellowships and grants, including those from the Rockefeller Foundation, the Ford Foundation (International Studies Association), and the Eleanor Roosevelt Institute. His publications include several articles on environmental studies and foreign affairs in such journals as *Diplomatic History*, *Environmental Review*, *The Historian*, *Journal of American Culture*, and *Prologue*; a monograph dealing with George E. Waring, Jr.; and a book entitled *The Shadow of Pearl Harbor: Political Controversy over the Surprise Attack, 1941-1946* (1977). In 1978 he was named general editor of the Texas A&M University

Press Environmental History Series. At the present time, he is completing a book-length study entitled "Environmental Challenge in the City: The Refuse Problem and Municipal Reform, 1850–1920."

Stanley K. Schultz received a Ph.D. in 1969 from the University of Chicago and is currently associate professor of history, director of undergraduate studies-history, and chairman of the American Institutions Programs at the University of Wisconsin-Madison. He has also been visiting assistant professor at Columbia University. Schultz has received several academic honors, including the Organization of American Historians' Pelzer Prize, and fellowships from, among others, the Harvard Law School and the Social Science Research Council. In 1978 he received an invitation through the Council for the International Exchange of Scholars to attend the first all-India conference on urban history. Among his several publications, including numerous articles, are *The Culture Factory: Boston Public Schools, 1789-1860* (1973), which is part of the Urban Life in America Series of Oxford University Press, and *Cities in American History* (1972), which he co-edited with Kenneth T. Jackson. Aside from his work in progress with Clay McShane, he is completing a study of housing patterns in the United States.

Raymond W. Smilor received a Ph.D. in history from the University of Texas at Austin in 1978. His dissertation is entitled "Confronting the Industrial Environment: The Noise Problem in America, 1893-1932." He has received fellowships from the National Science Foundation and Resources for the Future, Inc. His major areas of interest include American social and political history and environmental studies. He has published articles in *American Studies*, *Environmental Review*, and *Journal of American Culture*. He has taught American history at the University of Texas at Austin, St. Edward's University, and Austin Community College. In 1978-79, he was engaged in the completion of a study for the National Science Foundation that dealt with scientific and technological interface between the United States and the Soviet Union. He is currently a research fellow and program director for cultural, ethical, and institutional studies at the Institute for Constructive Capitalism, Graduate School of Business, University of Texas at Austin.

Joel A. Tarr is professor of history, technology and urban affairs and director, Program in Technology and Humanities at Carnegie-Mellon University. He received a Ph.D. in history from Northwestern University in 1963 and has been on the faculty of Carnegie-Mellon since 1967. He holds a triple appointment among the College of Humanities and Social Science, the School of Urban and Public Affairs, and the Carnegie Institute of Technology. His major interests include urban problems, technology and society, and applied history. He has received numerous honors, including fellowships and grants from, among others, the Andrew W. Mellon Foundation, the General Electric Foundation, and NSF/RANN. Among his many publications are *A Study in Boss Politics: William Lorimer of Chicago* (1971); (editor), *Retrospective Technology Assessment* (1977); (editor), *Patterns of City Growth* (1975); *The Automobile and the Smoky City* (1975); *Growth, Stability, and Decline in an Urban Area: One Hundred Years of Hazelwood* (1975); and numerous articles in such journals as *Agricultural History*, *American Heritage*, *Business History Review*, *Futures*, *Mid-America*, *Pacific Historical Review*, *Pennsylvania History*, and others.

Terry F. Yosie is a doctoral candidate in the Carnegie–Mellon University Doctor of Arts Program in History. His dissertation is a study of the evolution of wastewater systems and wastewater policy in Pittsburgh, 1800-1959.